*The life and death of*

# TIN PAN ALLEY

*Books on American popular music*
*by David Ewen*

*A Journey to Greatness:*
*The Life and Music of George Gershwin*
*Richard Rodgers*
*The World of Jerome Kern*
*Panorama of American Popular Music*
*History of Popular Music*
*Complete Book of the American Musical Theater.*
*American Popular Composers*
*The Story of America's Musical Theater.*
*The Life and Death of Tin Pan Alley*

FOR YOUNG PEOPLE

*The Story of George Gershwin*
*The Story of Irving Berlin*
*The Story of Jerome Kern*
*With a Song in His Heart:*
*The Story of Richard Rodgers*
*Leonard Bernstein*

# The life and death of

# TIN PAN ALLEY

The golden age of American popular music

## DAVID EWEN

Funk and Wagnalls Company, Inc., New York

*Contents*

# Foreword

Many people still refer to the American popular-song industry as "Tin Pan Alley," even though Tin Pan Alley no longer exists. Surely this in itself is eloquent testimony to the contribution Tin Pan Alley made to our popular music, to how sizable a segment of American popular-music history Tin Pan Alley was.

Strictly speaking, Tin Pan Alley was not a period in popular-music history at all, but rather a part of New York geography. Tin Pan Alley was a street—Twenty-eighth Street in Manhattan. From the beginning of 1900 until post World War I, so many of New York's music-publishing houses moved to Twenty-eighth Street, between Fifth Avenue and Broadway, that it rightly came to be known as the street of songs. It was from Twenty-eighth Street that the Remick house issued "In the Shade of the Old Apple Tree" and "Shine On, Harvest Moon" in the first decade of the 1900's. It was there on Twenty-eighth Street that Harry von Tilzer reaped a harvest by publishing his own songs "Wait 'Til the Sun Shines, Nellie," "Down Where the Wurzburger Flows," and "On a Sunday Afternoon." For some years the Shapiro-Bernstein house was just a stone's throw from Von Tilzer's (a geographical fact with poetic justice since Von Tilzer and Shapiro and Bernstein had once been publishing partners and, as such, had earlier reaped a joint harvest with Von Tilzer's ballad "A Bird in a Gilded Cage"). F. A. Mills was also on the same street; as Kerry Mills he had written the cakewalk classic "At a Georgia Camp Meeting." Also on Twenty-eighth Street were the publishing houses of Charles K. Harris, who had become wealthy with "After the Ball," and Leo Feist, who, in 1914, gave America its greatest World War I song, George M. Cohan's "Over There."

It is not difficult to laugh at Tin Pan Alley and its many foibles. This was a place where a corset salesman and a necktie salesman joined forces to become topflight publishers on whose decision rested the fate of songs; where one of the street's greatest creative figures was a composer who could play the piano only in a single key; where one hit song after another had to be dictated by its creator because he knew nothing about musical notation; where somebody who had had training in harmony and orchestration was looked upon askance and suspiciously; where lifting somebody else's melodic ideas, far from being frowned upon, yielded fabulous rewards; where lyrics were most often fashioned out of bromides, clichés, and bad prosody by semi-illiterates. This was a place where a composer could write a hymn to marital bliss while he himself was enjoying single-blessedness, and rhapsodize over Tennessee and Carolina without once setting foot below New Jersey.

This was the place that could produce a ballad about an apple tree in Central Park—a park that had no apple trees.

Tin Pan Alley has provided food for the satirist. When Richard Rodgers, Lorenz Hart, and Herbert Fields were just neophytes in the theater, they wrote a Broadway farce about Tin Pan Alley titled *The Melody Man*, which opened on May 13, 1924. In this Lew Fields played the role of a serious Austrian composer who earned his living doing hackwork in Tin Pan Alley until he achieved the heights of success by lifting a melody from his own ambitious *Dresden Sonata* and converting it into the pop tune "Moonlight Mama." A few years after that, Broadway boasted an even more vitriolic commentary on Tin Pan Alley ways—and the means by which a hit is made—through *June Moon*, a play by George S. Kaufman and Ring Lardner, which was based on the latter's short story, "Some Like It Cold."

Yes, it is easy to dismiss Tin Pan Alley with a smirk and a wisecrack—but for one significant and salient fact. Tin Pan Alley was the place where young composers grew up to success, and at times to greatness, from the most humble beginnings as piano demonstrators, song pluggers, arrangers, salesmen, stock clerks. George Gershwin, aged fifteen, demonstrated songs for Remick. The boy Irving Berlin plugged songs for Harry von Tilzer at Tony Pastor's Music Hall. Ernest R. Ball was a piano demonstrator for the Witmark brothers. Harry Ruby was a staff pianist and song plugger, first for Gus Edwards and later for Harry von Tilzer. Jean Schwartz was the song plugger for Shapiro-Bernstein. Jerome Kern, as a young man, worked as a stock clerk and salesman for T. B. Harms.

Their ascent in the music business, frequently to the heights, came only after these men had spent their formative years in Tin Pan Alley, learning their trade, sizing up their public, understanding what made a song "tick." What these and others like them would have become had there been no Tin Pan Alley is just idle and futile speculation. It is hard, however, to conceive how, under any other system of song production, creative figures in popular music such as Gershwin, Kern, and Berlin could have been much better, more prolific, or more successful.

All day long on Twenty-eighth Street pianos were strummed and thumped inside the converted four-story brownstone houses that lined both sides of the street. The piano demonstrators sat in their cramped cubicles trying out new songs for the performers who could bring them to the public. Outside the publishing house loitered the song plugger. Like the "pullers-in" of the cloak-and-suit district farther downtown, the plugger kept an eye alert for possible customers. Espying a vaudevillian, musical-comedy star, restaurant orchestra leader, minstrel, or anybody else capable of bringing a song to an audience, the plugger would use all the powers of his charm and persuasion to convince the performer to enter his establishment and listen to its new tunes. In an effort to keep leading performers from other houses, one publisher after another began to rent out office space as rehearsal rooms. Besides bringing in some additional income, this practice was valuable as an efficacious method by which the firm's songs could be brought, hot off the press, to a performer.

Soon after the turn of the twentieth century, Twenty-eighth Street was baptized "Tin Pan Alley." The credit for this goes most often to Monroe Rosenfeld, a colorful character who dominated early Tin Pan Alley history for a number of years. How did he happen to name the music-publishing row "Tin Pan Alley"? He was planning a series of articles on American popular music for the New York *Herald,* in or about 1903, when he went to the fountainhead for material. Visiting the offices of Harry von Tilzer, at 45 West 28th Street, he happened to hear Von Tilzer's piano, whose advanced age was betrayed by its raspy tones. To Rosenfeld, the piano sounded like the clashing of tin pans. "Tin pan music," remarked Rosenfeld, rolling the phrase on the tip of his tongue as if it were a choice liqueur. "Why," he said at last, "this whole street is a tin pan alley."

That was the title he used for his articles—"Tin Pan Alley"; and that was the name by which Twenty-eighth Street was henceforth known. Many years later, Harry von Tilzer insisted that it was he, and not Rosenfeld, who had coined the name for the Rosenfeld articles. Since Rosenfeld never did have any qualms about lifting somebody else's material without due credit, this may actually have been true. In any event, Monroe Rosenfeld was the first to use the phrase in print, and thus to popularize it, even if he had not concocted it.

But Tin Pan Alley became much more than just a street of music-publishing houses. It was, in actuality, an epoch in American popular music that started in or about 1885, long before Monroe Rosenfeld used his neatly coined phrase to identify it. And it ended long after Rosenfeld was gone and forgotten—sometime around 1930. During this era, a new way of life was conceived for American popular music: a way of writing songs, publishing and promoting them, and keeping them alive in public interest. Tin Pan Alley was not only the place but also the means by which some of America's most famous melodies came into being, oftentimes manufactured, as if on an assembly belt, to meet specific public needs or to cater to a public's fancy or whim. Tin Pan Alley invented the science of marketing songs, of making audiences everywhere song-conscious. Tin Pan Alley translated music into business—big business.

Tin Pan Alley was something else, too. It was a mirror

to and a voice of America during a period of formidable growth and change. The fads and fashions, the fluctuating mores, tastes, and moral attitudes, the current events and economic crises, the passing moods and social forces—all that made up American social history—were caught, fixed, and interpreted by Tin Pan Alley in words and music that were on everybody's lips.

Isaac Goldberg was intrigued enough by this phenomenon to step out of his favorite fields of psychoanalysis, Latin-American literature, contemporary drama, and philology to study the phenomenon of Tin Pan Alley. More than thirty years ago he wrote in his book *Tin Pan Alley:* "It made a genuine contribution to the raw material of music. What Charlie [Chaplin] has been to the movies; what our comic strip has been to the gay arts; what the skyscraper has been to architecture—this Tin Pan Alley has been to the minor music of the continents. To the blaring pandemonium of the circus, to the crude caricature of the minstrel show, we must add a distinctly American contribution, the less and less accidental beauty—if at times a crude and uncouth beauty—of the Tin Pan Alley song."

This book is the story of the birth, the growth, the decline, and the fall of Tin Pan Alley. Of course, Tin Pan Alley is only one aspect of the history of American popular music—but a major aspect. Our story begins before the name of Tin Pan Alley was coined, because the traditions of Tin Pan Alley were then established. Our book is the story of outstanding popular songs, of remarkable popular composers, of publishers and song pluggers with remarkable initiative and drive, and of performers who carried songs to audiences. Our book is also, in its way, a passing commentary on a half-century of American life as reflected in song.

"It may be just a street to many, but to some of us it

was a religion" was a line Eddie Foy used in his vaudeville act. He was referring to Broadway, but he could have been talking about Tin Pan Alley.

——D. E.

*The life and death of*

# TIN PAN ALLEY

# 1

## "Turn back the universe and give me yesterday"

There would have been no Tin Pan Alley if a new generation of song publishers had not come into being in or about 1880. These publishers had the courage to invade what thus far had been a conservative stronghold, and they had the foresight and the imagination to introduce into their business a new aggressive method of operation.

While there had always been publishers to issue popular songs and popular-song lyrics, most of the song hits before 1880 came from music-publishing establishments specializing in serious music and in instruction books for students; others came out of print shops and music stores.

Stephen Foster was published by Firth, Pond and Company in New York until it was dissolved in 1863; and Firth,

Pond and Company had been organized in 1831 to publish materials for serious musicians and students.

After 1837, the Oliver Ditson music store, in Boston, became one of America's leading publishers of classical music and instruction books. This firm also brought out, however, a good deal of popular material, including "The Battle Hymn of the Republic" and "Tenting on the Old Camp Ground" during the Civil War, the dusky ballad "Nicodemus Johnson" in 1865, and Harry Kennedy's tearjerker, "A Flower from Mother's Grave," in 1878.

Two other publishers of comparatively serious music in Boston brought out minstrel-show tunes on the side. They were C. H. Keith and John F. Perry, publishers of Dan Emmett and James Bland, respectively. John Church Company, still another Boston outfit, issued, together with their staples, the popular nonmilitary Civil War ballad "Aura Lee" and one of the leading sentimental ballads of the 1870's "I'll Take You Home Again, Kathleen."

Root and Cady in Chicago was also a publisher of musical classics, as well as a music shop, until it became a power in the song industry by issuing George F. Root's "Battle Cry of Freedom" in 1863 (George F. Root was a brother of one of the firm's partners). And Carr's was just a music store in Baltimore when in 1814 it published for the first time the song that was later to become America's national anthem—"The Star-Spangled Banner."

These were just a few of the publishing houses scattered all over the country who issued serious music with one hand and popular songs with the other. All such houses followed a pattern of operation that for many years left little room for initiative or experiment. These publishing executives sat in their offices waiting for successes to hatch. Composers, performers, even the public had to beat a path to their doors. To go out in search of song material, to manufacture songs for specific timely purposes or events, to find performers and even bribe them to introduce such songs, to devise ingenious strategy to get a public sufficiently interested in the songs to buy the sheet music—all this was not then in the philosophy of conducting a music-publishing venture. Song hits happened. Publishers themselves did little or nothing to create them.

A few early American song hits point up the rather apathetic way in which publishers seemed to go about their business. Measured by sheet-music sale—the yardstick that the industry used for many years—Stephen Foster's "Swanee River" and "My Old Kentucky Home" were substantial successes for their time. The *Musical World* of 1852 reported that "the publishers keep two presses running and sometimes three, yet they cannot supply the demand [for 'Swanee River']." "My Old Kentucky Home" sold over 50,000 copies of sheet music in less than a year after its publication in 1853. The publishing house of Firth, Pond and Company thus hit pay dirt, although it had done very little hand digging of its own. It was Stephen Foster himself, not his publishers, who interested the minstrel Ed Christy in using these songs in his shows.

The Hutchinsons—a popular troupe of singers touring the country in the middle 1850's—made "The Battle Cry of Freedom" a national success. But it was accident, not the planning of the publishers, that led the Hutchinsons to sing this patriotic ballad. The Hutchinsons had come across the song by sheer chance a few days after it had been introduced in Chicago by the Lombard Brothers.

The song chronicles of this period overflow with accounts of singers accidentally stumbling over numbers that they then introduced and made famous. The premières of many another popular song came about because their composers, such as Dan Emmett and Henry Russell, were performers as well. Certainly, the publishers took full advantage of the interest in sheet-music sale aroused by performance by popular singers. But finding ways and means of getting such performances, or stimulating public interest, did not come within the sphere of their activities. Advertising of popular songs was completely unknown. Promotion and song-plugging were nonexistent. To pay a performer to sing a song would have been regarded by some of these older die-hard publishers as an indiscretion only a degree higher than street soliciting.

But in or about 1880—and continuing right through the 1890's—a new concept of popular-song publishing was being crystallized. This unconventional, even revolutionary, concept could have come only from young men with the iconoclasm and the recklessness of the novice. Some of these new publishers had been printers, and some had worked as salesmen in other businesses. They came to popular-music publishing to seek out a rich area they shrewdly felt could reap a harvest if properly fertilized and tilled. Many of these new publishers were themselves song-writers who had grown weary of earning fifteen or twenty-five dollars from a number which later brought fortunes to the publisher. As publishers of their own creations, these neophytes would stop at no length to get their work across to audiences.

One of the first of the new publishing breed was Frank Harding, who took over the direction of his father's publishing establishment on the Bowery in New York City in 1879. Frank Harding represented the new age of music publishing for two reasons. He specialized in popular songs and through them became successful; and he was one of the first in the industry to realize that song composers had to be nursed and coddled into writing hits.

He had learned the music business by operating a hand printing press for a number of years in his father's firm, after which he became his father's assistant. Once he took over the control of the business, Frank Harding broke precedent by shattering the insularity of music publishing. He made his office a hangout for the city's composers and lyricists. They came there to drink liquor, play poker, or just to gab. But along the way they also wrote songs for Harding. Realizing that there was no stimulus so potent to creation as thirst, Harding would pay his writers the price of several rounds of drinks each time they handed him a manuscript. "It was no use giving them more than ten dollars at a time," he explained. "A man could get damned drunk on ten dollars. I used to buy beautiful songs from J. P. Skelly for from six to twenty-five dollars, excellent manuscripts." Skelly, James Thornton, Charles Graham, Monroe Rosenfeld—we'll talk a good deal more about them in pages to come—were some of those who could usually be found loitering around Harding's office. Thornton's celebrated ballad "My Sweetheart's the Man in the Moon" was published by Harding; so were Joseph J. Sullivan's "Where Did You Get That Hat?" and J. W. Kelly's "Throw Him Down, McCloskey."

T. B. Harms and Willis Woodward were two other young publishers to concentrate successfully on popular songs and to bring a new vision to their endeavor. Between 1881 and 1883, the firm of T. B. Harms had several minor hits to its credit, the most important of which was Frank Howard's "When the Robins Nest Again" in 1883. Introduced by Howard himself (a famous minstrel with Thatcher, Primrose, and West), this song immediately became a huge favorite with minstrel-show audiences.

The T. B. Harms company did not hit its full stride until Alex and Tom Harms, both of them perspicacious and indefatigable promoters, began tapping the New York musical theater for publications. Some publishers before Harms had issued stage music—William A. Pond, for example (successors in 1863 to Firth, Pond and Company) had released most of the songs that David Braham wrote for the Harrigan and Hart extravaganzas. But T. B. Harms exploited the sheet-music distribution of stage music more extensively than any publisher had done up to this point. Between 1885 and 1891, the firm published several songs from *Shane na Lawn* and *Wang*, the latter a spectacle starring DeWolf Hopper. Then, in 1892, Harms became the first Tin Pan Alley publisher to discover that the rights to the sheet music of a successful Broadway musical production were almost as profitable as striking oil. This valuable lesson was learned by Harms through *A Trip to Chinatown*, an extravaganza that had the longest run (650 performances) of any stage presentation in New York theatrical history up to this time; it also toured the country for more than a year. Among its songs—most of which were written by Percy Gaunt—were three winners in "Reuben, Reuben," "Push Dem Clouds Away," and "The Bowery." In fact, it was "The Bowery"—far more than Loie Fuller's sensational butterfly dance or the singing of J. Aldrich Libbey —that enabled *A Trip to Chinatown* to settle down for a long and prosperous run after a shaky beginning at the box office. For several weeks the show had floundered. Then, to bolster the material, Percy Gaunt wrote "The Bowery" and slipped the song into a scene in which Harry Conor impersonated a rube from the sticks who was surrounded by Bowery drunks and thieves. After he had delivered the six verses and chorus, the thunder of approbation compelled him to sing it again from the beginning. "The Bowery" is still remembered—one of a handful of songs by which the city of New York or districts of it have been immortalized.

In 1892, Harms published "The Bowery," "Reuben, Reuben," and "Push Dem Clouds Away," and sold what for that time was the astronomical figure of several hundred thousand copies of each of the three numbers. This was the first time in Broadway history, and in that of American popular music, that a stage production provided such a source of revenue for a publisher. Henceforth, following the lead of Harms, publishing houses would reach out to the musical theater ever more hungrily to cash in on its best musical numbers.

The sentimental ballad proved as rich a source of financial rewards for the house of Willis Woodward & Company as the musical theater was for Harms.

The sentimental ballad was, to be sure, nothing new in the 1880's. As a matter of fact it was as old as America itself. America's first sentimental ballad and the Revolutionary War came hand in hand. "The Banks of the Dee"—John Tait wrote the lyrics and adapted them to the familiar Irish melody, "Langolee"—described a Scotsman's sad farewell to his lass before embarking with the British troops for the colonies. After that, the sentimental ballad flourished in the 1830's mainly through the efforts of Henry Russell, a visitor from England. He began his career as an American popular-song composer while he was touring the country as a concert singer. In his lyrics and music, Russell shed many a tear over a tree, Mother, an old family clock, a ship afire, alcoholics, the insane, and a gambler's wife. "The Old Arm Chair," one of Russell's most popular, is probably America's first "mammy" song. "Woodman, Spare That Tree!" was one of the most widely sung and best loved sentimental ballads before the Civil War.

After Russell's time, hardly a year passed when men did not sing to women who sighed, a sad tale of woe narrated by a popular ballad. These were some of the more celebrated of these songs: "Darling Nelly Gray" in 1856; "Aura Lee" in 1861; "When You and I Were Young, Maggie" in 1866; "Sweet Genevieve" in 1869; "Grandfather's Clock" in 1876; "A Flower from Mother's Grave" in 1878; and "Why Did They Dig Ma's Grave So Deep?" in 1880. (In 1956, Elvis Presley borrowed the melody of "Aura Lee" for his song "Love Me Tender," which he introduced in the motion picture of the same name, and recorded for Victor in a disk that sold more than a million copies.) To these, of course, must be added the sentimental ballads of Stephen Foster and those by other composers inspired by the Civil War.

Many a mighty publishing establishment in Tin Pan Alley, and many a fortune, was built on the foundation stones of the sentimental ballad, whose greatest era opened in 1890. Before 1890 it was Willis Woodward that became one of the first establishments to help bring about this development by concentrating its prime efforts on such ballads. One of the first releases of the then newly organized firm of Willis Woodward was "White Wings" by Banks Winter. Winter himself had previously introduced his song at Huber's Gardens, a German beer hall on Fourteenth Street. Though the song was well received, it found no takers along publisher's row—that is, not until Pat Howley, an employee at Willis Woodward, accepted it for publication in 1884. The song became a huge success after Banks Winter tried it out in Boston with the Thatcher, Primrose and West Minstrels. Soon after that it was heard and acclaimed at Niblo's Gardens in New York. There was still another hit ballad in the Willis Woodward catalogue in 1884—Jennie Lindsay's "Always Take Mother's Advice." Charles Graham's "If the Waters Could Speak as They Flow" was one of Willis Woodward's best-selling songs of 1887.

That year of 1887, as a matter of fact, proved providential for the Woodward publishing house. For in that year it released "The Outcast Unknown," thereby acquiring under its roof perhaps the most successful creator of sentimental ballads of his time, Paul Dresser.

His name originally was Paul Dreiser, and he was the brother of Theodore Dreiser, one of America's most distinguished novelists. Paul was born in Terre Haute, Indiana, in 1857. In his boyhood he learned to play the guitar and the piano. Because his father wanted him to become a priest—and because his own inclinations drew him to the stage—Paul ran away from home when he was sixteen and joined a medicine show that marketed a "wizard oil." One year later he became a member of a troupe making one-night stands, and from there he went on to a stock company by whom he was billed as "the sensational comique."

Already Paul Dresser was writing songs. His first, "Wide Wings," was issued by a small Indiana firm with profit to neither publisher nor author. Several of his other songs were grouped into the *Paul Dresser Songster* by a small Chicago publisher. Then, in 1885, while appearing as "Mr. Bones" with the Billy Rice Minstrels, Dresser started writing sentimental ballads for that company.

Dresser, a man who quivered with sentimentality in every tissue and muscle of his huge body, would burst into tears at the sound of a touching song, and especially at one he had written. Inspired by a frustrated love affair, he produced in 1886 the words and music of "The Letter That Never Came," which he sold to T. B. Harms for a few dollars. Though this ballad did not do well, Pat Howley of Willis Woodward was astute enough to buy Dresser's very next ballad, "The Outcast Unknown." The song brought in a profit. Now convinced he had a "find" in Dresser, Howley urged the composer to give up acting in minstrel shows and to become a staff composer at Willis Woodward. The wisdom of Howley's offer was proved decisively with two extraordinarily successful ballads issued by Willis Woodward in 1888 and 1891: "The Convict and the Bird" and "The Pardon Came Too Late."

If the Willis Woodward firm was directly responsible for the successful appearance of Paul Dresser in American popular music, it was also instrumental (though indirectly) in the founding of a new publishing organization. Because that house became one of the most adventurous in the early history of Tin Pan Alley, and was to set some of the patterns that would govern the Alley for many years, this achievement by Willis Woodward was no minor one. This is how it came about.

Willis Woodward had begun the practice of bribing performers to do his songs. He asked young Jay Witmark, a successful performer of ballads in variety and minstrel shows, to include in his repertory "Always Take Mother's Advice." Mainly due to Jay Witmark's effective rendition, the ballad amassed considerable sales. When the time of reckoning arrived, Willis Woodward, in place of the sizable sum he owed Witmark, presented him with a twenty-dollar gold piece. In retaliation, Jay Witmark swore he would enter publishing to become Willis Woodward's chief competitor.

At that time, together with his brothers Isidore and Julius, Jay Witmark operated a little printing establishment at his home on West Fortieth Street. This firm did miscellaneous printing jobs such as Christmas cards and advertising throwaways. It now occurred to Jay that if he was able to make songs into hits by singing them, he ought to go into music publishing and work this magic for himself. There was one obstacle, however: the Witmark boys had no songs to publish. The mother of invention—necessity—compelled them to produce one of their own. Seizing upon an announcement in the papers that President Grover Cleveland was to marry Frances Folsom, Isidore Witmark wrote the instrumental number *President Cleveland's Wedding March*, hoping that the publicity attending such an event might work to the sales advantage of his brain child. By the time the wedding ceremony took place at the White House in 1886, the young Witmarks had printed a "de luxe edition" of their march, ready for immediate distribution; they were the only publishers with such a timely item. They could hardly have realized it at the time, but with their maiden effort the Witmarks had begun a trend: to manufacture popular songs for a specific event.

Thus the house of M. Witmark and Sons stepped boldly into the publishing arena. (The letter "M" in the name stood for Marcus, the boys' father. Marcus had no interest in the firm, but his signature was needed for all business documents since the Witmark boys were all under age.)

The march did well enough to convince the Witmarks that they were in the song-publishing business for good. The better-established houses referred cynically to the newcomer as "The Hatchery," because its proprietors were just fledglings; indeed, Willis Woodward prophesied (with more bitterness than vision) that the Witmark establishment would collapse in less than six months. But having started out on a solid footing with a minor hit, the Witmark boys had no intention of losing ground.

Their second publication was an Isidore Witmark song, "I'll Answer That Question." Since Jay's experiences as a singer had taught the boys that the best way to make a song successful was to get it featured by some prominent performer, Isidore set for himself the task of placing his new song to its best advantage. He finally got Mademoiselle Renée—a foreign music-hall star then touring America—to use the song in her act. (Mademoiselle Renée became the wife of the Broadway producer William A. Brady and the mother of Alice Brady, star of stage and screen.) In the same persuasive way Isidore Witmark induced Daniel Sully, a vaudevillian, to interpolate the firm's "Sassy Nolan," into his comedy routine. "Sassy Nolan" sold even better than the preceding Witmark songs, not only because of Sully's popularity but also because Sully, whose act was also called "Sassy Nolan," helped swell the sheet-music sale by purchasing forty-five thousand copies for distribution among his friends and wellwishers.

It was not long before M. Witmark and Sons outgrew its little printing shop at home. In 1888 it opened an office for song publishing at 32 East 14th Street. It was not the first music-publishing house to come to the vicinity of Union Square. Willis Woodward had preceded them there by setting up shop in the Star Building on Thirteenth Street. But if the Witmarks were not the first, they were certainly among the first to come to Union Square. Here, too, they proved pioneers. For Union Square was about to become the mecca of American popular music, the birthplace of Tin Pan Alley.

There was still another way in which the Witmarks broke new ground. When Isidore Witmark published his own songs, he was in the vanguard of a new species soon to dominate the popular-song industry—the composer-publisher. Paul Dresser was just one of several composers who were about to combine their songwriting efforts with publishing. This may well be the reason that a more dynamic approach to the distribution, popularization, and promotion of songs had begun to emerge. As the creator, manufacturer, and distributor, the composer-publisher was powerfully motivated to pull out all the stops in getting his songs heard.

In Chicago, a publisher named Will Rossiter, and a composer named W. R. Williams, were one and the same person. Rossiter possessed a keen sense for promotion. He became a prime mover in the early attempts of young publishers to bring songs to performers and audiences—instead of waiting for performers and audiences to come to them. He was one of the first to invade retail shops with his songs and sing them to anybody who would stop to listen. He was also one of the first to advertise his songs in theatrical trade journals.

Then there was Charles K. Harris in Milwaukee, best-known as the creator of "After the Ball," one of the most popular sentimental ballads ever written. But his significance in popular music rests just as securely on his achievements as a publisher. Born in Poughkeepsie, New York, in 1867, Harris spent his boyhood in Milwaukee, where he improvised a banjo from an empty oyster can and some strands of wire and taught himself to play minstrel-show tunes. When a vaudevillian gave him the present of a real banjo, Harris became so adept on it that he was soon making public appearances as singer and banjoist.

Harris was about sixteen when he saw *The Skating Rink*, a musical show starring Nat Goodwin. That performance fired him with the ambition to write a song for Goodwin to sing in the show. With the help of a friend, Harris completed "Since Maggie Learned to Skate," which he somehow managed to get Goodwin to use in his musical. Encouraged by this accomplishment, Harris was stimulated into writing more songs. These included "Creep, Baby, Creep" and "Let's Kiss and Make Up." He badgered every performer within the vicinity of Milwaukee to use his songs in their acts, even succeeding on one or two occasions. Meanwhile, since he had to make a living, he taught kids the banjo, worked as a bellhop, and clerked in a pawnshop.

His first published song was "When the Sun Has Set," which M. Witmark and Sons contracted for on a royalty basis. Harris' first royalty check amounted to eighty-five cents. Harris knew at once that if he were to make a living as a songwriter it would be as a publisher of his own compositions. In or about 1885, therefore, he convinced two of his friends to invest $500 each and join him in publishing his songs. He rented a one-room office at 207 Grand

Avenue in Milwaukee for seven dollars and fifty cents a month. His monthly overhead was another $2.50. At the end of the first year the new firm cleared $3,000 profit. Buying out his partners, he opened new and larger quarters in the Alhambra Theater Building; soon after, he was able to open a branch office in Chicago.

Then, in 1892, he wrote the song that was to be a climactic event in Harris' career as songwriter-publisher as well as in the early history of Tin Pan Alley. This ballad, "After the Ball," was born one evening when Harris, who was then twenty-five, was visiting Chicago. While attending a dance there he happened to witness a poignant scene. A young couple near him was quarreling. Hot words were exchanged. The young man left in a huff. Harris found himself thinking: "Many a heart is aching after the ball." And thus the idea for a song ballad was hatched.

Back in Milwaukee, he developed a complete story line —through three sixty-four-bar verses and a thirty-two-bar chorus. At a ball a young man catches his sweetheart kissing a stranger. Convinced that she is unfaithful, this young man leaves the ball without allowing his sweetheart to offer explanations. He never sees her again. Only many years later does he discover that the man his sweetheart kissed was her long-lost brother. Now an old man, the untrusting lover describes this episode to his little niece in explanation of why he has never married.

The ink was hardly dry on the manuscript paper when Harris welcomed a visitor to his publishing office. Sam Doctor, a vaudevillian, had wandered in to seek a slow waltz for his act. Harris turned over to him the newly completed ballad "After the Ball." Sam Doctor introduced the song in vaudeville in 1892. Unhappily, during his performance he forgot the words and helplessly stood on the stage, gaping with embarrassment and without emitting a sound. The laughter in the audience drowned out the music and turned the première of Harris' ballad into a fiasco.

Harris was now able to place his song in Charles Hoyt's fabulous extravaganza *A Trip to Chinatown* by the simple expedient of paying its singing star, J. Aldrich Libbey, $500 in cash and a percentage of the song's royalties. This, incidentally, was one of the earliest significant examples of a practice that was dubbed and denounced in the 1950's as "payola." Once Libbey's support had thus been purchased, Harris went on to coax the orchestra leader, Frank Palma, with a box of fine cigars, to orchestrate the song.

The song did not have much relevance in the production. It was slipped into the second act, set in San Francisco's Chinatown, and was delivered by Libbey dressed in evening clothes. But despite its inappropriateness, the ballad was an immediate sensation. Harris himself described the night it was introduced in his autobiography *After the Ball*. After Libbey had rendered the first verse and chorus the "audience remained quiet for a full minute and not a sound was heard. I was ready to sink through the floor. He then went through the second verse and chorus, and again complete silence reigned. I was making ready to bolt, but my friends . . . held me tightly by the arm. Then came the third verse and chorus. For a full minute the audience again remained quiet, and then broke loose with applause. . . . The entire audience arose and, standing, applauded wildly for five minutes."

Harris now became convinced he had a solid winner, especially when Isidore Witmark offered him the then-unprecedented sum of $10,000 for publication rights. But the song was not for sale. A few days after the sheet music was ready, the Oliver Ditson music store of Boston sent in an order for seventy-five thousand copies. To meet it, Harris had to go out and buy a printing press. When orders came from music stores all over the country, other presses had to be summoned into action. Within a year, Harris' publishing house was earning as high as $25,000 in a single week from "After the Ball." Additional stimulus to the sheet-music sale came when Helene Mora, a popular "female baritone," decided to use it in her vaudeville act. Then, at the World's Columbian Exposition in Chicago in 1893, John Philip Sousa offered a band arrangement of it that grew so popular that he had to include the song on virtually every one of his programs.

In time, "After the Ball" sold more than five million copies of sheet music, a sale without precedent in American popular music. Harris says in his autobiography that the song earned for him more than ten million dollars. Single-handedly, "After the Ball" made Charles K. Harris a power as a song publisher and one of the most celebrated creators of sentimental ballads in the 1890's.

Harris wrote a good many ballads after that: "Fallen by the Wayside," "I'm Trying So Hard to Forget You," "There'll Come a Time," "Better than Gold," "I've Come to Say Good-by." Some were passingly successful; most were failures. Only one has survived: "Break the News to Mother," a ballad that acquired a permanent place in American popular music as one of the representative songs of the Spanish-American War.

But Harris never did write a ballad to equal the popularity of "After the Ball," a fact that caused him no little anguish and bitterness. But he should have found consolation in the fact that his importance in American popular music did not spring exclusively from the record-breaking sale of his ballad. When Harris opened his first publishing office on Grand Avenue, he hung a shingle outside his door that read: "Charles K. Harris—Banjoist and Songwriter—Songs Written to Order." *Songs written to order*—the phrase is well worth italicizing. If there is any single moment at which Tin Pan Alley can be said to emerge it was at the moment that Harris so boldly painted that phrase on his shingle. By advertising that he was in the business of manufacturing songs to order, Charles K. Harris in Milwaukee had become the father of New York City's Tin Pan Alley.

# 2

## "There's no business like show business"

The movement of popular-music publishers toward New York City's Union Square, begun just before 1890 by Willis Woodward and M. Witmark and Sons, continued throughout the 1890's. The trail blazers were joined by the better-established houses as well as most of the newcomers.

This was the first time that the popular-music-publishing business—formerly scattered all over the United States—became centralized. This, then, was the real beginning of Tin Pan Alley.

There were sound practical reasons why publishers should now want to settle in or near Union Square. The song industry had become fully cognizant of the importance of the entertainment world to the conduct of its affairs. The older publishers as well as the neophytes wanted to center their activities, and their very presence, in what was then the entertainment capital of America.

By 1890, here in Union Square could be found Tony Pastor's Music Hall, the foremost vaudeville theater in America. Its footlights were continually throwing their luminous glare on such fabled celebrities of show business as the Four Cohans, Lottie Gilson, the first Pat Rooney, May Irwin, Weber and Fields, Eddie Foy, Emma Carus, Maggie Cline, Ben Harney, Lillian Russell, and many others. In Union Square was located the Union Square Theater in which in 1886 Lillian Russell had dazzled her audiences with the operetta *Pepita*, the music of which was the work of her husband, Edward Solomon. Also in the Square, the Academy of Music was still the home of grand opera, even though in 1883 it had found a formidable competitor in the then newly opened Metropolitan Opera House "uptown" on Thirty-ninth Street.

In Union Square there was a proliferation of burlesque and sporting houses, beer halls, penny arcades, restaurants. Across the street from Tony Pastor's was the Dewey Theater, favored home of burlesque shows, and Theiss's Alhambra, for varied forms of live entertainment. A few doors from the Alhambra stood the street's most celebrated restaurant, Luchow's, to this day a landmark on Fourteenth Street. Huber's Prospect Gardens Music Hall (a replica of an English music hall, even though its staff was mainly German) catered to its faithful clientele at the corner of Fourth Avenue and Fourteenth Street.

Just a short distance from East Fourteenth Street were clustered a number of theaters in which minstrel-show and variety troupes performed regularly. Just around the corner from Irving Place and fashionable Gramercy Park were two hotels—the Trafalgar and the Academy—which, however rundown and weatherbeaten, were the homes of visiting entertainers.

In the Union Square of 1890, as elsewhere in the United States, one form of stage entertainment was on its way out and another was on its way in.

On a sharp decline was the minstrel show, which had been flourishing since 1846 when its format had been set and established for all time by Ed Christy and his Minstrels. The end men, Mr. Tambo and Mr. Bones, became for years just about the most famous pair of characters in the American theater. The sight of these performers—faces blackened by burnt cork; dressed in frock coats, striped trousers, white gloves; with large flowers in the lapel—was calculated to arouse in audiences anticipations of nostalgia, gaiety, and hilarity: gay double-entendres; puns; absurd answers to provocative questions, repartee; solo comedy songs and sentimental ballads; choral numbers; dances; and walkarounds (the last being the strut of a performer around the stage during the presentation of the concluding musical number). All this was blended into a wonderful triple melange: the "olio," the fantasia, and the burlesque. The "olio" consisted of variety entertainment with a standardized pattern; the fantasia, with no standard format, permitted individual performers to strut their stuff; the burlesque satirized some of the highlights of the earlier two parts.

During the first half-dozen years of its activities, the Ed Christy Minstrels gave more than twenty-five hundred performances. Its success inevitably inspired imitation. All over America, minstrel troupes sprang up like wild mushrooms. Cool White (John Hodges) was the head of one group; many considered him America's foremost minstrel after Ed Christy himself. The Bryant Minstrels was organized and led to success by Dan Emmett, the most important popular composer in America before Stephen Foster. Other groups included the Virginia Serenaders, the Ethiopian Minstrels, the Harrington Minstrels, the Ordway Minstrels.

But by 1890 the demise of the minstrel show was imminent. With the growing intrusion of girls and sex into the musical theater, all-male companies began to lose their hold. A few troupes were still able to keep the hallowed traditions of minstrelsy alive: the Lew Dockstader troupe, for example, or Thatcher, Primrose, and West (later called Primrose and West), or the last of the great minstrels, George "Honey" Evans and Eddie Leonard.

While it flourished, the minstrel show did more than please its audiences for a half-century with the most delightful stage entertainment; it also immeasurably enriched the storehouse of American popular music. Some of America's finest popular songs had been written for—and were introduced and made famous by—these great dusky-faced minstrels. Dan Emmett's "Dixie," today remembered mainly as the leading song of the Southland during the Civil War, started out as a "walkaround" for the Bryant Minstrels in 1859. Emmett wrote other delightful and famous songs for the minstrel show, some of them only slightly less familiar than his "Dixie." Among these are "Old Dan Tucker" and "The Blue Tail Fly," the latter probably better known to most people today as "Jim Crack Corn." Cool White introduced "Lubly Fan" (occasionally identified today as "Buffalo Gals") with the Virginia Serenaders. One of America's first successful nonsense songs was largely made popular by the minstrel Billy Emerson— "Polly Wolly Doodle (author unknown). The first "hide-ho" song ever written was a minstrel-show tune called "De Boatman's Dance," introduced by the Virginia Minstrels. Stephen Foster wrote some of his immortal Negro ballads for Ed Christy, who was the first to bring them to their nationwide prominence—classics such as "Swanee River" and "My Old Kentucky Home." Some years after Foster, his most significant successor as creator of immortal Negro ballads, James A. Bland, himself a Negro, produced "Carry Me Back to Old Virginny," "Hand Me Down My Walking Stick," and "Oh, Dem Golden Slippers"—all of them staples in the minstrel-show repertory throughout the country. Banks Winter's "White Wings," as we said before, achieved its first success with the Thatcher, Primrose, and West Minstrels. And even as the minstrel show was gasping its last breaths, it had enough vitality to contribute several more permanent additions to our song literature—such favorites, for example, as songwriter Eddie Leonard's "Ida" and "Roly, Boly Eyes."

Eddie Leonard had just become a member of the Primrose and West Minstrels when, in 1903, he wrote "Ida." The manager of the company, Jim Decker, did not think highly of Leonard and was planning to fire him. When, therefore, Leonard insisted upon singing his new number, "Ida," in place of one previously selected for him, the company manager agreed as he fully expected this to be Eddie Leonard's last appearance. Singing with that slow drawl and those drawn-out vowels that were the salient characteristics of his style, Leonard created a furor. When he came back into the wings, Jim Decker told him: "Don't bother to pack, Eddie. You're staying with the company." Eddie Leonard now became the star of the troupe and stayed that way for over a decade. He always wore a white satin suit, white topper, and a frilled white shirt, a uniform that became as much a trademark of his as his slow drawl. His delivery of "Roly, Boly Eyes"—the last of his great song successes, published in 1912—was personalized by the way he drew out the words "eyes" to sound like "wa-wah-eyes." By the time "Roly, Boly Eyes" became popular, the minstrel show had lost its hold on theatergoers. But Eddie Leonard kept the song alive in vaudeville (where he was billed as "the last of the great minstrels").

While the minstrel show was dying out, vaudeville was beginning to reach a peak of national acceptance. It was to vaudeville, more than to any other branch of the musical theater, that the Tin Pan Alley of 1890 and the early 1900's owed its greatest debt. The history of vaudeville and Tin Pan Alley overlaps so frequently that it is hardly possible to speak of one without discussing the other.

Vaudeville (initially dubbed "variety") was a legitimate offspring of the minstrel show. Vaudeville, after all, was just a "fantasia" lifted out of the context of the minstrel show and stripped of minstrel costumes and burnt cork. The word "vaudeville" comes from *vau-de-Vire*, the French word that had taken on the meaning of "lively songs." The word "vaudeville" was used for the first time in the United States on February 23, 1871, at Weisiger's Hall in Louisville, Kentucky, when a troupe headed by H. J. Sargent presented a variety performance. In billboards and on programs the company identified itself as "Sargent's Great Vaudeville Company from Chicago." In the 1880's a touring company of variety artists also used the term "vaudeville" to describe its entertainment; and the first theater to call itself a vaudeville house opened during the same period in San Antonio, Texas.

One person above all others is now credited with establishing vaudeville as a favored form of stage entertainment. He was Tony Pastor (born Antonio Pastore), a one-time minstrel whose forte had been singing popular songs to his own banjo accompaniment. After leaving minstrel shows, Pastor joined a circus where he was a man of many roles: clown, ringmaster, comedian, singer, tumbler, bareback rider. From circus he graduated into variety entertainment, appearing in blackface and introducing a routine he made famous: singing topical songs (many of which he wrote himself) in which the events of the day were described in words and music. Later in his career, Tony Pastor devised a catch question and answer in one of his topical numbers that grew so popular that the words are believed to have carried Mayor Hewitt into New York's city hall. The sentences were: "What's the matter with Hewitt? He's all right!"

Tony Pastor opened his first theater devoted to variety entertainment in Paterson, New Jersey, on March 21, 1865. Pastor's aim was "wholesome entertainment" that every member of the family could enjoy. In those years (and for some time thereafter) only adult males and women of questionable reputation habitually attended the theater, which was regarded as disreputable. Pastor, however, was convinced that if he eliminated smoking and drinking inside the theater, disinfected the acts of smutty comedy, and covered female limbs, he could attract to show business a large new clientele—women and children. A clientele such as this could be counted on to keep the auditorium filled even on weekday afternoons when the menfolk were busy working.

His first experiment, however, did not prove too heartening. Women, still suspicious of the stage, stayed away, and children were still kept away. But Pastor apparently didn't lose heart. A year later he opened another variety theater, this time in downtown New York: the Tony Pastor Variety Theater or, as it was soon more popularly called, Pastor's Opera House. As bait to a female audience, he gave door prizes of groceries, kitchenware, dress patterns, toys. The women started coming, dragging their children with them. Before long all became delighted with the varied visual and aural delights found on Tony Pastor's stage—the jugglers, comedians, ballad singers, animal trainers, tap dancers, acrobats, one-act sketches, blackface minstrels. But it was the door prizes that initially established the popularity of variety with women folk. "I am quite serious," wrote James L. Ford in *Forty Odd Years in the Literary Shop*, "[in saying] that the most important moment in the history of the development of the theater in this country was that in which Tony Pastor first gave away his coal, flour, dress patterns to secure the patronage of respectable women."

In 1875, Tony Pastor moved to a different locale on Broadway. He stayed there six years. During this period, in 1878, he became the first producer of variety entertainment to tour parts of the United States. Then on October 24, 1881, Tony Pastor opened his Music Hall on East Fourteenth Street. His well-chosen bill included eight acts, among them an English music-hall singer, a monologist, a singer of comic songs, and an acrobat. He advertised his new house in the *Dramatic Mirror* as "the first specialty vaudeville theater of America, catering to polite tastes, aiming to amuse, and fully up to current times and topics." This was the place that almost at once became the leading vaudeville theater in America, the home of stars, the stage on which more than one formerly obscure and unknown performer scaled the heights.

When a little less than two months after the Music Hall opened, Lillian Russell made there her vaudeville debut—November 22, 1881—she was completely unknown. She had auditioned for Tony Pastor under her real name of Helene Louise Leonard. Pastor liked the way she looked—with her rich blond hair, voluptuous body, and hourglass figure. "She radiated a serene beauty and a calm confidence in her own loveliness," was the way Allen Churchill described her in *The Great White Way*. Tony Pastor also liked the way she sang, the way she "delivered with dignity or humor and sang in a voice which high-domed James

Huneker compared to a teakettle," in Churchill's words. "She was able to hit High C without apparent effort." But what Tony Pastor did not like was her name. He coined a new one for her, that of Lillian Russell, and booked her for his theater. And in doing so, he started her off on a career that would contribute much of the luster and glamour to the nineties.

Tony Pastor's huge success at the Music Hall inevitably invited imitators. Competitors appeared throughout New York: Proctor's on Fifth Avenue; Koster and Bial's on West Twenty-third Street; Hyde and Behman's on Adams Street in Brooklyn; later on, the Brighton Beach Theater in Brighton Beach, Brooklyn. Then in 1904, when Oscar Hammerstein built the Victoria on Forty-second Street, a new temple of vaudeville had come to New York, to remain without a rival until the Palace Theater opened on March 25, 1913. For almost twenty years, the Palace was the vaudeville showplace of America; and when the Palace stopped presenting top vaudeville, vaudeville was through.

Vaudeville spread out in ever-widening circles. B. F. Keith, a graduate from the circus, effected a minor revolution in 1883 by instituting continuous vaudeville (instead of two-a-day) at the Gaiety Theater in Boston. B. F. Keith was also responsible for opening a major vaudeville house in Boston—the Colonial, in 1893. The Majestic, the first million-dollar theater in America, opened in Chicago on January 1, 1906, under the direction of J. Murdock. The Orpheum in San Francisco brought top-flight variety entertainment to the West Coast.

It was not long after B. F. Keith had opened the Colonial that he went into partnership with E. F. Albee (another veteran of the circus) to start a chain of some seventy vaudeville theaters that spanned the whole country. In 1907, Keith joined with Proctor to form the Proctor

Amusement Company to manage several hundred vaude-ville theaters throughout the United States. Still other vaudeville circuits were organized by Klaw and Erlanger, by Alexander Pantages, by Martin Beck. Thus by the early 1900's vaudeville became a centralized operation whereby an act could travel by a circuit route throughout the country without changing material for years. The circuit —whether that of E. F. Albee, Keith and Proctor, or the Orpheum managed by Martin Beck—now became a series of steppingstones whereby actors could become stars and songs could grow into hits.

Vaudevillians, carrying a song on a circuit touching every major American city and many of the smaller ones, became a powerful agency for its promotion. Publishers could always tell when a certain vaudeville headliner played in a specific city: by the sudden spurt of sheet-music business from that place. And, because a vaudevillain re-tained a single act for a number of years (or until the cir-cuit had been covered two or three times) a song could be kept alive in public interest for an indefinite period. The life span of a sheet-music publication was thereby ex-tended. Even the older and more conservative publishers became convinced that it was important to place songs in vaudeville acts. And it was from their early experiences with vaudeville that the younger publishers in Tin Pan Al-ley came to realize that the first problem in their business was to get a vaudevillian to use their songs.

Many of the leading song hits of the 1870's and 1880's had started out in vaudeville. Harry Kennedy's lachrymose ballad "A Flower from Mother's Grave" (its writing in-spired by the death of an infant) was first sung by the com-poser himself in Brooklyn in 1878 before its popularity was enhanced through his subsequent appearances in vaude-ville in the major cities. The first Pat Rooney began his successful career in vaudeville in 1883 with a soft-shoe dance to one of his own numbers, "Is That You, Mr. Riley?", that caught on at once. The still-familiar "While Strolling Through the Park One Day" credited to Robert A. Keiser, was introduced at Tony Pastor's in 1884 by the Du Rell Twin Brothers. Its fame grew by leaps and bounds as the Du Rells toured with it, initiating several routines that later performers would borrow—namely, interpolating a soft-shoe dance while singing the chorus and lifting the hat at the "ah" just before the end of the number. In 1888, Joe Flynn wrote "Down Went McGinty" about an accident-prone Irishman and introduced it in his vaudeville act at Hyde and Behman's on Adams Street. His partner Sheridan sang the verse and chorus, after which Flynn repeated both with dramatic gestures. It was not long before "Down Went McGinty" became one of vaudeville's best-known and most frequently sung comic numbers. Maggie Cline gave a lusty presentation of John W. Kelly's "Throw Him Down, McCloskey" at Tony Pastor's in 1890. Striding athletically across the stage, as she swung her hips and tossed her powerful voice across the footlights (all the while accompanied by backstage noises and shouts), Maggie Cline electrified her audiences with this musical description of a brawl in which a small fellow triumphed over a fighter twice his size. A few years later Vestra Victoria, the English comedienne, sang "Daddy Wouldn't Buy Me a Bow-wow" at Tony Pastor's, and her use of ridiculous baby talk made it one of the leading comedy numbers of the time.

Second in importance to vaudeville (as far as placement of songs went) was burlesque. "To place a ballad . . . in a burlesque show was the infallible method in the nineties, and long afterward, of establishing a hit and insuring great profits," wrote Bernard Sobel, burlesque's distinguished historian. "The runs were long and by the time one show after another presented a song the whole country knew the tune by heart. Thus composers and song publishers went to great lengths to place their numbers and displace competitors."

The beginnings of burlesque in America came in 1869 when Lydia Thompson and her British Blondes appeared in *Ixion* at Wood's Theater in New York. The elaborate plot was just an excuse to exhibit expensive sets and costumes, songs, dances, humor, and most of all, girls in tights. The girls in tights, of course, stole the show and created a furor. Stimulated by the success of *Ixion*, Michael Leavitt produced a new kind of entertainment for America called *Mme. Rentz's Female Minstrels*. It combined elements of the minstrel show, vaudeville, and extravaganza, to which was added the interest of girls in flesh-colored tights. Other girls wore gowns slashed down the side to reveal legs and thighs. "New York hadn't seen anything like it," Pauline Markham, one of these girls, recalled later. "Every time my leg made its appearance outside the cut skirt it was greeted with great guffaws from some of the men present."

Michael Leavitt scored such a hit with this production that he decided to make it an annual showpiece for New York. He now called his entertainment the Rentz-Santley Shows—the "Santley" in the title being Mabel Santley, his most celebrated beauty. Season after season he mounted burlesque shows that in pretentiousness of production and costuming, and in the lavish exhibition of female beauty and limbs, anticipated the *Ziegfeld Follies*. These shows, explains Bernard Sobel, were "substantial entertainments with a great deal of rough-and-tumble humor. Tights were plentiful but nudity was undreamed of. There were no hootch-dancers, and aside from the occasional double entendre, little salaciousness. The dancing, though not as expert as it is today, was good." The hootchy-kootchy dancer—and after that the strip tease—were later refinements of burlesque. Meanwhile, out of these Rentz-Santley productions there stepped forward the first female performer to be dubbed the "Queen of Burlesque." She was May Howard, who in time became the manager of her own burlesque company (and the wife of Paul Dresser). But the May Howard company was not the only important successor to Rentz-Santley. Between 1870 and 1880, companies like the Ada Richmond Burlesquers and Ada Kennedy's African Blonde Minstrels became exceedingly popular. In Chicago, Sam T. Jack operated for many years a burlesque company of his own. Various other burlesque troupes flourished elsewhere in the country: at Butler's Standard in St. Louis; at the Theatre Comique in Washington, D.C.; at Pence Opera House in Minneapolis; at the Park Theater in Detroit; at the Academy of Music in Pittsburgh.

As had happened with vaudeville, circuits soon sprang up that enabled companies to tour from city to city and which placed various companies and theaters under a single managing head. There was the Traveling Variety Managers' Association of which Samuel A. Scribner was the president; the Eastern Circuit of House Managers, George Krauss president; in the West, the Empire Association, with J. L. Kernan and James J. Butler as directors; and, finally, in 1900 the Columbia Circuit founded by Sam Scribner.

It was in burlesque that amateur nights first became an attraction in American theaters—fertile ground not only for the aspiring young performers but also for music publishers seeking a place in which to spot songs. This development took place at Miner's Bowery Theater in New York in the early 1900's. Friday night became traditional for these amateur performances, and there, one evening in 1908, the boy Eddie Cantor earned his first five dollars in show business.

It was in burlesque that many a later star cut his eye

teeth as a performer—Bert Lahr, Fanny Brice, W. C. Fields, Sophie Tucker, Leon Errol, Jack Pearl, Bobby Clark, Gypsy Rose Lee, Joe Cook, to name just a few. And it was in burlesque, of all places, that the father of modern arrangements got his musical start and his first musical experiences—Frank Sadler, who in the 1910's did most of the arrangements for Jerome Kern's musical comedies.

While few new songs were written for burlesque, and few were introduced there, burlesque was nevertheless a beehive of song activity and helped many a song grow to popularity and stay there a long time.

Besides minstrel shows, vaudeville, and burlesque, American theatergoers were entertained in the 1880's and 1890's by such other forms of the musical theater as the operetta and the extravaganza. These were seen in Union Square at the Alhambra and the Union Square Theater, and within a short distance, at the Globe, the Theatre Comique, the Bijou, the Standard, the Broadway, and the Fifth Avenue. Though the musical theater was still partial to foreign importations—and particularly to the comic operas of Gilbert and Sullivan, the opéra-comiques of Offenbach, and the operettas of Johann Strauss II and Suppé—American composers and librettists were starting to get heard.

One of the earliest American musicals in which the entire score was written expressly for the production (rather than being made up of adaptations and interpolations) was *Evangeline*, an extravaganza produced in 1874. E. E. Rice wrote all the music for this spectacle based on the poem of Longfellow. Then in 1887 there came the first successful comic opera by an American—Willard Spencer's *The Little Tycoon*, which enjoyed a several-year run in New York and Philadelphia. Between 1878 and 1885, David Braham, an American composer of English birth, became the first to write complete scores for a series of musical productions. Braham wrote all the music for the Harrigan and Hart burlesques that came to be known as the "Mulligan" series. These were set in New York and were filled with recognizable New York characters involved in everyday situations, complications, and problems.

Little by little, then, American songwriters were beginning to invade the American musical theater—sometimes with complete scores, more often with single songs. Some of the leading hits of the 1880's—which emerged from neither the minstrel show nor vaudeville—were first heard in operettas and extravaganzas. "Remember, Boy, You're Irish" was one of several Irish ditties that William J. Scanlan wrote for *Shane na Lawn*, and it penetrated the sheet-music market through the presses of T. B. Harms. "Drill, Ye Tarriers," probably by Thomas Casey (others insist that its creator is unknown), was quietly slipped into the second act of the Charles Hoyt extravaganza *A Brass Monkey*, at the Bijou Theater in 1889, where it was sung by a trio dressed up as tarriers (construction men). It brought down the house, and during the next few years it was often heard in vaudeville, most often in Maggie Cline's lusty and uninhibited presentation. From Braham's various scores for the Harrigan and Hart burlesque extravaganzas came such popular ditties as "The Skidmore Fancy Ball," "The Babies on Our Block," and "My Dad's Dinner Pail," all with lyrics by Edward Harrigan. And we have already seen what happened to "After the Ball," after J. Aldrich Libbey interpolated it in *A Trip to Chinatown* in 1902.

The stage was not the only place where a song could pass from performer to audience in the 1880's and 1890's. From downtown Chatham Square and the Bowery up to Thirty-fourth Street—but with a particular concentration in the Union Square area—there could be found numerous saloons, beer halls, wine cellars, restaurants and other places where good fellows could get together. In those days when good fellows gathered they gave voice to songs.

Some of these places boasted only a piano; some had a small ensemble; some a full-sized orchestra. Some featured a singing star whose name was inextricably linked with that of the place where she or he appeared. Many employed singing waiters. Minnie Schulte, a voluptuous blond, drew patrons into George Huber's Prospect Gardens, of which her husband was the proprietor. Maude Nugent was for many years the main attraction at The Abbey on Eighth Avenue near Thirty-fourth Street, where she introduced her own song "Sweet Rosie O'Grady." Herman's, also on Eighth Avenue but nine blocks below The Abbey, had a large orchestra and several specialty acts. The Atlantic Gardens on the Bowery near Canal Street, favored by a German clientele, featured the country's first woman orchestra; later on, Jessie Lindsay created a furor there with her performances of "Daisy Bell" (or "A Bicycle Built for Two"). The Winter Garden in Union Square had a six-piece ensemble. Before Ben Harney became a headliner at Tony Pastor's, he played piano rags at McGurk's on the Bowery or at McGlory's Armory Hall on Hester Street. And before James Thornton became famous for his sentimental ballads, he was a singing waiter at Bal Mabile in Greenwich Village.

There was a good deal of singing at home, as well as in public places; this was the main reason the song business started to boom in the early 1890's. Since the genteel womenfolk of that period still looked suspiciously on musical shows and public eating-and-drinking-places, a good deal of entertainment had to be concentrated in the family parlor. The most popular form of such entertainment was the singing of current hits from sheet music, the singers grouped around the family piano (and later the player piano). The males liked nothing better than to collaborate in some close harmony: the tenor voice sang above the melody; the second tenor carried the tune; and the other two voices filled in the harmony. This type of male singing soon came to be known as barbershop quartets—though it originated not in barbershops but in the home. Barbershop-quartet singing became such a favored pastime in the 1880's and 1890's that it is hardly possible to bring up a picture of that period without evoking the image of four males—garters holding up the sleeves of shirts, gold teeth gleaming below flowing mustaches, hair parted in the middle—chanting the strains of "Sweet Adeline" or a like ballad.

In order to sing and play the current hits, people had to buy sheet music. The market for sheet music started to grow active in the 1880's, and in the 1890's it developed so extensively that department stores had to install sheet-music counters. In the early 1900's newspapers began publishing supplements containing the words and music of some current hit songs, and department stores were printing songs to distribute as throwaways as a means of advertising. In the early 1880's a hit song might reach a fifty-thousand-copy sale, but by the 1890's a sale of less than a quarter-million copies was not regarded highly, while several songs hit the jackpot with a sales figure touching and passing the million mark. Charles K. Harris' "After the Ball" is usually regarded as the first popular song to sell well over a million copies. In fact, by selling more than five million copies, "After the Ball" became the first song to indicate that popular music had become a giant industry.

# 3

## "Cry me a river"

Tin Pan Alley was built on the foundation stones of sentimental ballads. What had happened to Charles K. Harris'
"After the Ball" in 1892 was to be repeated again and again
by many other publishers and composers. A single ballad
would transform a menial publishing establishment into an
empire, and an unknown and impoverished composer into
a tycoon.

It is fitting that the sentimental ballad prospered as it
did in Tin Pan Alley in the 1890's. This was essentially a sentimental era. It paid lip service to morality, virginity, and
basic virtues in unctuous phrases. It regarded the home, the
wife, the family as sacrosanct; the mother, as a boy's best
friend; a sister or a daughter, beyond the touch of sordid
realities. Man was the sovereign of his domain. He made

the rules that his womenfolk obeyed. He might invade places forbidden to his wife, daughter, or sister. He might toast—with champagne in slippers in fancy restaurants—women who lived on the other side of respectability; he might even consider it the ultimate in sophistication to cavort with the glamorous female stars of the stage. But this in no way interfered with, or was regarded as a contradiction to, his sanctimonious attitudes at home. His wife lived in a world of her own. Possibly as a reaction to the way in which her husband entertained less moral companions away from home, his wife made a fetish of respectability. She swathed herself in a multitude of garments, her skirt floating atop layer upon layer of petticoats; her corset strapped around her body like protective armor; her peek-a-boo shirtwaist and mutton sleeves permitting little flesh to be seen. To her, the women of the night spots—for all their finery and diamonds—were unfortunate, to be regarded with a mingling of pity and contempt, because so few of them would ever know the blessings of marital life, children, and the security and peace that respectability brought.

The 1890's was a sentimental era, but it was also a gay one, with a gloss and a glitter that often concealed the rough and scabrous edges below the surface. America might suffer bank failures and depressions; but in Chicago the World's Columbian Exposition of 1893 was the magnificent window-dressing to convince the rest of the world that this country was riding on the crest of prosperity toward ever greater power and significance. On October 9, 1893, when the country was in the depths of an economic collapse, almost three-quarters of a million people visited the Exposition, whose importance, said Harry Thurston Peck, lay "in the fact that it revealed to millions of Americans whose lives were necessarily colorless and narrow, the splendid possibilities of art, and the compelling power of the beautiful."

There was prosperity and plenty—for the few. The exploitation of America's limitless resources by an oligarchy had begun. The age of trusts, industrial kings, and utility magnates was at hand. The *nouveaux riches* had risen from humble origins to become men of consequence in the social and financial worlds. They were ready to play hard, live intensely, and spend lavishly.

Ornate display was the order of the day, symbolized by the potted palm in hotels and public places, a suggestion of opulence. Tiger rugs, Oriental weapons as decorations, Biedermeier-type furniture, all contributed a touch of luxury and flamboyance to the home. Even greater magnificence could be encountered in the newer hotels. The Imperial, which opened on Broadway and Thirty-second Street in 1890, marked a new day for America in architectural magnificence—with its green marble Palm Room, marble lobby with gilt decorations, and sweeping staircase.

Overeating and overdrinking was as much the rule of the day as overdressing and overindulgence in diamond displays. Diamond Jim Brady prided himself as much for his gastronomic feats as for the diamonds that he wore to such excess. Pleasure was king; glamour, queen. The hunt for good times among the affluent brought on an unprecedented prosperity to any place providing good entertainment and good food; and the fetish for glamour helped to make goddesses of such stage stars as Lillian Russell.

The ballads of the 1890's reflected the era by sentimentalizing over home, virtue, parental and filial devotion, while lamenting over those who followed a life of sin or sold themselves for gold. In all these songs, virtue was ever its own reward, and vice always met its just punishment.

Between the two polar points separating virtue and vice lay an extensive field for song fertilization: the constancy or fickleness of lovers; the pathos of misunderstandings and separations; the pathetic plight of abandoned wives or children; the tragedy of death. Many of these ballads not only squeezed every ounce of sentiment they could from a given situation, but also went on to build a complete story of woe —with the beginning, middle, and end of a short story— through a succession of verses.

That these songs were an echo of the mores of the times was one of the reasons why sentimental ballads of the 1890's went out of their way to glorify the pure and excoriate the wicked. Another reason lay in the fact that the greatest single market for sheet music was the family circle spending evenings around the piano singing ballads. Since women—carefully sheltered from the unsavory world outside their protected households—dominated this audience, the songs had to make a direct appeal to their moral standards and had to satisfy their partiality for tear-provoking sagas.

Four composers dominated the world of the sentimental ballad in the 1890's, but none was more significant than Paul Dresser, whose "The Pardon Came Too Late" in 1891 was one of the first great song successes of the decade. Like Charles K. Harris before him—and many a composer after him—Dresser soon came to realize that there was much more money in publishing than in songwriting. As the staff composer for Willis Woodward he was casting about for a way in which he might get more profit from his songs. F. B. Haviland, an employee at the Oliver Ditson publishing house, and Pat Howley, the manager of Willis Woodward who had brought Dresser to the firm, finally became the instruments whereby Dresser became his own publisher.

Haviland and Howley had for a long time been discussing the possibilities of setting up an independent publishing operation of their own. When they felt the time was ripe for such an adventure, they invited Dresser to come along with them as a partner and staff composer. Early in the 1890's the three men formed the George T. Worth Company, with a capital of about two hundred dollars, and opened a one-room office at East Twentieth Street. The name "George T. Worth" was a blind, concealing the identity of the proprietors; since neither Howley nor Haviland wanted as yet to give up their respective jobs, they did not want their bosses to know they had set up a competitive business. But Howley soon discovered he needed all his time and energy for his new firm; and when Howland's association with the firm of George T. Worth was uncovered by Ditson, he was forced to give up that job and concentrate on his own publishing venture. In 1894, the new establishment assumed the name of Howley, Haviland and Company. Paul Dresser's name would be affixed to those of Howley and Haviland a few years later.

The year of 1894 was also the one in which the newcomers had their first song hit, "The Sidewalks of New York." Its lyricist, John D. Blake, was a salesman in a hatter's shop who liked writing verses. One day, Charles Lawlor, a vaudevillian, entered the shop humming a melody. When Blake learned that the tune was original with Lawlor and expressed interest in it, the composer suggested that Blake write a lyric for the melody. "Something about New York," he suggested to Blake as an afterthought. Between his selling chores at the shop, Blake scribbled down his verses. Lottie Gilson—dubbed "the Little Magnet" because she was such a draw at the box office—liked the song and introduced it in 1894 at the Old London Theater in the Bowery. It was so well received that she had to repeat both verse and chorus, and at the repetition of the refrain the audience joined in. Pat Howley bought the song from its authors for a straight cash fee and issued it in 1894. The sheet-music sale soared at once, and Lottie Gilson's renditions in vaudeville houses around the country kept the sales going for the next few years. Since that time, the song has become the one with which the city of New York is most often identified in music. During the 1924 Democratic convention, Alfred E. Smith adopted it as his presidential campaign song. An alert reporter, seeing how many of the coatless delegates were rallying to the Smith candidacy under the stimulus of the tune, decided to find out what had happened to its writers. Lawlor was dead. But Blake was found performing in a little obscure vaudeville theater in Brooklyn. Asked by the reporter if he had read in that day's papers that "The Sidewalks of New York" had been adopted as Al Smith's campaign song, Blake turned an expressionless face toward the interviewer. He did not have to answer: the interviewer now realized that Blake was blind. In 1933, the New York *Herald Tribune*, learning that Blake was penniless, created a fund to clothe, house, and feed him, and continued to support him until his death two years later.

During the first half dozen years or so following the issue of "The Sidewalks of New York," Howley, Haviland and Company published a number of other songs that sold well. But it was because of Paul Dresser's ballads that the new firm had to seek larger quarters on Thirty-second Street; and it was due to Dresser's ballads that Howley, Haviland became a major power in Tin Pan Alley. As long as Dresser remained productive and successful, so long did Howley, Haviland remain a major institution in the Alley. Their big song of 1895 was Dresser's ballad "Just Tell Them That You Saw Me," which grew so popular that the title developed into a popular catch phrase among newspapermen, entertainers, and sophisticates; a manufacturer profited from this Dresser success by producing buttons with the phrase printed across the face, which gay blades everywhere wore on their lapels.

In 1896 the Dresser hits included "He Brought Home Another" and "I Wonder If She'll Ever Come Back to Me"; in 1897, "If You See My Sweetheart" and "On the Banks of the Wabash"; in 1898, "The Old Flame Flickers"; in 1899, "The Curse of the Dreamer" and "I Wonder Where She Is Tonight"; in 1900, "I'd Still Believe You True." He also produced war songs during the Spanish-American conflict, and postwar songs when it was over. Dresser's importance to his publishing house was acknowledged in 1901 when its name was officially changed to Howley, Haviland and Dresser and a larger percentage of the profits was assigned to him. Almost as if in celebration, Dresser went on to write and publish no less than six hit songs in 1901, including the still-familiar "Way Down in Old Indiana." (This song is not to be confused with the later ballad "Back Home Again in Indiana," with words by Ballard MacDonald and music by James F. Hanley, published in 1917.)

His most famous ballad was "On the Banks of the Wabash," still the most popular number about the state of Indiana. Theodore Dreiser, the composer's brother, once wrote that it was he who had suggested to Paul the Wabash River as a subject for song treatment, since rivers had done particularly well in such literature; Dreiser even maintained that he had helped Dresser with the lyric. But Max Hoffman, Witmark's orchestrator, gives quite a different account, and the one now considered authoritative. (This account appears in *Story of the House of Witmark: From Ragtime to Swingtime* by Isidore Witmark and Isaac Goldberg.) "I went to his room at the Auditorium Hotel [Chicago] where, instead of a piano there was a folding camp organ, Paul always carried with him. It was summer. All the windows were open and Paul was mulling over a melody that was practically in finished form. But he did not have the words. So he had me play the full chorus over and over again at least for two or three hours while he was writing down the words, changing a line here and a phrase there, until the lyric suited him. . . . When Paul came to the line 'through the sycamores the candlelights are gleaming,' I was tremendously impressed. . . . I have always felt that Paul got the idea from glancing out of the window now and again as he wrote, and seeing the lights glimmering on Lake Michigan. . . . The song was published precisely as I arranged it. . . . During the whole evening we spent together, Paul made no mention of anyone's having helped him with the song."

Dresser was a huge man, weighing over three hundred pounds. He wrote most of his songs on an organ at one or the other of two Broadway hotels he made his New York home over a period of many years—the Gilsey House on Twenty-ninth Street and the Marlborough on Thirty-sixth. He liked nothing better than to play one of his new numbers for a singer like Dick José, whose dulcet voice was admirably suited to Dresser's ballads and who had introduced a good many of them, including "Your Mother Wants You Home, Boy," "Calling to Her Boy Just Once Again," "Every Night There's a Light," "He Fought for a Cause She Thought Was Right," "I Wonder Where She Is Tonight," and "In Dear Old Illinois." While singing his own ballads, whether to José to to somebody else, Dresser would become so moved by the pathos of his own ballad that frequently he would burst into sobs and have difficulty finishing.

"He seemed to have a peculiar fondness for the twilight hour," Paul's brother Theodore Dreiser revealed, "at which time most often he might be found thrumming one or another strain, until at last some particular one might capture his fancy and presently he might be in tears.

The sighings over home and mother and lost sweethearts and dead heroes that were here!"

Dresser lived in grand style, entertained regally, spent money recklessly, and was always ready with a generous handout. He earned somewhere in the neighborhood of half a million dollars and spent every cent of it. Then things started to go in reverse. Beginning with 1902 the sales of his ballads slipped badly. By 1903 the Dresser songs were doing so poorly that the firm of Howley, Haviland and Dresser would have been in deep trouble had it not issued Theodore Morse's hit song "Dear Old Girl," the income from which kept the firm from bankruptcy. Finally, in 1904, Haviland left the organization to form a new company of his own in partnership with Theodore Morse. He called the firm F. B. Haviland, opened offices at Thirty-seventh Street and Broadway, and started business with the outstandingly successful Morse song "Blue Bell." Meanwhile, Howley, Haviland and Dresser carried on as best it could with Pat Howley and Paul Dresser—at a more modest location in the Holland Building. But its days were numbered, and in 1905 they called it quits.

Dresser now went into publishing for himself in a two-room place on Twenty-eighth Street. He was convinced that he still was able to write a ballad capable of rehabilitating his fortunes. Though completely impoverished, he continued to appear in Tin Pan Alley in sartorial elegance, wearing a dapper frock coat and silk top hat. His was the confident air of a man not only long accustomed to affluence but also of one convinced it would return before many more days. He kept on insisting to his colleagues in the Alley that his next hit would be the greatest of them all. Nobody believed him. Those whom he had so long wined and dined, and to whom he had loaned money so generously without asking for its return, deserted him.

Even his personal life had become bankrupt. He had

married May Howard—the first of the burlesque queens —whose extra-marital indiscretions began almost as soon as she had pronounced her marriage vows. Then she deserted both him and their infant child for another man. Dresser sublimated his bitterness (as one might have expected) in a sentimental ballad, "The Curse," which he never published. Then tracing May's whereabouts, he sang his ballad to her and through its tearful sentiment effected a temporary reconciliation. But May was beyond reformation. An attempt to resume a normal marital status collapsed. Dresser now rewrote "The Curse" and assigned to it the kind of happy ending he himself was fated never to enjoy. Now entitled "The Curse of the Dreamer," it was published in 1899 and became a huge success.

If his marital life sounds like the text of one of his ballads, so do his last days. Dresser *did* have one more big song hit in him. It was "My Gal Sal," which in time rivaled even "On the Banks of the Wabash" in popularity and financial rewards. "It's the best song I've ever written," he kept telling his skeptical colleagues. "It's a million-copy hit, but I can't push it because I'm broke." He published it in 1905. It was introduced in vaudeville by Louise Dresser, a popular singer whom Paul had discovered and helped make successful, which was why she adopted his name. From there, it went on to exceed Paul Dresser's own enthusiastic prognostication. It sold not one but several million copies. But Dresser did not live to witness the victory. He died a pauper in his sister's home in Brooklyn on January 30, 1906. Had his death been the subject of one of his ballads, surely the diagnosis of his last fatal illness would have been heartbreak.

In 1942, Paul Dresser's biography was filmed in Hollywood, with Victor Mature playing the composer; the script was by his brother Theodore Dreiser. It was named "My

Gal Sal" after the song Dresser did not live to see grow
famous.

During its heyday between 1895 and 1902, Howley,
Haviland (and later on, Howley, Haviland and Dresser)
published a number of highly impressive numbers by composers other than Dresser. In 1896 one of its leading songs
was the ballad "In the Baggage Coach Ahead," the work of
Tin Pan Alley's first successful Negro composer, Gussie
Davis. Davis was a man able to profit from his experiences.
While sweeping the floors of the Cincinnati Conservatory
of Music, where he worked as a janitor, he picked up dribs
and drabs of musical knowledge. He soon put these to use
by writing ballads. The first to get published was "The
Lighthouse by the Sea," issued by a small Cincinnati printer
in 1886. When the sheet music was displayed in the printer's windows, Davis would stand outside day after day
pointing out the display to passers-by he had stopped with
the comment: "See that? That's *me*." In 1887 he wrote and
had published "Wait Till the Tide Comes In."

His first hit was "The Fatal Wedding" in 1893, a pathetic saga about a wedding interrupted by the arrival of
the groom's real wife—with her baby. The baby dies in
her arms, and the groom commits suicide. After the double
funeral, the two women go to live with one another. "The
Fatal Wedding," introduced by a minstrel-show troupe in
Cincinnati, proved a sensation and remained such in renditions in vaudeville theaters all over the country. An inter-
esting musical feature of this ballad was the fact that it
quoted a musical excerpt from Mendelssohn's Wedding
March.

In 1894, Davis tried to capitalize on the success of "The
Bowery" by writing a competitive number called, "Only
a Bowery Boy," but it didn't do too well. A year after that,

he wrote the lyrics to "Down in Poverty Row"; the music was composed by Arthur Trevelyan, an Englishman. This number was one of the selections most often asked for that year at the Bal Mabile in Greenwich Village, where pert Bonnie Thornton was the favorite performer.

Davis' varied experience served him well when he set out to write the song that brought him fame—"In the Baggage Coach Ahead"—and which helped make Howley, Haviland and Dresser affluent. Davis had once been employed as a Pullman porter when, on one of his train rides, he came upon a child crying bitterly. When he inquired about the trouble, the child, between choked sobs, informed him that its mother was in the baggage coach ahead —in a coffin. A fellow porter, to whom Davis described this pathetic incident, was impelled to write a poem about it. Some years later, after Davis had left his railroad job to become a songwriter, he came upon this poem. In an age that seemed to find morbid delight in ballads about deaths, coffins, and graves, the poem appeared to Davis as ideal material for a song. Thus he wrote "In the Baggage Coach Ahead" and sold it outright to Howley, Haviland for a few dollars. Pat Howley induced Imogene Comer, "queen of song" as she was billed in vaudeville, to use it on the circuit. She kept it in her act three years—three years of sheet-music sales that reaped a fortune for the publishers, but nothing, beyond the pittance that had originally been paid, for its creator.

Among the large sales amassed by Howley, Haviland in 1898 and 1899 were those from two numbers written by Monroe Rosenfeld: "Gold Will Buy 'Most Anything" and "She Was Happy Till She Met You." Long before he had devised, or helped to devise as the case may be, the name of Tin Pan Alley for the song industry, Monroe Rosenfeld laid some of the groundwork for the music industry through his successful ballads. He had come from Cincinnati in the early 1880's on the advice and encouragement of the publisher Frank Harding. A man of varied talents, Rosenfeld started to earn his living in New York by writing pieces for the newspapers. After that, at different periods, he found employment as a press agent, a writer of short stories, an arranger and adapter of songs, and a composer. He also earned extra dollars by selling song ideas to writers, composers, and publishers.

He was a man who drank nothing stronger than water and who could take women or leave them strictly to themselves. But one vice held him mercilessly in its grip. He was a chronic horse better—and a chronic loser. To raise money for this expensive hobby he sold many of his songs for a few dollars apiece, just enough to bring him to the track and to place one or two bets. He was not beyond lifting other people's songs or lyrics and palming them off as his own work on unsuspecting publishers; nor did his conscience ever trouble him when he sold the same song to two different publishers in return for a small cash consideration from each. He even evolved his own technique in selling songs. He would interest one publisher in a suitable idea for a ballad and receive from him an advance of, say, twenty-five dollars. For half that amount he commissioned some other impoverished writer to do the number for him.

When all else failed in bringing him cash, he would be driven to extremes. In one instance he passed off a fraudulent check. When the police closed in on him, he jumped out of a second-story window and permanently injured his leg. He managed to elude arrest, but he paid for his indiscretion by going around with a perceptible limp for the rest of his life. He always wore bell-bottom sailor trousers in an effort to conceal his deformity.

Rosenfeld's first big year as a songwriter came in 1884 with two numbers issued under pseudonyms, and with "Up the Golden Stairs," soon to become a favorite in minstrel shows. A fourth, "Good-by, My Boy, Good-by," had the largest sheet-music sale a Rosenfeld song had thus far enjoyed.

The tune of his hit song in 1886, "Johnny, Get Your Gun" (a phrase well remembered by George M. Cohan when many years later he wrote "Over There") had been lifted bodily from an earlier jig, "Johnny, Get Your Hair Cut." His greatest success in the 1880's came with the sentimental ballad, "With All Her Faults I Love Her Still." This melody was pilfered from a song written some years earlier in Germany by Theodore Metz, which Rosenfeld had heard Metz play at Wilson's Pavilion in Harlem. Metz's amazement, as well as anger, therefore, can be fully appreciated when—as musical director of the Primrose and West Minstrels—he was handed the music of "With All Her Faults" and was told that it was Rosenfeld's song. Nevertheless, it was with that company that this ballad was introduced by Dick José, and it was here that it first became popular.

When Rosenfeld's big hit in 1894, "And Her Golden Hair Was Hanging Down Her Back," first appeared, the sheet music credited him as composer. But the melody actually was the work of Felix McGlennon—Rosenfeld had just been the arranger. On the other hand (perhaps to even the count), the sheet music of Rosenfeld's "Take Back Your Gold" in 1897 named Louis W. Pritzkow as lyricist. But it was Rosenfeld who had written the lyrics. He had bribed Pritzkow, a popular minstrel, to use the song in his show by giving him both the cash and the credit for doing the lyrics. "Take Back Your Gold" was one of the songs that first brought Emma Carus to recognition in vaudeville—the robust and dynamic shouter of songs who used to preface her act with the line "I'm not pretty, but I'm good to my family!" Emma Carus plugged "Take Back Your Gold" incessantly in her act, possibly as a way of pay-

ing back Rosenfeld an old debt. For it was Rosenfeld who
had discovered her and who, because he liked the quality
of her speaking voice, urged her to become a professional
singer. In time she became a star of stars in vaudeville; few
if any could belt out a ragtime tune the way Emma Carus
did.

Rosenfeld had two other hits in 1897, both duly credited
to him. One was "I Don't Care If You Never Come Back,"
which Bert Williams made familiar to vaudeville audiences
when he was a member of the team of Williams and
Walker. The other was one of the best-loved sentimental
ballads of the 1890's—"Just for the Sake of Our Daughter."
Rosenfeld's last published song, for which he produced
only the lyrics, was also a hit, "Down Where the Silv'ry
Mohawk Flows," in 1905.

Rosenfeld sold his songs, or his ideas for songs, to any
publisher willing to lay out a few dollars. It is for this reason that something from his pen—sometimes just the
words, sometimes only the music, and occasionally both—
appeared on the lists of most of the leading publishing
houses in Tin Pan Alley. He himself was broke as long as
he lived, and he died broke. But several publishing houses,
including Howley, Haviland, made fortunes from his song
efforts.

Dresser, Davis, and Rosenfeld were three successful
composers of sentimental ballads in the 1890's. Jim Thornton was a fourth. He had come to Tin Pan Alley by way
of a saloon, the Bal Mabile on Bleecker Street, at which he
had been employed as a singing waiter. The patrons there
liked the easy way he projected his voice in popular tunes,
the rapport he was able to create with them. Thornton
was a big, likable, gregarious fellow who drank liquor in
prodigious quantities but never lost his charm or dignity
even when under the influence of alcohol. He had a seemingly inexhaustible fund of stories and jokes. John L. Sulli-

van, the boxing champion, liked nothing better than to spend nights in bars with him, engaging in formidable drinking bouts while listening to Thornton's tales.

While working at the Bal Mabile, Thornton fell in love with one of its female entertainers, little Lizzie Cox, known as Bonnie. She was a girl with two hobbies: she loved art, and she collected diamonds. (Eventually her jewel collection was second only to that of Lillian Russell among theaterfolk.)

When Bonnie loved something or somebody, it was intensely and permanently. That's the way it was when she married Jim Thornton. His drinking habits, his extravagance, his weakness for staying out all night with Sullivan and other friends tried her temper severely; but these indiscretions never made her doubt for a moment that she loved her man.

Through the years it was Bonnie who in one way or another was the source and inspiration of some of Thornton's finest ballads. And Thornton's very first song, "Remember Poor Mother at Home" (which he sold to a publisher for $2.50!), was introduced by Bonnie at the Bal Mabile.

In 1889, Thornton left the Bal Mabile to begin a new career in vaudeville; there he appeared in an act with Charles B. Lawlor, the composer of "The Sidewalks of New York." On stage and off, Thornton always wore a Prince Albert coat and formal striped trousers. With his reserve and dignity he had the look of an undertaker, but there was nothing funereal about his vaudeville act. It was made up of a side-splitting monologue and hilarious virtuoso feats at the piano. It was for this act that Thornton created his first important song, "Upper Ten and Lower Five." His first big hit followed soon after that—and owed its existence to Bonnie. One evening she implored him to come home straight from the theater instead of making the rounds of saloons. When he refused, she asked him lightly if she was still his sweetheart. Just as lightly, Thornton replied: "My sweetheart's the man in the moon." He decided to use the phrase both as a title and as the material for the lyric of a new ballad, which he wrote with Bonnie's small vocal range in mind. He himself introduced it in the Orpheum Theater in San Francisco, but it was Bonnie who made it popular, after her first performance of it at Tony Pastor's.

Thornton's hits now came thick and fast. In 1894 he wrote "She May Have Seen Better Days," which T. B. Harms published. A year later Frank Harding issued "The Streets of Cairo"; for this Thornton lifted a hootchy-kootchy tune made popular at the Chicago world fair. In 1896 he had no less than four substantial hits to his credit, including "On the Benches in the Park" and "It Don't Seem the Same Old Smile," the latter introduced by Helene Mora in vaudeville. Though the sales for these and other Thornton songs were large, he realized little enough for his efforts. He invariably sold one of his songs for fifteen or twenty-five dollars to realize enough money with which to pick up the check in the saloon.

The song by which he is still remembered, and which sold over a million copies, is "When You Were Sweet Sixteen," written in 1898. Once again Bonnie was responsible for its existence. Asked by Bonnie if he still loved her, Thornton replied quickly: "I love you like I did when you were sweet sixteen." She told him that his answer had the makings of a good musical number, and he agreed. Bonnie sang it for the first time in vaudeville, after which it became a favorite of barbershop quartets and silver-toned tenors. This ballad was also involved in a lawsuit. Thornton had sold it outright to two different publishers—Witmark (who issued it) and Joseph W. Stern, who insisted he was the legal owner of the copyright. The matter was finally straightened out with a handsome settlement paid by Witmark to Stern.

If Thornton wrote numerous songs to get the price of several rounds of drinks, he also, in reciprocity, used his bouts with liquor as a way of getting ideas for songs. He even wrote ballads about his experiences in taking cures in alcoholic clinics in White Plains, New York—"When I Took the Keely Cure" and "Curious Cures."

He kept on writing his ballads in the 1900's, his last success being "There's a Mother Waiting for You" in 1903. But he soon had to realize that no longer was there an audience for sentimental ballads. When he did so, his creative flow stopped. A brief moment of vanished glory returned when he appeared on Broadway as himself in the Jerome Kern musical comedy *Sweet Adeline*, in 1929. But by then there were few indeed who remembered that he had once written "When You Were Sweet Sixteen" and "My Sweetheart's the Man in the Moon."

# 4

## "You're not the only pebble on the beach"

New publishers kept springing up all the time, in or near Union Square. Frequently they had little capital and even less experience in the music business. Yet these newcomers had initiative, energy, and drive—in place of experience and money—and these qualities served them well. The newer firms were responsible for instituting many of the procedures in writing, publishing, marketing, and promoting songs that were to become the bone, tissue, and muscle of Tin Pan Alley.

One of the most significant of these new arrivals was Joseph W. Stern & Company. It was organized by Joseph W. Stern and Edward B. Marks in 1892 with a capital of about $100. Stern was a necktie salesman; Marks sold sewing hooks and eyes and whalebone. Neither had any musical training. As Marks revealed later on in his book *They All Sang:* "Joe could play the piano with one hand and fake with the other like nobody's business, but he hadn't fooled around with the music end of the game. . . . I don't play any instrument and I can carry a tune a little farther than Equipoise can carry the Empire State Building. . . . Where there was a wedding or birthday party in the family I used to write rhymes for the occasion. Sometimes I even won little prizes for verses."

In his free time, Marks used to loiter around Fourteenth Street because he liked to rub elbows with stage folk and professional songwriters, many of whom he got to meet and know in the various neighborhood saloons. In this way he became acquainted with Polly Holmes, an Irish character comedienne then appearing at Tony Pastor's. One day she asked him to write a comedy number for her. He complied with "Since McManus Went Down to the Track," about a horse-playing bricklayer. Marks got George Rosenberg, an active arranger along music row with a hole-in-the-wall office on Fourteenth Street, to produce a melody for his lyric. Polly Holmes sang it at Tony Pastor's and got a big hand. To Marks it meant the beginning of a career as lyricist.

Marks now redoubled his songwriting efforts. Upon advice from Frank Harding, the publisher, he sought out Will H. Fox, the then-popular vaudeville comic who billed himself as "Paddy Whiski" and who did a burlesque on Paderewski, then one of the most famous concert pianists in the world. In his act, Fox favored an outlandish costume that included baggy trousers, a woman's shirtwaist, one rubber boot with a price tag still attached to it, one low shoe exposing a white sock, and an enormous yellow wig. At the piano he made a shambles of virtuosity by playing at times with toes and nose and by performing the kind of digital pyrotechnics that Chico Marx would do in a later day. During these outlandish concerts Fox would keep muttering all kinds of nonsensical comments, sometimes to himself, sometimes to his audience. He was, in short, a piano-playing comic, the first successful one in vaudeville.

"This funny fellow," Harding told Marks, "writes good tunes on the side, things like 'The Broken Home.' If you can get him to write melodies for your lyrics you'll be getting yourself a good partner. That's the shortest route to success for a lyricist like yourself—a good composer."

Marks made the rounds of those night spots to which Fox was most partial, finally locating the comic at Callahan's near the Bowery. Somehow he managed to persuade Fox to start a collaboration. Their first efforts were "Break the News to Mother Gently" (whose title anticipated a similar one by Charles K. Harris by a number of years) and "I'd Live Life Over in the Same Old Way." Harding published both items, and both were failures.

Marks' first success came with "December and May," the sad love story of an elderly bachelor and his young sweetheart—one of the earliest "December-May" songs from Tin Pan Alley. William Lorraine wrote the music, Harding published the song in 1893, and Lydia Yeamns introduced it the same year at Tony Pastor's. She scored such a huge success with it that she made it a basic part of her repertory and kept on singing it for a quarter of a century. This ballad was one of Tony Pastor's particular favorites; he always asked Lydia Yeamns to include it in her act whenever he booked her for his Music Hall.

Measuring his own profits from this song with those realized by his publisher, Marks came to the forceful realization that he had better go into publishing for himself. While selling on the road, he crossed paths with Joe Stern, a necktie salesman who enjoyed writing tunes. They struck up a friendship, and after that a writing partnership. One day in 1894, stuck in their hotel in Mamaroneck, New

York, during a blinding rainstorm, they stumbled upon a poignant news item in the day's paper. A lost child, wandering about the city streets, was found by a policeman, who turned out to be her long-lost father. Here, they knew immediately, was grist for their mill. They rushed down to the hotel parlor, which boasted a piano, and pieced together the words and music of "The Little Lost Child."

Marks convinced his collaborator that the wisest thing for them to do was to publish the song themselves. They rented a little office in the basement of a building on Fourteenth Street and Second Avenue. Then they translated a capital of about $100 into a desk, a chair, and a deposit with a local printer. The new firm called itself Joseph W. Stern & Company, Marks' name being omitted because he did not as yet want to jeopardize his job as a salesman.

The day the printer delivered the sheet music to their office—and even before the proud authors-publishers had a chance to open the bundles—Della Fox dropped in to see them. She was an established star on Broadway, having appeared with De Wolf Hopper in such outstanding extravaganzas as *Wang* and *The Panjandrum*, and a vaudeville headliner. She had happened to be walking along Fourteenth Street when she became attracted to the new and shiny sign of the Joseph W. Stern & Company. As this was a new publishing outfit, Della Fox felt it might be able to provide her with some fresh song material for her vaudeville act. Stern and Marks enraptured her with their rendition of "The Little Lost Child." She forthwith introduced it in vaudeville. The song's tremendous popularity, however, did not begin with Della Fox's performance; it really caught on when Lottie Gilson started to sing it in vaudeville. She invariably stopped the show with it, and was compelled to repeat the refrain several times before her audiences would be satisfied.

But publishing a sensational ballad that sold between one

and two million copies of sheet music was not the only way in which the new firm of Joseph W. Stern left its impress on Tin Pan Alley. Since they themselves had been salesmen, both Stern and Marks came to the early realization that sheet music could be sold in the same way neckties and whalebone were marketed. The house of Joseph W. Stern became the first to utilize a salesman on the road to visit all local shops and distributors that handled sheet music. As long as Stern and Marks themselves continued going on the road with neckties and sewing hooks, they carried a supply of their latest published songs with their other samples. Then when the fabulous success of "The Little Lost Child" made it possible for them to give up their outside jobs for good and concentrate on the song business, they made it a practice to travel several times a year around the country with a full sample case of their sheet music.

Before long, Joseph W. Stern & Company became the first publishers to issue orchestrations as well as piano copies of their publications. Until Stern and Marks embarked upon this new and unorthodox practice, performers had to pay out of their own pockets for the orchestrations of numbers they wanted to use in their act. Their reluctance to try out new numbers was broken down once they could get orchestrations free. With remarkable perspicacity, Stern and Marks realized how much more easily they could get their numbers played and sung if orchestrations were available gratis. Consequently, one of the first things they did—once the money started to roll in and their firm was on a solid footing—was to lift George M. Rosenberg from his hole-in-the-wall office and pay him a fulltime salary to orchestrate every Joseph W. Stern song. Besides being one of the first significant orchestrators in Tin Pan Alley, Rosenberg (or "Rosey" as he was known in the trade) contributed the "Honeymoon March," a two-step in the style of

Sousa, to the Stern catalogue in 1894. One of the reasons this piece did as well as it did was the unusual way Stern and Marks found to promote it. They took down the name of every bride and bride-to-be listed in the engagement and wedding announcements in the papers and sent each a copy of the march; it was not long before the march became a much talked-about composition.

In their first year of operation, Stern and Marks published the love ballad "Somebody Loves Me," by Hattie Starr, the first successful woman composer in Tin Pan Alley. (This song is not to be confused with the far more familiar ballad of the same name by George Gershwin.) She had come to New York from the sticks, bringing this song with her. Originally it was written in a fast tempo. When she showed it to Josephine Sabel, then appearing at Koster and Bial's, the singer suggested changing the tempo to a slow waltz time. Hattie Starr made the necessary revision, and Sabel sang it, and with such success that Edward B. Marks bought the publication rights.

Another successful number issued by this company during its first years was a "mammy" song by Dave Marion, "Her Eyes Don't Shine like Diamonds." Curiously enough, though this was a mawkishly sentimental ballad, its success was due primarily to a comedy team in vaudeville, the Russell Brothers, who included it in their act for a change of pace.

But the biggest hits to come out of Joseph W. Stern & Company in the 1890's were the ones Stern and Marks themselves wrote. Soon after they had published "The Little Lost Child," Stern and Marks wrote and published "His Last Thoughts Were of You." This was introduced by Minnie Schulte at George Huber's Prospect Gardens Music Hall, and was later successfully presented by Lottie Gilson in vaudeville. Two years later Stern and Marks wrote and published (and Lottie Gilson introduced it at

Proctor's Fifty-eighth Street Theater) the greatest triumph Stern and Marks were to achieve both as songwriters and as publishers—the sentimental ballad "Mother Was a Lady."

Where "The Little Lost Child" had been inspired by a news item, "Mother Was a Lady" was the direct result of an episode witnessed by the songwriters. They were dining with Meyer Cohen, popular singer of ballads, in a German restaurant on Twenty-first Street. At a nearby table, two brash young women were harassing and insulting a waitress. She was in tears as she exclaimed, "My mother was a lady!" Then she added: "You wouldn't dare to insult me if my brother Jack were only here!"

Meyer Cohen remarked that in this incident lay the embryo of a wonderful sentimental ballad. Marks took the cue. In his lyrics he developed a pathetic story about a waitress who was being subjected to insults by a salesman. Only later does the salesman discover that the waitress is the sister of his best friend. In atonement for his cruel behavior, the repentant drummer begs the waitress for her hand in marriage.

The several-million-copy sale of "Mother Was a Lady" enabled Stern and Marks to seek larger quarters. In 1896 they moved a few blocks north from Union Square, to 45 East 20th Street. Delighting in their affluence, they equipped their new offices with a piano besides outfitting a reception room in which composers and lyricists could congregate and performers in search of new material could be entertained.

Affluence inevitably increased the prestige of Stern and Marks. Even established composers now started to beat a path to their doors. In 1895, Gussie Davis brought them "Down In Poverty Row." James Thornton sold them "Don't Give Up the Old Love for the New" in 1896, and in the same year Harry Braisted and Stanley Carter brought them "You're Not the Only Pebble on the Beach." The latter, introduced at the Casino Roof Garden by Lottie Gilson, became such a favorite that before long everybody was using the title in conversation as a token of disapproval. Harry Braisted and Stanley Carter also contributed to the Stern list a fine sentimental ballad, which they wrote on a dare. During a discussion of Paul Dresser's ballads, one of Harry Braisted's friends insisted that writers of comedy songs could never do a ballad. Harry Braisted, supported by Stanley Carter, took up the challenge, since they were known primarily for their lighter songs. The result was "She Was Bred in Old Kentucky," which Lottie Gilson sang with huge success.

In 1897, Thornton returned to Stern with "There's a Little Star Shining for You" and Monroe Rosenfeld sold them a sentimental ballad that became one of his best sellers, "Take Back Your Gold." In 1898 the company manager of Joseph W. Stern, Max S. Witt, wrote one of the leading numbers put out that year—"The Moth and the Flame." It had been inspired by Clyde Fitch's play of the same name, and Helene Mora sang it for the first time in *Pleasure Palace*.

Apart from their own creations, Stern and Marks enjoyed their greatest publishing success before 1900 with a song that came to them as a result of their newly won position in Tin Pan Alley. One day, in 1896, Maude Nugent visited them with a number she had written and introduced at The Abbey on Eighth Avenue. The song was "Sweet Rosie O'Grady." She sang it for Marks, while Stern painstakingly picked out the melody on the piano. Both men liked it. But they were also convinced that the market was saturated by numbers whose titles carried a girl's name. Haughtily, Maude grabbed her manuscript from the piano and left in a huff. With a sudden and inexplicable change of heart, Marks followed her. He caught up with her on

Fifth Avenue just as she was making a beeline straight for Howley, Haviland. "I'll buy it, I'll buy it," he kept shouting at her. He brought her back to the office and consummated a deal whereby for the consideration of one hundred dollars in cash he acquired all the rights!

Maude Nugent never earned another penny from the music sales of "Sweet Rosie O'Grady." There are those who feel she did not deserve even the hundred dollars Marks paid her, doubting seriously that she had written it in the first place. These skeptics, pointing to the facts that never before or after did she produce another successful song and that her husband, Billy Jerome, was a professional and successful songwriter, hinted that he had probably written the song and gallantly permitted his wife to palm it off as her own.

To Joseph W. Stern & Company the question of whether Maude Nugent did or did not write "Sweet Rosie O'Grady" was purely academic. What interested the publishers exclusively was that the song kept the profits pouring into the company. Most of the leading ballad singers of the day were using it in their acts; there was hardly a vaudeville hoofer who did not at one time or another perform a buck-and-wing to its strains.

In 1943, "Sweet Rosie O'Grady" lent both its title and its tune to a successful screen musical starring Betty Grable. But years before that, in 1918, the song had an offspring in "The Daughter of Rosie O'Grady"—words by Monty C. Brice, music by Walter Donaldson. Pat Rooney, Jr., introduced it at the Palace Theater in 1919 and after singing the number, he did a waltz clog to it. The song and the waltz clog from then on became a Pat Rooney trademark.

Joseph W. Stern & Company also brought out the first fruit of a composer soon to make his mark both in Tin Pan Alley and within the Broadway musical theater—John Stromberg. His first published song, "My Best Girl's a

New Yorker," was released by Stern in 1895. Before becoming a songwriter, Stromberg had worked for a number of years as an arranger for M. Witmark & Sons. Once published, "My Best Girl's a New Yorker" came to the notice of Weber and Fields, the comics then planning the production of extravaganzas and travesties in their own music hall. They liked Stromberg's song well enough to ask him to be both their conductor and composer. This relationship lasted half a dozen years. In that time Stromberg wrote all the music for Weber and Fields productions at the Music Hall, beginning with *The Art of Maryland*, which opened on September 5, 1896.

Though Stromberg had been given his start as a composer by Joseph W. Stern, the big Stromberg hits coming out of the Weber and Fields burlesques were released first by a new publishing venture started by Weber and Fields themselves, then by M. Witmark & Sons. These hits included: "Kiss Me, Honey, Do" (or, as it is sometimes called, "Dinah"), introduced by Peter F. Dailey in *Hurly Burly*; "When Chloe Sings a Song" from *Whirl-i-gig*, with which Lillian Russell made a stunning debut as a Weber and Fields star by singing a "coon song" for the first time in her career; "Keep Away from Emmaline," the big hit number from *Hurly Burly* with which Fay Templeton made her debut at the Weber and Fields Music Hall; "Ma Blushin' Rosie," one of the greatest song triumphs to come out of these extravaganzas, introduced by Fay Templeton in *Fiddle Dee Dee* (the song later became a big favorite with Al Jolson, who revived it in the motion picture *Jolson Sings Again* in 1949); and the song that is always associated with Lillian Russell, which she sang in *Twirly Whirly*, "Come Down, Ma Evenin' Star."

"Come Down, Ma Evenin' Star" was not only Stromberg's most famous ballad but also his swan song. Its manuscript was found in his pocket when his dead body was discovered in a New York apartment in 1902. He had apparently committed suicide, depressed by chronic bad health. When Lillian Russell started to sing the number on the opening night of *Twirly Whirly*, she broke down midway and was unable to continue. Thereafter, "Come Down, Ma Evenin' Star" became her song of songs. When, in 1912, Weber and Fields were temporarily reunited in a musical production of which Lillian Russell was a star attraction, her poignant rendition of "Come Down, Ma Evenin' Star" so stirred the audience that there was not a dry eye in the audience by the time she finished.

Though neither Stern nor Marks could have guessed it at the time, their publication of "Those Lost Happy Days" by Leo Feist in 1893, launched the career of a man soon to become one of their most dynamic publishing competitors. Feist was a corset salesman turned songwriter. In 1893, after he tried in vain to get Stern and Marks to take him as a partner in their firm, he started to print his own songs, found musicians to introduce them, and went out to the shops to peddle the sheet music. Once he had accumulated $200 he rented a two-room office near Union Square as the base for his publishing efforts. His first hit came in 1894, his very first year of publishing, with Monroe Rosenfeld's ballad "And Her Golden Hair Was Hanging Down Her Back." Later on, Leo Feist brought out even greater hits— "Anona," which Mabel McKinley made popular in vaudeville, and the cakewalk "Smokey Mokes." Before the 1890's had ended, Leo Feist's firm was one of the more progressive institutions in Tin Pan Alley. It became the first house there to flaunt a slogan on all its publications. It read: "You Can't Go Wrong with a Feist Song."

Among the other new publishers to spring up in or near Union Square in the 1890's was Shapiro-Bernstein. Its founders—Lew Bernstein and Maurice Shapiro—were partial to ballads with extended story lines in the style of "After the Ball" and "Mother Was a Lady." They encouraged performers in vaudeville to present such songs in semi-dramatized versions. From the inception of its operations, Shapiro-Bernstein instituted a policy of getting stage stars to sing their songs by means of tactful, though not always inexpensive, bribes. Lottie Gilson, for example, was once presented a diamond ring valued at $500.

Still another of the significant younger firms in Tin Pan Alley during this period was an importation from Detroit, Whitney-Warner. In 1894 it transferred its main offce to Union Square, adopting the new name of Jerome H. Remick and Company. One of its first publications was a hit, the whimsical number by Anita Owen "Sweet Bunch of Daisies" that Phyllis Allen helped make popular. Before long, Remick was to be one of the major strongholds of hit songs in the Alley.

While new firms were gaining a foothold in Tin Pan Alley, some of the older ones were solidifying their own positions. As the 1890's were turning the corner, M. Witmark & Sons was being built up into a major company, largely through Charles Graham's ballad of 1891 "The Picture That Is Turned to the Wall." Graham was an alcoholic who became a victim of his weakness, dying in a ward in Bellevue Hospital in 1899. His first song came in 1887, "If the Waters Could Speak as They Flow," published by Willis Woodward. The Witmarks bought some of his songs before acquiring the biggest hit of Graham's career "The Picture That Is Turned to the Wall." It was inspired by a scene from Joseph Arthur's melodrama *Blue Jeans*, in which a farmer turns a picture of his wayward daughter to the wall as a symbol of permanent renunciation. Graham amplified on this theme in "The Picture," selling the final product to Witmark for fifteen dollars. It was still in manuscript when Andrew Mack, a beloved Irish tenor, dropped in upon the Witmarks in search of a new number. When he failed to find anything he liked among the publications, he began browsing through the yet unpublished manuscripts and found "The Picture." He seized upon it and introduced it in *The City Directory* at the Bijou Theater. After that Julie Witmark—still a successful performer in vaudeville, minstrel shows, and extravaganzas—took it into his repertory and plugged it all over the country with assiduity and perseverance, for which he and his brothers were rewarded bountifully. Isidore Witmark himself conceded the significance of the song's success in the book *From Ragtime to Swingtime*, which he and Isaac Goldberg wrote. " 'The Picture That Is Turned to the Wall' was more than a financial success for the Witmarks. It brought them a coveted prestige. Formerly they had sold sheet music by the hundreds of copies; now they knew sales in the thousands. . . . Jobbers who scorned to deal with 'children' were camping on their doorsteps for copies. Dealers who had refused them displays now buried other songs beneath 'The Picture.' Singers whom they had been obliged to chase now chased them."

Graham's hit after that, "Two Little Girls in Blue," was not a Witmark publication; Spaulding and Kornder purchased it for release in 1893. Graham insisted that the idea for the song came to him while shaving. Looking out of the bathroom window he caught a glimpse of two little girls dressed in identical blue clothes coming home from school. He further maintained that his inspiration came so suddenly that, unable to find a pencil, he grabbed some soap and scrawled on a mirror the song title, some key words, and a few notes of the chorus.

Such an origin may well be a figment of the composer's imagination. But it is no legend that in writing his song Graham tried to create another "After the Ball." The similarity between these two numbers is too striking to be coincidental. In both ballads the story pivots on the axis of a huge misunderstanding. Graham's lyrics tell the tale of two sisters who marry two brothers. The couples quarrel, and the sisters are separated. This leads to a permanent separation. As in "After the Ball," the whole story is told by a heartbroken old man—to a nephew this time instead of a niece. Even the melody carries reminders of "After the Ball." Derivative though it was, "Two Little Girls" became one of the song triumphs of the early 1890's.

Since success always breeds success, the Witmarks found once they had become a power with "The Picture That Is Turned to the Wall," their catalogue sprouting hit after hit. In 1898, they acquired John Stromberg's "Kiss Me, Honey, Do" and other songs from the Weber and Fields extravaganzas, having purchased the publishing house of Weber, Fields and Stromberg for $10,000. That was also the year when they published Jim Thornton's "When You Were Sweet Sixteen." In 1899, Witmark issued Chauncey Olcott's "My Wild Irish Rose," which Olcott himself—since 1896 a Broadway star in musicals of his own writing—introduced in *A Romance of Athlone*. However successful this ballad may have been, it was only the harbinger of bigger and better things to come in the field of Irish balladry. Most of these bigger and better things came in the early 1900's, when the Witmarks began publishing the works of Ernest R. Ball.

While "Why Did Nellie Leave Home?," which the Witmarks released in 1891, was not even a minor success and did nothing to further their financial interests or to solidify their security, it belongs with one of their major publishing achievements in the 1890's. The reason? Simply that "Why Did Nellie Leave Home?" was the first published song by a brash young upstart by the name of George M. Cohan, then a member of the successful vaudeville team The Four Cohans, which included his father, mother, and his sister, Josephine. In this act, besides singing, he did buck-and-wing dances, sentimental recitations, a bootblack specialty number. He wrote a good deal of his own material, including the words and music of some of the songs. Despite his youth (he was only thirteen)—or, perhaps, because of it— the boy Cohan was, as Witmark later recalled in *From Ragtime to Swingtime*, a cocky, self-assured, opinionated youngster, sure of himself and his gifts. "When he was not arguing with the theaterfolk, he was tramping the streets of New York with unrecognized masterpieces under his arm. He was no more afraid of publishers than he was of managers. . . . Everybody in those days was swell-headed to Georgie, except the ardent, impatient boy who made the ready diagnosis. He would pass the Witmark offices and call the brothers 'big stiffs'—to himself. 'Just goes to show how smart those babies in there are, publishing all that bum material written by a lot of hams, and here am I, the best songwriter, and walking right by their door with four or five sure hits under my arms.' "

Unfortunately for the Witmarks, they did not realize that there was a good deal of truth in what Cohan was saying about himself and his songs. Having done so badly with "Why Did Nellie Leave Home?" the Witmarks lost interest in him. In 1895, when Cohan had his first minor hit— with "Hot Tamale Alley," which the dynamic May Irwin sang in vaudeville—and in 1898, when he had a major success with "I Guess I'll Have to Telegraph My Baby," other publishers profited from his talent.

The house of Witmark, then, was responsible for some of the highly successful songs of the 1890's and for the early fame of several well-esteemed composers. But the influence of the Witmarks on Tin Pan Alley was felt in several other directions as well—through the introduction and development of some of the methods that soon became basic with their competitors.

Witmark was the first publishing house to distribute free "professional copies" to performing artists. Such copies were printed without the usual trade covers and on cheaper stock paper. A free generous handout of such songs to all members of the acting and singing profession spelled a good many more performances for these numbers, and by a greater number of artists, than had been the practice when these performers had to buy their own sheet music.

Witmark ushered in a new era in the orchestration of popular songs by hiring Frank Sadler, the burlesque-house musician. Sadler was the first in Tin Pan Alley to introduce new instrumental effects and unusual harmonies in his orchestral adaptations of popular tunes. A new world of song presentation was thus opened up. Jerome Kern conceded more than once that during his impressionable years in Tin Pan Alley and on Broadway Sadler's orchestrations had enormous influence. Sadler's successful orchestrations also encouraged other publishers to hire gifted orchestrators of their own.

Witmark was one of the first houses to become interested in ragtime—not only in piano rags and ragtime songs but even in a ragtime primer. (The significance of this will become clearer when we discuss the importance of ragtime in Tin Pan Alley.)

Witmark was also the first publisher to open up a music library in Tin Pan Alley. This happened in 1898. When the Witmarks did this, they took an ad in the New York *Dramatic Mirror* that announced that they were offering "for sale or to hire the largest collection of vocal concert numbers and excerpts in America . . . music of every description, arranged, transposed, copied, lithographed."

# 5

*"East side, west side,
all around the town"*

The most significant advances made by the younger firms in Tin Pan Alley were in the field of song exploitation. An altogether new and logical concept was now crystallized: that song hits were not born but made; that it was possible to sell songs with high-pressure methods. Song-plugging, as this practice came to be called, was the reason the younger firms were able to sell their songs in hundreds of thousands, whereas their predecessors sold them only in thousands; why a million-copy sale, a phenomenon before 1890, was achieved by each of these new enterprising firms not once but many times.

Many and varied were the methods devised to get songs performed and liked. Often serving as their own pluggers, publishers like Pat Howley, Edward B. Marks, Joseph W.

Stern, Tom Harms, Julie Witmark, and Leo Feist would make the rounds of saloons, brothels, night spots, theaters and restaurants all around the town, from early evening to dawn. No place in which a song could possibly be heard was off limits. "In the nineties," explained Edward B. Marks in *They All Sang*, "a publisher had to know his way about the night spots. It was important to get his wares before the bibulous public, so he had to spend a large part of his time making the rounds for plugs and more plugs. In his wanderings he saw as broad a cross-section of New York as any man—even broader than a wine agent because the song plugger hit spots where champagne would have been considered an effeminate affectation. Sixty joints a week I used to make; Joe Stern, my partner, covered forty. What's more, we did it every week."

Marks went on to explain: "The line ran from the Bowery—Miner's, the London, Atlantic Gardens—up to Fourteenth Street (Tony Pastor's and the Alhambra) and west to Huber's (not yet a museum), and then north to The Abbey, the Haymarket, and Koster and Bial's. The songs were started where the liquor flowed and released the impulse to sing. . . . The way to get a song over was to get it sung in the music halls by a popular singer. The publisher was his own salesman, making the rounds of the night spots and plugging his wares. I took along Louis the Whistler to insinuate the tunes. I bought beer for the musicians and jollied the headliners."

The publisher would carry under his arm a batch of chorus slips—sheets of paper with the refrain of a song printed on it and a request for the public to join in the singing. Beer was by no means the only commodity with which to buy a performer's favor. Boxes of cigars, free dinners, a pretty but inexpensive bauble for females, were also distributed freely, now in one place and now in another, among orchestra leaders, singing waiters, café-house singers, vaudevillians, and so forth. Even the managers of dog acts expected little presents before they used certain songs for entrance or accompanying music. Naturally, the celebrated stars of the Broadway musical theater and vaudeville had to be bought with more expensive gifts—later on with cold cash.

In or about 1893, a new method of song plugging came into existence that flourished for a number of years. This practice called for publishers to plant singers, usually boys, in the audience of a theater. When the stage performer completed a number, the singer would rise in his seat (as if spontaneously) and, with the finger of the limelight pointing to him, he would raise his voice in a repetition of the refrain. The applause of the audience would then encourage him to sing the refrain several times—until the melody was planted firmly in the memory of the listeners. Some say this practice started with Gus Edwards, then fourteen years old, who was to become one of Tin Pan Alley's leading songwriters and publishers and one of vaudeville's foremost headliners. The boy Edwards was hired to sit in the balcony of Hurtig and Seamon's burlesque theater in New York and join the stage performers in singing ballads such as "The Little Lost Child," "Don't Send My Boy to Prison," and "A Mother's Plea for Her Son." He scored such a hit with his tender piping voice that Tin Pan Alley released a number about him—"A Song in the Gallery."

The singing stooge in vaudeville and burlesque became one of Tin Pan Alley's most significant allies in the plugging of songs. In the early 1900's the boy Irving Berlin worked as a singing stooge for Harry von Tilzer by appearing at Tony Pastor's Music Hall. He was part of the act "The Three Keatons," whose youngest member was Buster, later one of the most famous comedians of the silent screen.

There was still another way in which stooges, preferably boys, could get placed by publishers in vaudeville and burlesque houses. In the 1890's and the early 1900's theaters used to hire waterboys to serve patrons with drinking water. It did not take publishers long to think of planting singers in this job. Joe Santley (later on of the famous vaudeville team of Santley and Sawyer) first put his feet inside a theater by working as a "waterboy" at Proctor's Fifth Avenue—actually he was being paid to plug Witmark songs. He would join in singing the refrains of such songs as "Absence Makes the Heart Grow Fonder" and "When You Were Sweet Sixteen." Santley long insisted that the first time that Jim Thornton's ballad "When You Were Sweet Sixteen" was sung publicly anywhere was when he himself introduced it at Proctor's as a waterboy.

When boy singers proved so valuable for plugging songs, publishers began raiding synagogue and church choirs. Ben Bloom, later Remick's ace song plugger, was lifted from a synagogue choir to become a boy singing stooge in vaudeville; and Al Jolson got his start in show business the same way.

One of the ways in which child singers soon came to be used (not exclusively, of course, since older singers were also employed for the same purpose) was in connection with song slides. This was a new way of popularizing songs by means of stereopticon slides. It first became popular early in the 1890's, and remained a favorite attraction in vaudeville and movie theaters for many years thereafter.

The idea of "song slides" was conceived by George H. Thomas. He was an electrician employed in a Brooklyn theater then presenting *The Old Homestead*, a play in which the ballad "Where Is My Wandering Boy Tonight?" was sung. An unusually dramatic effect was produced during the performance of the ballad by having the house lights lowered and by flashing a picture on a screen showing a drunkard seated at a bar, his head resting wearily on his arms.

One day, while watching this effect, Thomas wondered why it wasn't possible to dramatize other popular songs by flashing a series of slides on a screen. He came with his idea to Joseph W. Stern & Company and sold them a plan to give the then recently published "The Little Lost Child" a song-slide treatment. Stern and Marks provided the funds to pay a photographer to take pictures in a Brooklyn police station, in which different episodes of the ballad were depicted. Thomas's wife played the part of the lost child's mother; an actual policeman played himself; and a child actress was recruited to perform the role of the little lost girl.

The song slides of "The Little Lost Child" were exhibited for the first time during the intermission of a show put on by the Primrose and West Minstrels in 1894. May Allen sang the ballad while the pictures were being flashed on the screen. The stunt worked far beyond the wildest hopes of anybody connected with it. The audience loved it.

Soon song slides were being used all over New York City and then throughout the United States. Their influence on audiences gave such a phenomenal boost to sheet-music sale that publishers scrambled over one another in the rush to get their songs dramatized in slide pictures. The De Witt C. Wheeler Company went into the production of song slides in a big way. Singers started to specialize in this field, and many a boy or girl started his (or her) theatrical career acting in song slides, including Georgie Jessel, Fanny Brice, and Eddie Cantor.

At first, publishers were quite happy to give away these slides free to any theater wishing to use them—in return for the publicity and promotion received. But song slides became such a basic part of the show, and were so eagerly sought after by audiences, that publishers felt they could charge a modest fee of from between five and ten dollars for a set of slides. Sometimes as many as a thousand sets of slides of a single song were being rented out at the same time to theaters all over the country.

# 6

## *"The world is singing my song"*

Despite the immense popularity of the sentimental ballad in the 1890's, other kinds of songs, some of which were highly successful, were being produced in Tin Pan Alley in those years.

Still in a more or less sentimental vein—though much less so than dramatic ballads like "After the Ball" and "Mother Was a Lady"—were nostalgic little waltzes that projected a simply expressed sentiment rather than narrating an elaborate tale. In that style were such songs as "Daisy Bell" and "The Band Played On."

"Daisy Bell" (perhaps better known by its alternate title "A Bicycle Built for Two") was written by the Englishman Harry Dacre soon after he came to the United States in 1891. He arrived with a bicycle among his belongings, for which he was required to pay duty. Billy Jerome, a Tin Pan Alley lyricist, met him at the pier and remarked wryly: "It's lucky you don't have a bicycle built for two, otherwise you'd have to pay *double* duty." The phrase "bicycle built for two" stuck in Dacre's mind. He used it for the first song he wrote in America. Nobody in Tin Pan Alley was at first interested in it, since in 1891 cycling still had a limited appeal for Americans. But in England, where the song was introduced by Kate Lawrence, it struck home and became an instantaneous favorite.

Then, late in 1891, a revolution took place in the construction of bicycles in the United States. The former high wheel was made smaller, the frame was dropped, pneumatic tires were introduced. All this added up to a vehicle easier to handle and safer to ride. Women began leaving their kitchens to go cycling—encouraged by doctors who said the sport was beneficial to health and by ministers who maintained it was beneficial to the soul.

With cycling a national fad, "Daisy Bell" caught on. Tony Pastor was the first one to sing it in America—at his Music Hall. T. B. Harms published the song in 1892, and Jennie Lindsay caused a sensation when she sang it at the Atlantic Gardens on the Bowery. After that it seemed that the whole country was on wheels—and singing "Daisy Bell."

"The Band Played On" was inspired by the German brass bands that were roaming the streets of New York City in return for whatever coins appreciative listeners wished to shower upon them. Words and music were written by John E. Palmer after he had heard one of these bands playing outside his apartment. When Palmer's sister made a move to close the window he exclaimed: "Let the band play on." His sister replied: "That's a good song title for you." If this story is to be believed, Palmer agreed and went to work at once.

He showed his song to the vaudevillian Charles B. Ward. After Ward made some corrections and minor changes, he bought it from Palmer for a few dollars. Ward then published the song himself in 1895, taking credit for the music while crediting Palmer only with the lyrics. Ward introduced the song in a Harlem Theater. After that he used his influence among his stage friends to get it heard in leading vaudeville houses. The New York *World* also became interested in it, publishing both words and music in one of its Sunday issues and using its columns to publicize it. This was the first instance in which a Tin Pan Alley product was successfully promoted by a newspaper. The song sold a million copies within a few years, and Ward (much to Palmer's chagrin) was made wealthy by it.

Maude Nugent's sweet, ingenuous waltz "Sweet Rosie O'Grady" is representative of another genre that flourished in Tin Pan Alley in the 1890's—the Irish ballad. Since 1880, wave upon wave of immigrants had swept into America from Ireland. As their numbers swelled in the big cities, so did their influence. Irish names, the Irish accent, Irish idiosyncrasies invaded the musical theater and the popular song. Harrigan and Hart, in their series of extravaganzas about the Mulligan family in the 1880's, provided probably the most celebrated and the most significant caricatures of the Irish in the American theater up to that time. The same kind of flavor and color that made the characters, situations, and dialogue in these extravaganzas so thoroughly Irish could be found in the songs that David Braham wrote for these productions.

Irish songs became even more popular in the 1890's than they had been a decade earlier. In the 1890's David Braham enriched his collection of successful Irish ditties with some of the best he ever wrote, among which were "Maggie Murphy's Home," "The Last of the Hogans," and "Danny by My Side." The last of these became such a favorite of Governor Alfred E. Smith of New York that he sang it in 1933 as part of the ceremonies celebrating the fiftieth anniversary of the opening of the Brooklyn Bridge.

Among the other outstanding songs of Irish interest to come out of Tin Pan Alley in the 1890's were: "Paddy Flynn," which Maggie Cline delivered with so much vitality in vaudeville; "Sweet Katie O'Connor," whose composer Harry Dacre was obviously throwing a covetous eye on the success then being achieved by "Sweet Rosie O'Grady"; Joe Flynn's "I Never Liked O'Regan"; J. W. Kelly's "Throw Him Down, McCloskey"; Chauncey Olcott's "My Wild Irish Rose"; and the "Irish Jubilee" by James Thornton and Charles Lawlor.

German dialect songs were also popular, although not quite so much as the Irish ones. This sudden interest in German characters, accents, and mannerisms was also the result of an influx of European immigration into the new world. In their music-hall extravaganzas, Weber and Fields gave their incomparable portrayals of Dutchmen. Joe Weber was short and stocky; Lew Fields, by contrast, was tall and thin. Both men wore flashy and greatly oversized checked suits and ridiculous derbies. Each cultivated little tufts of hair on his chin to suggest a beard. Both spoke in a thick German accent that accentuated the humor of their absurd dialogue and the ridiculous situations in which they constantly found themselves.

Possibly as a result of the influence of Weber and Fields, German characters were favored in burlesque and vaudeville in the 1890's. Before he became a successful composer and publisher, Harry von Tilzer did a German comedy act with George Sidney at Tony Pastor's Music Hall. In tune with this trend were such songs as "Kaiser, Don't You Want to Buy a Dog?" made popular by the German comic Gus Williams, also at Tony Pastor's.

Comic and nonsense songs also had their share of the spotlight in Tin Pan Alley. Vaudeville comics favoring the Irish brogue featured such standbys as "Down Went McGinty" and "Throw Him Down, McCloskey." Others had preferences that traversed a wide arc: Joseph J. Sullivan's "Where Did You Get That Hat?," which the composer himself introduced at Miner's Eighth Avenue Theater and then sang all over the country; "Daddy Wouldn't Buy Me a Bow-wow," introduced by its composer Joseph Tabrar; "When I Do de Hootchy-kootchy in de Sky," with a bow on the part of its author, Gussie Davis, in the direction of the Chicago world fair; "Do, Do, My Huckleberry, Do" and "Put Me Off at Buffalo," both of them the work of the Dillon brothers, who introduced them in their vaudeville act.

Nonsense songs had always been favored in the minstrel show, from "Zip Coon" and "Jump Jim Crow" to "Polly Wolly Doodle." They went over even better in vaudeville; "Zizzy, Ze Zum, Zum"—usually sung with the accompaniment of absurd facial contortions and awkward body gestures—became popular in 1898. Perhaps the most successful nonsense song of the 1890's was one whose lyrics were sheer gibberish—"Ta-ra-ra-bom-de-ray." It is hardly possible to hear its strains today without visualizing a line of chorus girls throwing their garters at men in the audience (the height of stage naughtiness in the 1890's!). "Ta-ra-ra-bom-de-ray" came into Tin Pan Alley in 1891 through a publication of Willis Woodward, and it penetrated the American theater when Lottie Collins sang it boisterously at Koster and Bial's. Its emergence in New York, whether in publication or performance, was the end of a circuitous route that had its starting point in Babe Connors' place, a St. Louis brothel on South Sixth Street near Faust's Restaurant.

Babe Connors' place was famous for its immense, glittering chandelier, one of the most elaborate and ornate of its kind to be seen anywhere in St. Louis, for the diamonds its proprietress made an inextricable part of her daily costume, for the dozen or so octaroon girls, all of them imported from New Orleans. But its greatest single asset was its leading entertainer: a powerful singer known as Mama Lou, whom Orrick Johns once indecorously described as "a gnarled, black African." Mama Lou wore a costume that in a later year became identified with Aunt Jemima of pancake fame: calico dress, gingham apron, a bandanna on her head. Mama Lou was big, fat, old, and ugly—that is, until she opened her mouth to sing. Then she—and the entire place—became transfigured. She seemed to dig deep inside her entrails for the songs of her race that she emitted like some mighty lamentation. She was one of the first to sing Negro spirituals to a white clientele in a night spot. She was also one of the first to deliver "Frankie and Johnny," now a part of American folklore. And she was the first of a dynasty of singers who were to make the blues an art form—her successors being Bessie Smith and Ma Rainey.

One of the numbers that always electrified her clientele was "Ta-ra-ra-bom-de-ray." This was a lusty tune with lusty lyrics. Some are convinced she wrote both, but whether she did or not, she made the song so much her own by her presentation of it that everybody identified it with her. When Paderewski once listened to her, he was so taken with both her rendition and the song that he went over to the piano and played it back to her.

Henry J. Sayers was another who heard her sing "Ta-ra-ra-bom-de-ray" at Babe Connors'. He was a publicity man for the show troupe the Tuxedo Girls and thought the number would suit his company. "I had never tried my hand at songwriting," he later explained, "but I thought that with a few changes I would clean up the stuff. When I showed it to the boss he almost threw me out of the office. 'This is unprintable, unsingable, untouchable,' he shouted. I had to admit that even with my changes the verses were filthy. I decided to rewrite the lyrics entirely. But they fell flat and remained that way three years."

Sayers eventually sold his version to Willis Woodward, who, upon issuing it in 1891, credited Sayers as composer and lyricist. Before the song became popular in New York, it created a sensation in London through Lottie Collins. In her extraordinarily effective presentation, she sang the verse with the greatest of propriety. Then the chorus line delivered the refrain with shrieking voices and high kicks. The correspondent for the New York *Herald* reported from England on February 28, 1892: "London has gone stark mad over the refrain. It has become a hideous nightmare. Everywhere, from Belgrave and Mayfair to Housditch and Whitechapel. In drawing rooms and hovels one hears 'Ta-ra-ra-bom-de-ray,' and there is hardly a theater in London in which the refrain is not alluded to at least once during the night. . . . If you go to the House of Commons lobby, it is probable that it is the first thing that greets your ear, and one expects no other reply from the bus driver, newsboys, hawkers, and policemen." The first sheet-music release in London was sold for a dollar a copy. Then a competitor flooded the market with the music priced at two cents apiece. After that it was given away free with each purchase of tea.

Lottie Collins then brought it back to the United States. She magnetized audiences at Koster and Bial's in the same electrifying way that she had done in London—and with the same ultimate results. "Ta-ra-ra-bom-de-ray" became the rage of New York City, then of the country. It is still intermittently revived on the musical stage and the films in stories about the 1890's.

Two other vigorous tunes came out of Babe Connors'

place in St. Louis. One was the melody of "A Hot Time in the Old Town," which Theodore Metz claimed was his. Metz was the bandleader of the McIntyre and Heath Minstrels. According to his account, while touring with his company in 1886, he witnessed from a train window a fire being put out by some Negro children in Old Town, Louisiana. A minstrel near him remarked: "There'll be a hot time in the Old Town tonight." Metz felt that in this comment he had the makings of a good minstrel-show number. After Joe Hayden had prepared the lyrics, Metz completed the music; and Willis Woodward published the song in 1886. The music was used as a march for the McIntyre and Heath Minstrels when they paraded through the streets before showtime; and with the lyrics, it was used as the opening chorus of their show. "A Hot Time in the Old Town" acquired a new status, and an increased fame, when it became one of the favorite tunes of the Spanish-American War. American soldiers in Cuba sang it loud and often, in anticipation of going home. The Rough Riders, under Theodore Roosevelt, adopted it as their song. But Theodore Roosevelt himself thought little of the song and maintained that it did not deserve its popularity.

Though to this day Metz's name appears on the sheet music as the composer of the song, it is more than probable that he helped himself to a melody he had heard Mama Lou sing in St. Louis. A number of his contemporaries insisted that they heard the melody there long before it was published.

Just as Metz was credited with being the composer of "A Hot Time," so in 1895 Charles E. Trevathan was credited with being the creator of "The Bully Song," or "The New Bully." But many of Trevathan's colleagues maintain that, like Metz, he had picked up his tune at Babe Connors' establishment.

Trevathan was a sportswriter who liked playing the guitar. He was aboard a Chicago-bound train with May Irwin, the famous vaudevillian and musical-comedy star, when, to amuse himself, he started to strum the melody of "The Bully Song." As he did so, he improvised lyrics. May Irwin was delighted with the number and told Trevathan she would like to sing it on the stage. Trevathan then wrote out the melody for her, with some accompanying words. May Irwin, with her big voice and even bigger delivery, threw a song across the footlights as though it were being ejected from the mouth of a cannon. "The Bully Song" was tailor-made for her dynamic style. From then on this was the song with which she was always identified. It was her tour de force when she sang it in *The Widow Jones*, a Broadway musical that opened on September 15, 1895. And it was due entirely to her success with this song that she came to be known as "the stage mother of ragtime."

Many other songs of the 1890's were as uninhibited, as noisy, and as abandoned as were "Ta-ra-ra-bom-de-ray" and "The Bully Song." Most of these more vigorous numbers were either songs about the Negro or by Negroes. Through the years, since the Civil War, the minstrel show had been the frame for Negro songs and dances. After that, this kind of song material could also be found in vaudeville shows. Tin Pan Alley took these Negro songs, increased the tempo, strengthened the beat, and added the salt and spice of syncopation.

This robust kind of popular tune required a vigorous presentation on the part of such human dynamos as May Irwin, Imogene Comer, or Lottie Collins. They shouted rather than sang, felling an audience in front of them with their vocal power and personal dynamism the way lumberjacks bring down a tree with swings of the axe. These—and such successors as, say, Emma Carus and Sophie Tucker

—made excessive use of rubatos in their singing, almost as if they were deliberately trying to stay out of key and rhythm.

These interpreters of Negro songs came to be known as "coon shouters" because what they sang were called "coon songs." The use of the reprehensible term "coon" for singer and song was the consequence of the fact that the word "coon" appeared in the titles of some of the earliest of these numbers: for example, Paul Allen's "New Coon in Town," published in 1883, introduced by the composer and his vaudeville partner Lester; in 1888, "The Whistling Coon" by Sam Devere, a black-face vaudevillian and one of the foremost banjoists of his time (he always invited the audience to join in the refrain when he sang his hit tune); in 1893, "Little Alabama Coon," by Tin Pan Alley's first woman composer, Hattie Starr.

May Irwin contributed a success of her own to the "coon song" repertory when, in 1893, she wrote "Mamie, Come Kiss Your Honey" and introduced it in *A Country Sport*. But if there is any single year in which the national vogue for "coon songs" can be said to have started it was 1896, the year in which two classics were written and first became popular: Ernest Hogan's "All Coons Look Alike to Me" and Barney Fagan's "My Gal Is a High Born Lady."

Ernest Hogan was a Negro vaudevillian who late in his life voiced regret and shame that he had ever written "All Coons Look Alike to Me," the song that made him famous. Like so many other intelligent Negroes he regarded "coon songs" as demeaning to his race. Actually, save for the use of the word "coon," there was nothing in Hogan's song that in any way was derogatory to the Negro. Its theme was *not* that every Negro looks like every other Negro. The Negro heroine in this song is merely explaining why she is rejecting her persistent suitor—all suitors are the same to her. Hogan himself introduced the song and made it popular. Rupert Hughes once described his performance as "simply fascinating" because of "its impudent determination to keep out of key and out of time."

Barney Fagan, the composer of "My Gal Is a High Born Lady," was one of vaudeville's best known buck-and-wing artists. Later on he was the stage director of the Primrose and West Minstrels. One day, while cycling along Lake Michigan in Chicago, he was attracted to the peculiar rhythm produced by a broken pedal banging against his wheel. The rhythm suggested a syncopated tune. The finished product—Fagan wrote both words and music—was sold to Witmark for a hundred dollars. Witmark published it in a highly effective arrangement by Gustav Luders (later on, a successful composer of Broadway operettas). Charles Haverly introduced it with the Haverly Minstrels, but it was Clara Wieland who first made it successful, at Koster and Bial's.

One of the earliest classics of syncopation—Kerry Mills's "At a Georgia Camp Meeting"—was written as a protest against, and a reaction to, the "coon song." Frederick Allen Mills, as he was officially named, studied the violin with private teachers and then worked as head of the violin department at the University of Michigan School of Music. In 1893 he opened his own violin studio in Ann Arbor and occasionally gave violin recitals. It was not long before he made the transition from serious to popular music by writing the syncopated tune for the piano "Rastus on Parade," which he identified as a "two-step march." He published it himself in 1895, using the name of Kerry Mills as composer—under F. A. Mills, he was the publisher.

Kerry Mills liked to haunt the offices of publishing houses, and in them he had often heard May Irwin and Imogene Comer rehearse new "coon songs." The style of both the songs and the singers repelled him, because he felt that both put the Negro in an unfavorable light. This impelled him to write a song more realistic about Negroes. Using a religious camp meeting in the South as his subject, he wrote "At a Georgia Camp Meeting." Since every publisher turned it down, he had to issue it himself just as he had previously done with "Rastus on Parade."

Dave Genaro, of the vaudeville team of Genaro and Bailey, liked the song and introduced it in vaudeville. When he finished singing verse and refrain—and before repeating the refrain a second time—he did a peculiar type of Negro strut which was to become popular in vaudeville and minstrel shows as the "cakewalk." "These were strutting steps," explains Sigmund Spaeth, in his *History of Popular Music in America*, "with the dancers leaning backward as far as possible, business and by-play with canes and high hats, and so forth."

The "coon song," the "coon shouter," the syncopated tunes of Kerry Mills, and the cakewalk carry us to the threshold of ragtime—a musical style whose impact on Tin Pan Alley was no less decisive than that of the sentimental ballad a decade or so earlier. But that is a later story.

## 7

## *"Bring on the Follies girl"*

A new century had arrived. It was rich in achievements and richer still in promises for the future. America had just emerged from the brief Spanish-American War victoriously, with flying banners and few casualties. It was about to extend its sphere of influence by leasing for perpetuity the Canal Zone on the Isthmus of Panama for the building of a canal linking the Atlantic and Pacific oceans.

Internally in the United States, expansion was the keynote. Industry, now grown to prodigious proportions, had created the billion-dollar trust. It was flourishing in spite of the efforts of the Sherman Antitrust Act to limit its giant growth. A survey early in the 1900's disclosed that more than five thousand organizations had been consolidated into three hundred trusts—one of the most powerful of these being U. S. Steel. These trusts were controlled by just a handful of financial barons, headed by the Rockefellers and the Morgans.

Prosperity was everywhere. In the West the successful application of science to agriculture had helped make the soil fertile and facilitated cultivation. Railroads linked hitherto widely separated and far-flung cities. In the South the rise of new factories and the development of natural resources increased job opportunities. In the East a fabulous extension of business opportunities came as the result of the invention of the automobile, telephone and telegraph, and the wider use of electricity. Exports to Europe soared as the demand for American-made machines and products exceeded the supply.

Growth and expansion penetrated into every possible area. The development of public education and growing literacy brought new strength to the press and made it a powerful instrument for the molding of public opinion. (Had not the press already proved its potency in 1898 by fomenting a war?) Large-circulation magazines and best-selling novels reached a larger public than ever before. The age was so sure of itself and its strength that it could now accept frank criticism: the "muckraking" magazine article and book were becoming popular.

It was an age able to think in terms of immense size—symbolized, perhaps, by the building of New York's first skyscraper, the Flatiron Building, in 1902. It was an age encouraging speed, first with the trolley car (in Boston in 1898), then with the subway (in Boston and New York in 1898 and 1900, respectively), finally with the automobile (14,000 of them on the road by 1900). As movement accelerated, man's age-old dream of flying was reaching fulfillment: In 1903 the Wright brothers lifted their airplane from the ground at Kitty Hawk.

Everyone seemed conscious of the promises of the new

age; recognized how industry was continually opening new horizons; saw how seemingly limitless were the opportunities for favorable speculation and the amassing of wealth. Money was spent even more freely than in the 1890's, and by many more people. In an attempt to reap some of the economic harvest, con men, gold-brick merchants, and the city slicker enjoyed a heyday. People lived more opulently, lavishly, ornately than ever. They dressed more flashily. The dandy of the 1880's and 1890's was replaced by the dude with his loud-colored vest, peg-top trousers, stiff collar, and a hat, either derby or straw, that was attached to his coat lapel with a cord.

The national ego bulged; Americans were becoming increasingly chauvinistic. John Philip Sousa sang the praises of America's might and majesty in his stirring marches, of which "The Stars and Stripes Forever" in 1897 almost assumed the august status of a national anthem. Jack London, Edith Wharton, Frank Norris explored American backgrounds, experiences, and characters for their novels. Walter Damrosch wrote an American opera *The Scarlet Letter*, produced in 1896; and Edward MacDowell and Henry F. Gilbert tried to realize *American* symphonic music by using the melodies and rhythms of the American Indian. American drama was beginning to emerge from the cocoon with William Vaughn Moody's *The Great Divide* in 1906. Putting a forceful finger on American achievement, the Hall of Fame was instituted at New York University in New York, and the first volume of *Who's Who in America* was released, both in 1900. Charles Dana Gibson glorified the American girl in cartoons, as Ziegfeld was doing on the stage. In 1907, George M. Cohan—a real Yankee Doodle Dandy—strutted up and down the stage, a flag draped around his body, singing the praises of his country.

*

Like everything else in the United States, the musical theater was undergoing a radical metamorphosis. The slow-moving, static, girl-free minstrel show was on its way out. In its place came the revue, essentially vaudeville in fancy dress. The expanding American economy, with its partiality for gilding the lily, dictated that costume designs and staging be sumptuous; and to this dictation, the revue gave ready response.

The first revue—it was called *The Passing Show*—opened at the Casino Theater in 1894. It was the brainchild of George W. Lederer, who created it because he had become convinced that vaudeville, mounted with the magnificence of an extravaganza, could find a select audience willing to pay a far higher price of admission than the twenty-five and fifty cents charged by Tony Pastor. Lederer built up a program decked out with beautiful show girls posing in "living pictures," spectacles, acrobatic acts, sketches, songs. He brought down the curtain on a sensational divertissement that held the audience spellbound.

Like every other successful venture, *The Passing Show* inspired imitation. *The Merry Whirl* came in 1895, followed by *In Gay New York* in 1896, and *All of the Town* in 1897. By the end of the century the revue was a Broadway institution. It did not now have long to wait for a producer who combined showmanship with a dash of genius, imagination with a sprinkling of daring, taste with a flair for extravagance. Such a producer, destined to make the revue a true reflection of the times in the grandioseness of its concept and the magnificence of its realization, was Florenz Ziegfeld. His production—the *Ziegfeld Follies*.

Ziegfeld was a man who loved beauty in all its manifestations and deified it. No price, he felt, was too high to pay for its glorification, no obstacle too insurmountable for its successful fulfillment. Though his only experience in show business had been as manager of Sandow the Great, the strong man at the Chicago world fair of 1893, Ziegfeld soon was driven by the dream of producing an American show for Anna Held, the Parisian star. Penniless and without a reputation, he went to Paris and actually convinced her to sign a contract. Then he went about the necessary business of raising the funds for a sumptuous production. It was called *A Parlor Match* and it came to the Herald Square Theater on September 21, 1896. Here Anna Held sang "Won't You Come and Play With Me?" She was not a striking beauty, as Marjorie Farnsworth points out in *The Ziegfeld Follies.* "She had a plump little figure laced in at the waist until her hips jutted out horizontally. . . . She was a tiny girl, a little over five feet in height, with a halo of light brown hair and a nose a little too long to agree with an artist's ideal." But, Miss Farnsworth adds, "to Americans she was the epitome of Gallic spice and naughtiness." Her large, luminous dark eyes—filled with a baby innocence, "mischievous with a trace of naughtiness"—provided a tantalizing contrast to the suggestiveness of the lyrics, which her piquant French accent made all the more provocative.

She became Ziegfeld's wife in 1897, and continued to star in other lavish Ziegfeld productions. In *Parisian Model* she sang "Delightful to Be Married" and "I Just Can't Make My Eyes Behave"; in *Miss Innocence,* "I've Lost My Teddy Bear"; in *The Little Duchess,* "Maiden with the Dreamy Eyes." She consistently smashed the box-office records previously established at the Casino Theater by Lillian Russell—a fact that went a long way to prove that she was now Lillian Russell's successor as the darling of the stage. In fact, in line with this development, Lillian Russell's opulent figure—with its generous curves and ample swells—no longer was regarded as the criterion for feminine beauty. Women now sought to acquire the slim, petite, boyish contours of Anna Held. Whatever Anna Held did —or whatever her publicity maintained she did—the public followed. Even the taking of milk baths! For Ziegfeld, already a master at attracting newspaper interest, had been ordering gallons of milk delivered to his door each day for Anna Held's baths. He announced that Anna Held's perfect, satinlike skin was the product of these milk baths; he even brought reporters into the privacy of her bathroom to see for themselves how her skin was soaking in the milk. The stories that followed in the papers induced a new bathing cult among American womankind—who were already starving themselves in a desperate attempt to achieve Anna Held's "hand-spanned eighteen-inch waist."

By virtue of Anna Held's successes, Ziegfeld became a producer of wealth and influence. In the early 1900's he had the wherewithall to produce his stage masterpiece—the *Follies*. He wanted an American *Folies Bergères*—to create the most spectacular revue ever mounted in the United States, the setting for the most beautiful women ever to walk across an American stage.

On July 8, 1907 he presented the first such production—the *Follies of 1907*, at the Jardin de Paris (the roof of the New York Theater). There for the first time he glorified the American female with a chorus line of "Anna Held girls" in tableaux to stun the senses. One of these was a swimming pool routine simulating a motion-picture show.

That is how the *Follies* were born. For the next two decades, the *Follies* (or the *Ziegfeld Follies*, as the show was named in 1911 and after) became increasingly opulent in its productions; increasingly generous in the presentation of stars, either those of established fame or those it was about to make famous; increasingly lavish in the display of feminine beauty bedecked in the most stunning jewels and gowns. Ziegfeld produced the *Follies* the way he lived, in the grand manner of royalty. He would spend more than a thousand dollars for a gown that was worn in only a single scene and was on view for only a few minutes. He could discard, without so much as a moment's hesitation, a set that had cost him twenty-five thousand dollars because he had come to the sudden realization that it did not do justice to his conception. He paid fabulous salaries to attract the best talent the stage had to offer. In thinking in big terms, in executing big dreams, he refused to take into account the simple arithmetic of income and outgo; and that, in the end, proved his undoing.

The big parade of female pulchritude, the ornateness of scenery and costumes, the brilliance of individual performances—this is what made the *Ziegfeld Follies* the yardstick by which all other revues were henceforth measured, the standards toward which they would all aspire.

In 1908 the production number "The Taxicab Girl" made audiences gasp—girls, in abbreviated dress, appeared wearing headlights, red tin flags, and a sign reading "For Hire." As they thus flitted about the stage, Gertrude Vanderbilt sang "Take Me Around in a Taxicab." Female beauty was further glorified in a spectacular number inspired by the popular cover girl of the day, "The Nell Brinkley Girl," and in another number, "Merry Widows of All Nations," which was stimulated by the American success of Franz Lehár's operetta *The Merry Widow*.

This was also the year in which Nora Bayes made her *Follies* debut. She was already a star by that time, the aristocrat of lady vaudevillians, the queen of the "coon shouters," the "Wurzburger girl," as she came to be known after scoring a major success with Harry von Tilzer's "Down Where the Wurzburger Flows." She strode majestically across the stage, usually with a fine lace handkerchief or a fan in her hand. She did not woo her audiences, as so many other female stars of the *Follies* did; rather, she subdued them with the weight of her personality and the volume of her vocal delivery. She had a husky, throbbing contralto voice that she herself described as "terrible" but whose effect on audiences was hypnotic. "She strode up and down a stage, putting over songs, clowning, swinging hips, pausing center stage (full spotlight) to deliver a sentimental recitative," describes Allen Churchill in *The Great White Way*. "In everything she did, Nora was a lady . . . 'Nora was heart, all heart, her act was full of heart,' an old-timer recalls. 'She sold songs where others just sang them,' an admirer has stated."

In her initial *Follies* appearance, Nora Bayes put her best foot forward with a song, written in collaboration with her husband, Jack Norworth, which was to displace "Down Where the Wurzburger Flows" as her song identification. It was "Shine On, Harvest Moon." When many years later the story of her life was filmed, with Ann Sheridan as Nora Bayes, it was titled "Shine On, Harvest Moon." And when, in 1931, the last of the *Follies* to be produced by Ziegfeld was seen in New York, "Shine On, Harvest Moon" was revived for Ruth Etting, as a reminder of a resplendent moment in *Follies* history and of a surpassing singing star, who had then been dead three years.

In 1909, Lillian Lorraine, aptly described as "the queen of Venuses" came to the *Follies*. Exquisite, petite, delicate, with soulful and enormous brown eyes and a perfect complexion, she was, as Sophie Tucker once described her, "an eyeful that knocked you cold." For her first *Follies* appearances, she sang "Nothing but a Bubble" in a sea of soap bubbles and "Up, Up, Up in My Aeroplane," as she soared in a little flying machine over her audience. Florenz Ziegfeld considered her the most beautiful woman he had ever seen—and proceeded to fall in love with her.

That edition in 1909 was one with which Sophie Tucker had a short and unhappy association. She was starred in a mammoth jungle scene singing "Moving Day in Jungle Town" and several other hit songs. She stopped the show cold during out-of-town tryouts—something Nora Bayes would not tolerate since she insisted that she, and she alone, stop the show with her songs. A compromise was reached whereby Sophie Tucker was left with just the one number "Moving Day in Jungle Town." But even that was taken away from her soon after the *Follies* opened in New York. Eva Tanguay, probably the greatest vaudevillian of her time—as well as the most uninhibited—was taken into the show, and Eva Tanguay wanted to do the jungle number. Thus Sophie Tucker was eased out of the production. She never again appeared in the *Follies*.

The song that enabled Eva Tanguay to become one of the leading, if not *the* leading, female vaudevillian before she came to the *Follies*—with a weekly income of about twenty-five hundred dollars the year round—was "I Don't Care." It was published in 1905, and she introduced it in her act soon after that. From then on her frequent singing of "I Don't Care" kept it as one of the biggest-selling numbers in Tin Pan Alley for about a decade. By virtue of that song she came to be known as the "I Don't Care girl." But she was also identified on vaudeville bills as "The Human Gyroscope" and "Miss Tabasco." She was a bombshell. As uninhibited as a typhoon, she blew in and out of the vaudeville bill howling her songs. She usually sang numbers written for her—"I Can't Help It," "Egotistical Eva," and "Whistle and Help Me Along"—and between her numbers she recited verses and injected double-entendres that made her act one of the most risqué in all vaudeville. She mocked everyone and everything, including herself. She did a takeoff on Salome, and forgot to use most of the veils; she poured champagne on her head; she showed off her beautiful legs. She wore the most expensive, distinctive, and at times the heaviest gowns on any stage; one of them was made up entirely of coins, weighed forty-five pounds, and cost more than two thousand dollars. She was a star of stars before Ziegfeld took her for the *Follies*, and she was a star of stars *in* the *Follies*.

In the *Follies of 1910*, Bert Williams became the first Negro to share the spotlight with white performers in a major Broadway revue. He, too, like Eva Tanguay, came to the *Follies* after starring in vaudeville. As the partner in the famous vaudeville team of Williams and Walker he was among the first Negro entertainers (as *Show Biz: From Vaude to Video* points out) "to break loose from the standard formula of colored acts—the chicken-stealing, crap-shootin', gin-guzzlin', razor-totin' no-account." He was a pantomimist and ad-lib artist second to none. He was also one of a kind in the rendition of Negro dialect songs, some of which he wrote himself. He had sung many such songs to national popularity in vaudeville, including "Nobody," "Let It Alone," "Somebody Lied," "I Don't Care If You Never Come Back," and "You're in the Right Church but the Wrong Pew."

Williams shone like a diamond in the *Ziegfeld Follies of 1910*, in which he made his bow singing "Late Hours," "I'll Lend You Everything I've Got Except My Wife," and his own classic, "Nobody." In the *Follies of 1911* he almost stole the show with "Woodman, Spare That Tree!" by Irving Berlin, and "Dat's Harmony." After that he was heard in the succeeding editions of the *Follies* with such songs as "You're on the Right Road but You're Going the Wrong Way," "Blackberrying Today," "My Landlady," and "You Can't Make Your Shimmy Shake on Tea." He also appeared in various comedy scenes (frequently in collaboration with Leon Errol), and in the *Follies of 1914* he presented his incomparable poker pantomime.

In all there were twenty-three editions of the *Follies*. In that time, Marion Davies, Nita Naldi, Harriet Hoctor, Mae Murray, and many others stepped out of the chorus line to become stars of stage and screen. Will Rogers, W. C. Fields, Leon Errol, Ed Wynn, Marilyn Miller were some of the many stars to brighten the stage of the New Amsterdam Theater.

If any one star is most closely identified with the *Follies* in general and Florenz Ziegfeld in particular, it was Fanny Brice. She appeared in every edition of the *Follies* between 1910 and 1923, except one. When Ziegfeld inaugurated his *Midnight Frolic* atop the New Amsterdam Theater, she was the star of that as well—frequently doing her act in the *Frolic* immediately after completing her show downstairs in the *Follies*. Some years after that, she became a principal performer in a radio show called the *Ziegfeld Follies of the Air;* she was featured in the motion picture *The Great Ziegfeld;* and she appeared in the *Ziegfeld Follies* when it was revived two years after Ziegfeld's death.

She had been Ziegfeld's discovery. Her earliest stage experiences came from amateur contests, the first of which was at Kenney's Theater in Brooklyn when she was fourteen. A gawky, lanky girl, with long legs, and none-too-attractive face, she was looked upon with amused skepticism whenever she entered one of these contests. But once she started to sing—and in those days she specialized in "coon songs" and ballads—she held an audience transfixed. She invariably won first prize, which, together with the pennies and nickels that the appreciative audience showered on her, came to as much as seventy-five dollars a week.

After changing her name to Fanny Brice (she was born Fanny Borach), she worked first as a singer of popular tunes for song slides at a movie house on Eighty-third Street and Broadway and then as a singer in burlesque. One evening the leading performers of her troupe were required to give a benefit performance in Arverne, Long Island. The manager of the company insisted that Fanny do a "specialty." The suggestion filled her with horror, she had no "specialty" in her repertory, she feared the lack might jeopardize her job. In her despair she went to Irving Berlin and begged him to provide her with a number or two. Berlin played two songs for her—one was a Jewish comedy song, "Sadie Salome," which he sang for her in a Yiddish accent, and the other was a ragtime piece, "The Grizzly Bear." Fanny Brice decided to try her luck with both numbers. "I had never had any idea of doing a song with a Jewish accent," she later confessed. "I didn't even understand Jewish, couldn't talk a word of it. But, I thought, if that's the way Irving sings it, that's the way I'll sing it. I learned them both in an hour, and the explanation for that is simple: youth and ambition."

She appeared at that benefit wearing a linen costume that fit a bit too tightly and had been starched too stiffly. As she delivered her two numbers, the costume began to rub her in all the wrong places. "It's gathering you-know-where, and I'm trying to squirm it away, and singing and smiling, and the audience is loving it. They think it's an act I'm doing, so, as long as they're laughing, I keep it up. They start to throw roses at me."

That's how Fanny Brice became a comedienne, and that's how she started doing Yiddish-type songs in which she was inimitable.

Ziegfeld saw Fanny perform in a burlesque show at the Columbia Theater on Broadway, summoned her to his inner sanctum and—miracle of miracles—hired her for the *Follies.* In the *Follies of 1910* Fanny Brice started off with a ragtime tune, "Lovey Joe." But what really brought the house down was her comic presentation of "Good-by, Becky Cohen," the first song by Irving Berlin to get into the *Follies.* The next day Ziegfeld tore up his contract with Brice, wrote a new one with a steep hike in salary, and made her a star. She remained a star—year in, year out. She parlayed a gawky physique, an awkward manner, an incomparable gift at mimicry and travesty, a Yiddish accent, and a talent at making funny faces and grotesque gestures into successes of the highest order. Her "specialties" were *sui generis*—comedy songs and routines introduced into the various *Follies* such as "Ephraham," "Second Hand Rose," "I'm a Vamp from East Broadway," "Ziegfeld Follies Rag," "Soul Saving Sadie," "Nijinsky," and "Modernistic Moe."

On one occasion, however, she also showed herself to be a tragedienne of song. In 1921, Ziegfeld had brought Mistinguette from Paris to sing the popular French ballad "Mon Homme." After she came and sang for him, Ziegfeld decided not to use her after all. Fanny Brice asked to do the number in a new American adaptation by Channing Pollack. At a rehearsal she sang it wearing an evening gown. Ziegfeld jumped from his place in the theater and tore the dress from her. He told her he wanted her to appear in rags, singing the song leaning against a lamppost on a dark stage. And that's the way Fanny Brice presented "My Man." Her audiences knew that she was singing her heart out because she was talking about herself and her ill-fated marriage to Nicky Arnstein, the convicted gambler and gangster, whom she loved deeply and devotedly.

Still another of the more consistent stars of the *Follies* who was a singing comedian without parallel was Eddie Cantor. He was the star in various editions from 1917 through 1927. Ziegfeld also produced around him several magnificently mounted and highly successful musical comedies, including *Kid Boots* and *Whoopee*.

Born Edward Israel Iskowitz in the lower East Side of New York, Eddie Cantor became an orphan at the age of two and from then on he was raised by his grandmother, Esther, who went from door to door as a peddler to support him. The child Eddie supplemented her meager income with pennies earned from singing and performing in the streets. When he was fifteen, he won first prize (five dollars) in an amateur contest at Miner's Bowery Theater. Soon after that he got his first job as a singing comedian with a burlesque company at a salary of fifteen dollars a week. Later he was employed as a singing waiter in Coney Island (Jimmy Durante was his pianist there), and with the vaudeville act of Bedini and Arthur, with whom, for the first time, he blackened his face.

His first big break came, in 1912, when Gus Edwards hired him to appear in his school-kid act in vaudeville, entitled that year *Kid Kabaret*. One of Eddie's routines was an imitation of Eddie Leonard doing "Ida." Since Ida Tobin was Cantor's boyhood sweetheart (whom he would marry in 1914), the song "Ida" had a personal meaning to him, and it remained one of his favorites. In another routine he wore a battered high hat, a Prince Albert coat, and white gloves, and carrying a book under arm, he sang "Waiting for the Robert E. Lee," in an accent half-southern half-Yiddish. The audience was his; it stayed that way for the next half-century.

In 1916, Cantor had a small part in *Canary Cottage*, a musical comedy playing in California. Ziegfeld spotted him there and called him to New York for an audition. Ziegfeld liked what he heard and saw and signed Cantor to appear in the *Midnight Frolic*, a revue atop the New Amsterdam Theater. Running nervously up and down the stage, clapping his hands, and his eyes almost popping out of their sockets through his white horned-rimmed glasses, Eddie Cantor sang "Oh, How She Could Yacki, Hacki, Wicki, Woo." Ziegfeld (who had a passion for sending telegrams even when the recipient was just an elbow room's away) wired him: "Enjoyed your act. You'll be here for a long time." He was. The next year, Ziegfeld brought him downstairs to the stage of the New Amsterdam for the *Follies of 1917*. Cantor had the audience in the palm of his hand as he sang "That's the Kind of Baby for Me." So great was the clamor of the audience that even after he had given twelve encores of the chorus, the din would not die down; and the next act—Tom Richards—had to start his performance through the noise. In his dressing room, Cantor was found sobbing, his head in his arms. His grandmother had died a few months earlier and thus had not lived to witness this triumph. Will Rogers consoled him by saying: "What makes you think, Eddie, she didn't see you—and from a very good seat?"

In later *Follies*, Cantor presented "You'd Be Surprised," "The Dixie Volunteers," "My Blue Heaven," "A Modern Maiden's Prayer," and "It All Belongs to Me" (among many other numbers), and helped them all to become the kind of hits they were.

While a good deal of the music for the various *Follies* was supplied by such regulars as Irving Berlin, Dave Stamper, Raymond Hubbell and Louis Hirsch, most of the hit songs through the years were the work of various individual composers, lucky enough to get their numbers interpolated into the various editions. Finding a slot in the *Follies* for one of its songs became for Tin Pan Alley a prime aim and a prime achievement. A preeminent star singing one of these items, or a stupendous production number of which it was the core, was, after all, the shortest possible cut to success.

Year by year, the hits kept coming out of the *Ziegfeld Follies*, much to the delight and to the profit of Tin Pan Alley: "Garden of My Dreams," which Lillian Lorraine introduced; "My Baby's Arms," "Tulip Time," and Irving Berlin's "A Pretty Girl Is like a Melody," all sung by John Steel; "Mr. Gallagher and Mr. Shean," a lively comedy number that Mr. Gallagher and Mr. Shean themselves presented; Ina Claire singing "Hello, 'Frisco"; Jose Collins in her winning presentation of "Peg o' My Heart" and "A Little Love, a Little Kiss"; Elizabeth Brice's charming way with "Row, Row, Row." These and other songs—"By the Light of the Silvery Moon," "Hold Me in Your Loving Arms," and Victor Herbert's "A Kiss in the Dark"—made the *Ziegfeld Follies* as much a gilded showcase for wonderful songs as it was for incomparable stars and beautiful girls.

## *"The lullaby of Broadway"*

Other forms of the Broadway musical theater, besides the revue, were opening new vistas and offering Tin Pan Alley richer opportunities for song exploitation. The American operetta, for example, was blooming into full flower in the first years of the new century.

Victor Herbert had had his first produced operetta in 1894, *Prince Ananias*; and his first major success came a year after that with *The Wizard of the Nile*. From then on, the American theater found in him a composer of such rare melodic invention and with such a trained gift for harmony and orchestration that many still regard him as our theater's first significant composer. Surely, Victor Herbert is the first composer for the American theater whose best music has survived and is still capable of affording audiences the same kind of pleasure it offered when first heard. He is also the first of our stage composers whose best operettas are still frequently revived, on the screen as well as on the stage.

Irish-born and German-trained, Herbert remained throughout his life a "European" composer, even though all his operettas were written in this country for American consumption. His melodies boasted an Irish sweetness and sentimentality; his harmonies and orchestrations had Germanic solidity. But, after all, the American operetta was essentially a European commodity—extensions of similar works by Offenbach, Suppé, Johann Strauss II, and Gilbert and Sullivan. The hands that created operettas for the New York theater might have been American; but the voice remained European. American operettas, like the European, called for texts with foreign or make-believe settings, synthetic plots, stock characterizations, and lilting Continental-type melodies, usually in three-quarter time. Herbert's operettas were no exceptions to this rule. *The Fortune Teller* in 1898, *Babes in Toyland* in 1903, *Mlle. Modiste* in 1905, *The Red Mill* in 1906, and *Naughty Marietta* in 1910 were all American-made—but with ingredients imported from across the Atlantic.

Herbert completed his first scores for the Broadway theater before he personally, and his influence, penetrated Tin Pan Alley. But beginning with "The Gypsy Love Song" and several other hit numbers from *The Fortune Teller*— all published by Witmark in 1898—his huge stature dominated Tin Pan Alley just as it did Broadway. In Tin Pan Alley he was looked upon with a mixture of awe and envy: because he had the god-given gift for lyricism to produce "Moonbeams," "March of the Toys," "Toyland," "Kiss Me Again," "I'm Falling in Love with Someone," "Ah, Sweet Mystery of Life," and many others; because the writing of such beautiful melodies came so easily to him;

because he was so prolific that he could work on three or four operetta scores at the same time, and yet always meet his deadlines well before the zero hour; because he was so thoroughly trained a musician that he was able to serve as conductor of a major symphony orchestra, on the one hand, and write ambitious concertos and opera, on the other; and because he was a man who always had the joy of life in him, who took as much delight in good wines and the culinary art as in music, and who had an inordinate capacity for making and keeping friends and inspiring affection as well as admiration.

Though born in Ireland—in the city of Dublin in 1859 —Herbert spent the impressionable years of his childhood in England. At the age of three, upon the death of his father, he and his mother went to live with her own father, Samuel Lover, at his home just outside London. As a writer of ballads and popular novels, including *Handy Andy*, Lover attracted to his place leading authors, musicians, and artists, thus providing the child Victor with a highly sophisticated setting in which to grow up and one in which his obvious gift for music could be properly nursed. That gift blossomed with his first piano lessons with his mother, and soon required more experienced instruction. In his eighth year, therefore, his mother took Victor to Stuttgart, Germany, where the boy received a thorough musical training at its conservatory.

After some additional study of the cello with Bernard Cossman in Baden-Baden, Herbert played that instrument in several major German and Austrian orchestras directed by such masters as Brahms, Liszt, Saint-Saëns among others. He now completed two large works for cello and orchestra—a suite and a concerto—which he himself introduced in Stuttgart between 1883 and 1885.

In 1886, he married Theresa Förster, celebrated German prima donna. Since she had contracted to appear with the

Metropolitan Opera for the season of 1886–1887, her young and handsome husband was hired to play the cello in the opera orchestra. They came to the United States early in September of 1886 to fulfil their respective duties at the Metropolitan Opera. Except for a brief visit to England, Herbert never again left the United States. He acquired American citizenship and completely identified himself with American music in every way—both as a conductor and composer. In 1893 he succeeded Patrick S. Gilmore as the leader of the famous Twenty-second Regiment Band; from 1898 to 1904 he was the principal conductor of the Pittsburgh Symphony; and beginning with 1904, he founded and directed salon orchestras bearing his name. As an American composer he produced such works as the *American Fantasia* based on our national songs and compositions whose melodies and rhythms were derived from the music of the American Indian. The climax of his career as a serious composer came in 1911 with the production of his opera *Natoma*. But by that time he had become one of the most successful and most significant creators of popular music for the American stage.

Herbert's first operetta was never produced. This was *La Vivandière*, which he had written for Lillian Russell. She finally succumbed to her qualms about appearing in a show written by a novice and she withdrew from the production. *La Vivandière* was never mounted, and Herbert's score has been lost. Soon after that, in 1894, William MacDonald, director of a light-opera company, engaged Herbert to do the music for *Prince Ananias*. Except for some kind words by the critics about Herbert's songs, *Prince Ananias*, which came to New York on November 20, was a dud. But with *The Wizard of the Nile*, a year later, Herbert possessed both a hit show and a hit tune, the latter in the waltz, "Star Light, Star Bright."

He wrote thirty-nine operettas and several hundred songs,

becoming the first musical giant of the American musical theater. Through his music, he influenced American operetta and the American popular song. Tin Pan Alley felt his impact not only through the high musical standards of his songs but also through his dynamic legal involvements, which changed the financial structure of the song industry.

The American theater boasted other kings of operetta besides Herbert in the 1890's and early 1900's. Most of them, however, differed from Herbert in that they served their musical apprenticeships in Tin Pan Alley before they turned to the stage. Gustav Luders was one of these. He had come from Germany when he was twenty-three. Soon after his arrival he was hired as an all-around utility musician for the Chicago office of the Charles K. Harris publishing firm. From there he went to Witmark's to work as an arranger. One of his jobs there in 1898 was to make a piano arrangement of Barney Fagan's "My Gal Is a High Born Lady." His own popular songs, some of which were published by Witmark—Isidore Witmark described them as "tunefully bright and gay"—were far less successful.

Then, in 1899, Luders did the score for *Little Robinson Crusoe*, his first operetta. This sent him off into a new career, and a highly successful one—within the theater. His first hit song was "The Tale of the Kangaroo," heard in *The Burgomaster* in 1900. With his practical training in Tin Pan Alley, Luders had no intention of abandoning a format that had finally brought him recognition. During the next few years Luders introduced into his operettas other songs, each of which had "The Tale" in its title: "The Tale of the Bumble Bee" in *King Dodo* in 1902; "The Tale of the Seashell" (and, just to vary the monotony, "The Message of the Violet") in *The Prince of Pilsen* in 1903; "The Tale of the Violet" in *Woodland* in 1904. All these numbers were issued by his former employer, the Witmarks.

*The Prince of Pilsen* was his triumph. It enjoyed an extended run in New York. After that it went on a tour throughout the United States besides making three return engagements to New York. Subsequently it was frequently revived. Jess Dandy was seen in the leading role of Hans Wagner more than five thousand times.

Luders' thirteenth opera was *Somewhere Else*, produced in 1913. It was such a fiasco on its opening night that it had to close down after only three performances. Luders took the defeat to heart—literally. He died of an attack one day after his show closed.

Karl Hoschna was another composer who started out in Tin Pan Alley and ended up in the musical theater as a creator of operettas. He came from his native Bohemia in his nineteenth year, after which, for two years, he played the oboe in one of Victor Herbert's orchestras. Then, obsessed with the unreasonable fear that the vibrations from the double reed of the oboe would affect his mind, he decided to give up that instrument for good and seek some other way of earning his living. He dispatched a pleading note to Isidore Witmark begging for a job "however menial" and "at any salary you care to pay." Hoschna's pitiful letter impressed Witmark who hired him as a copyist for fifteen dollars a week. Hoschna's early musical training at the Vienna Conservatory made him a valuable addition to Witmark's staff and he was soon assigned to do arrangements and to advise Witmark on manuscripts.

In 1902, Hoschna met Otto Hauerbach, a young advertising executive. (Later on, as Otto Harbach, he became one of Broadway's most distinguished and prolific librettists and lyricists, a position of distinction he retained for half a century.) Hoschna and Hauerbach started to work on operettas, but not until 1905 did one of their efforts reach the stage—*Belle of the West*, which was a dismal failure. They had two more setbacks before they emerged vic-

torious with *The Three Twins*, which starred Bessie Mc-
Coy (then only eighteen) when it opened in New York
on June 15, 1908. The production made Bessie McCoy an
overnight star, with songs like "Cuddle Up a Little Closer"
and "Yama-Yama Man" (for the rest of her career she
was identified as the "yama-yama girl"). Paradoxically, neither of these two songs, which made Bessie McCoy a star
and the show a box-office success, was part of the score
Hoschna originally wrote for his operetta. He had written
"Cuddle Up a Little Closer" some years before 1908 for a
vaudeville sketch; and "Yama-Yama Man" was hurriedly
created and interpolated into the operetta while it was in
rehearsal in Chicago.

Hoschna and Hauerbach joined their talents for a second
operetta triumph—*Madame Sherry* in 1910. This score
boasted a saucy little tune in "Every Little Movement Has
a Meaning All Its Own," sung with the accompaniment of
suggestive little undulations of the body, and with a good
deal of ogling at the men in the front rows. The song always inspired titters of embarrassment from the women in
the audience and ripples of delight from the men. In 1910,
and for a number of years after that, young people used to
consider themselves the acme of sophistication by whispering to their companions of the opposite sex—probably with
a wink and a smirk—that "every little movement has a
meaning all its own."

The revue and the operetta shared the spotlight with the
extravaganza in the American theater. First becoming popular in 1866 with *The Black Crook*—a show that introduced to the American stage undraped females, suggestive
dances, songs with sex innuendos as well as the most spectacular scenes yet seen in America—the extravaganza had
truly become a many-splendored thing by 1900. *The Wizard of Oz* in 1903—and its unashamed imitator in 1905,

Victor Herbert's *Babes in Toyland*—presented spellbinding tableaux, ballets, spectacles, and stunning stage effects. But ambitious though these productions were, they were destined to be completely outstripped in every department by the extravaganzas that came to the Hippodrome Theater beginning with 1905.

The Hippodrome Theater was a new house built at a cost of almost two million dollars, boasting the largest stage in the world, and some of the most complex and advanced stage machinery known anywhere. The theater opened for the first time on April 12, 1905, with a varied program comprising a circus show, ballet, and a "spectacular drama" entitled *Andersonville*. Later the same year the Hippodrome offered its first extravaganza, *A Society Circus*, in which the French clown Marcelline made his American debut. Other highlights of this production were two lavish spectacles, "Song of the Flowers" and "The Court of the Golden Fountains."

During the next decade, *Pioneer Days, Sporting Days, In and Around the World, Wars of the World*, and other extravaganzas introduced electrifying effects and prodigious scenes to stupefy the senses and defy the credulity of an early twentieth-century audience: airplane battles and auto races; earthquakes and tornados; the thundering of herds of deer and elephants across the plains; a city fire; rush hour at Grand Central Station in New York; and, most celebrated of all, a mystifying tank act repeated for a number of years in which chorus girls stepped down into a forty-foot-deep tank filled with water, never to reappear.

Every element of the musical theater was subservient to spectacle at the Hippodrome. Though these productions contained a good deal of music—at first, the work of Manuel Klein, after that, of Raymond Hubbell—very few hit songs came out of these shows. One, however, was a triumph, and it was the result of a huge misunderstanding.

When John Golden—then a songwriter, in later years the producer—was told that an Oriental singer would appear in *The Big Show*, in 1916, he somehow jumped to the conclusion that she was Tamaki Miura, the prima donna who had attracted a good deal of attention in Puccini's *Madama Butterfly*. He decided, therefore, to build up a little scene about Madame Butterfly, and for this he wrote the lyrics—to Hubbell's music—for "Poor Butterfly" about Cio-Cio-San. As it turned out, the performer was not Japanese—she was a Chinese-American vaudevillian, Haru Onuki. She was such a fiasco at the Hippodrome that after a few days she was replaced by Sophie Bernard, who was actually the one who first put "Poor Butterfly" across to audiences. Two months later a dance recording finished what Sophie Bernard had started—making "Poor Butterfly" one of the biggest hit songs of 1916. " 'Poor Butterfly,' " as John Golden later recalled in his autobiography, "was strummed, hummed, whistled and wept over by as many voices and hands as there are pianos, ukuleles, typewriters, and tenors in the land. I think I am safe in saying that T. B. Harms, the publishers, in all their experience, never had a bigger selling song, and I know I never had one which made more money."

But at the Winter Garden, where the extravaganza also held sway for more than a decade and made there its last splendid stand, performer and song had to share the limelight with spectacle and display. The Winter Garden opened on March 21, 1911, with a dual attraction. One half of the program consisted of a "Cook's tour through vaudeville with a Parisian landscape" entitled *La Belle Paree*. The other half was a "Chinese opera"—*Bow Sing*. At the opening night both presentations fell flat. Throughout each of the two spectacles the audience moved about restlessly, then started to cough and talk. The critics the next morning were devastating. On the second night the theater was three-quarters empty. Nothing, it seemed, could prevent a fiasco. Then on the third evening something happened on the stage that was not in the program. One of the performers in *La Belle Paree* stepped out of character, went to the edge of the footlights, and began to talk flippantly and informally to the few spectators scattered throughout the theater. "Lots of brave folk out there," he remarked, peering through half-closed eyelids into the dark auditorium. "Come to think of it," he added, "after the reviews we got, there's a lot of brave folk right up here on the stage." The audience started to chuckle. "That's better, folks! What do you say we get a bit better acquainted?" The audience applauded. "Tell you what I'm gonna do. I'm gonna sing some songs for you, if you'll listen." The applause grew louder. Then, for the following half-hour, the performer sang his heart out.

The next day everybody along Broadway was talking about the unrehearsed, improvised sequence. Lines started to form outside the Winter Garden box office. The show became a hit. And the performer who had brought the public into the theater became the cynosure of everybody inside the auditorium, once he stepped on the stage. That's the way it was to be for the rest of the run of *La Belle Paree,* and for every other extravaganza in which he would henceforth be starred at the Winter Garden.

Al Jolson was that performer, and the Winter Garden became his personal kingdom, where he ruled with song and laughter and carried on an uninterrupted love affair with his audiences.

He had been born Asa Yoelson in Washington, D. C., the son of a cantor. In his early boyhood he sang in the synagogue choir. Then one day he went into a local vaudeville theater where Eddie Leonard was the headliner. During his act Leonard asked the audience to join him in singing "I'll Leave My Happy Home for You." As if mesmerized, little Asa rose in his seat and sang—and everybody in the theater listened. That was the moment in which Asa knew where his destiny lay. He ran away from home, found a job as a singer, was caught and dragged home—this happened several times. Then he formed a vaudeville act with his brother, Harry, and a third partner, Fred E. Moore. They were described in the billing as "Introducers and Promoters of High-class Ballads and Popular Songs."

It was in vaudeville (at the Rockaway Theater in Long Island, New York) that Al Jolson, as he now called himself, blackened his face for the first time. His success in vaudeville brought him a contract with the Lew Dockstader Minstrels at a salary of seventy-five dollars a week. At first he was an end man, then he was given a spot in the olio; and then, at the Fifth Avenue Theater in February, 1909, he was allowed to do a single just before the closing. He wooed his audience with song and stories in such a way that the audience became his own. "Haven't seen a demonstration for a single act," reported Sime Silverman in *Variety*, "or any act, for that matter, as was given Al Jolson when he appeared next to closing in Dockstader's Minstrels."

He made an even closer contact with his audiences when he appeared in Hammerstein's Victoria later the same year. Midway in his act he shouted to the wings: "Bring up the house lights." He then sat down on the edge of the stage, his feet dangling into the orchestra pit, and started an informal chat with the audience. "Ya know, folks, this is the happiest night of my life. Yes, siree. I'm so happy . . . I want to sing and sing and sing. . . . Ya wanna lissen?" *Did it want to listen?* The audience wouldn't let him leave the stage.

It was on the strength of his success at the Victoria that Al Jolson was signed up by the Shuberts to appear in *La Belle Paree* for the opening of the Winter Garden. And it was as a result of his triumph in *La Belle Paree* that the Shuberts not only built their next extravaganza around him—*Vera Violetta* in 1912—but also inaugurated Sunday-evening concerts at the Winter Garden. There Jolson could keep the stage all to himself for the whole evening and sing to his heart's content.

The Jolson legend was now in the making. So were the routines that gave him his individuality. At the Winter Garden concerts he had a special runway built so that he could come ever closer to his audience, while singing a program that embraced between twenty and thirty songs. In *Honeymoon Express* he played for the first time a blackface character named Gus, a simple, well-meaning but often blundering underdog who, before the play was over, emerged as a hero. Gus would return again and again in later Jolson extravaganzas at the Winter Garden. Also in *Honeymoon Express*, a painful ingrown toenail compelled Jolson, in one of his numbers, to relieve the pressure on his foot by dropping on one knee. He stayed in that position as he sang. To give the impression that this accidental gesture was part of his routine, he swung his arms out toward the audience as if to take it in in one huge hug. The bended knee and the outstretched arms thenceforth became a Jolson trademark. In *Robinson Crusoe, Jr.* he occasionally abandoned story, setting, and character to take over the show by himself and create a rapport even more intimate between himself and his audience than he had been able to effect in the formal show. He would sing his songs, tell his stories, do ad-libs, take the audience into his confidence about his personal affairs. "You ain't heard nothin' yet," he would shout exuberantly when the audience went wild—and then he would go on to do a few more numbers. In *Sinbad* he sang about the Southland and about Mammy in a way that made the hearers believe he had discovered both.

As long as he held sway—all through the 1910's—he made song hits, more song hits than any other single performer of his generation. Along Tin Pan Alley it became a truism that to get Jolson to sing a song was to have a big hit on your hands. Publishers used cajolery, flattery, the intercession of Jolson's closest friends, to get him to sing their numbers. When these failed, bribery was called upon. One publisher gave him the gift of a race horse; others got him a cut in a song's royalties; still others listed him as a collaborating lyricist or composer. The trick was to get Jolson to use the new songs—and he used them aplenty. Some he introduced at his concerts; others interpolated into his regular Winter Garden show whether the song fit into the show or not. The songs he sang, and often made successful with a single rendition, became *Jolson* songs, so much so that any other performer singing them after that would find himself imitating Jolson's mannerisms. In *Honeymoon Express* he sang "You Made Me Love You"; in *Robinson Crusoe, Jr.,* "Where Did Robinson Crusoe Go with Friday on Saturday Night?" and "Yacka Hula Hickey Dula"; in *Sinbad,* "My Mammy," "Rock-a-bye Your Baby with a Dixie Melody," and George Gershwin's "Swanee"; in *Bombo,* "Toot, Toot, Tootsie," "California, Here I Come," "I'm Goin' South," "April Showers," and "Yoo-hoo." Still other songs to which he gave that old Jolson magic included "Avalon," "The Spaniard that Blighted My Life," "Everything Is Peaches Down in Georgia," "You Ain't Heard Nothin' Yet," "After You've Gone," "N'Everything," and "On the Road to Calais."

Musical comedy was a new kind of musical theater that was beginning to take shape in the early 1900's. It became as popular as the revue, extravaganza, and the operetta; and before long it would displace them.

Musical comedy was thoroughly American—just as the

operetta was thoroughly European. It borrowed something from the minstrel show, something else from burlesque, and other elements from revue and extravaganza. To these, it contributed American plot, characters, backgrounds, colloquial dialogue and lyrics, and the kind of tunes that were Tin Pan Alley's specialty.

Musical comedy, as distinguished from other and earlier forms of musical theater, emerged with George M. Cohan, a graduate of both vaudeville and Tin Pan Alley. As a creator of musical comedies, he wrote his own plays, lyrics, and melodies; and often he was the star performer. In everything he wrote and did he was the Yankee Doodle Boy who insisted he was born on the Fourth of July—though his birth certificate places the day twenty-four hours earlier! His theater was also Yankee Doodle, through and through. He populated his musicals with such American types as a jockey, a boxer, a United States Senator, a super-patriot, a manufacturer. Cohan's settings were New Rochelle, Broadway, Washington, D. C. He often filled his musicals with sermons on patriotism; and, so that nobody could fail to see how warmly he felt toward his country, he wrapped a flag around his waist and ran up and down the stage singing hymns to flag and country.

He was a performer with a cocksure manner—arrogance, impudence, and self-assurance. He wore his hat cockily over one eye, and he swung a bamboo cane. When he had a point to make, he directed a forceful forefinger to his audience. He sang out of the corner of his mouth with a peculiar nasal twang, and when he danced, it was with a halting kangaroo step. Often, by introducing a homely monologue, an informal speech, or some slangy salutations, he succeeded in forging a bond between himself and his audience.

When he wrote his musicals he remained himself—brash,

sentimental, sanctimonious, cocky, but, above everything else, American. One critic (James S. Metcalf) described him as a "vulgar, blatant, ill-mannered, flashily-dressed, insolent smart Alec." And to a great extent he was all of these things. It was also true that his plots were compounded of coincidences and improbabilities, that his characters were made of cardboard, and that his pet routines and songs had little relevancy to the story line he was developing. Yet, in spite of these limitations, he was a powerful force in the American musical theater because he introduced a vitality, vibrancy, gusto, irreverence, and informality that helped to lift the musical show out of its doldrums. As writer and performer, he was a human cyclone, before which the old shibboleths, formulas, and traditions in the American theater had to give way. *Little Johnny Jones* in 1904—in which Cohan himself appeared as an American jockey, inspired by Tod Sloan—may have been pure corn. But it introduced into the theater an invigorating breeze that swept away some of the cobwebs that had been gathering so long over operettas and extravaganzas and that dispelled some of the musty odors that had been collecting in all the nooks and corners. The same was true of *Forty Five Minutes from Broadway* in 1906 (the setting of which was New Rochelle, New York) and *George Washington, Jr.,* also in 1906, whose hero was a super-chauvinist.

His songs were sentimental, trite, homey, and obvious— just as were so many of the songs coming out of Tin Pan Alley at the time—but they boasted a colloquial style both in lyrics and melody that was fresh and new for the American theater. "Give My Regards to Broadway," "Yankee Doodle Boy," "You're a Grand Old Flag," "Mary's a Grand Old Name," and "So Long, Mary" were pure corn, and pure Cohan.

But the basic fact remains that with his lyrics, texts, and melodies, Cohan helped bring the American musical theater to the threshold of modernity, and that all the writers of musical comedies that followed him had to continue where he had left off.

# 9

## *"Music, music, music"*

In Union Square, M. Witmark and Sons had anticipated many of the later practices of Tin Pan Alley. Once again, in 1893, it became a pioneer by moving its offices out of the Fourteenth Street area to 49-51 West 28th Street. It was in the vanguard of a general movement on the part of publishing houses toward Twenty-eighth Street.

Publishers were moving uptown because show business was moving uptown. The Casino Theater, which had opened in 1882 (and which in the 1890's was the temple of musical productions in New York) was found in the Thirty-fourth Street district. So were the Herald Square Theater and the Manhattan Opera House, two other auditoriums in which musical shows were mounted. Nearby were the Knickerbocker and the Wallack theaters.

The finest restaurants were also drifting north. Delmonico's came to Forty-fourth Street and Fifth Avenue. Rector's migrated from Chicago to settle on Broadway between Forty-third and Forty-fourth streets. Café Martin, Café des Beaux-Arts, and the Metropole were some other luxurious eating and drinking places prospering near Forty-second Street.

Music publishers followed the trend. Howley and Haviland transferred to Broadway and Thirty-second Street; Leo Feist to Thirty-seventh Street. But most of the publishers followed Witmark's lead right into Twenty-eighth Street, between Fifth Avenue and Broadway. So did important out-of-town publishing houses, including Charles K. Harris from Milwaukee and Broder and Schlam from San Francisco. By 1900, Twenty-eighth Street knew the largest concentration of popular-music publishers any single street had known up to that time, Fourteenth Street not excluded. Two or three years more and Twenty-eighth Street would be baptized "Tin Pan Alley" by Monroe Rosenfeld.

It was on Twenty-eighth Street (in line with the over-all expansion taking place in all other facets of American life) that the song industry became big business. The year 1900 saw "A Bird in a Gilded Cage" selling two million copies of sheet music. By 1910 a five-million-copy sale had been realized several times—"Meet Me Tonight in Dreamland" made it in 1909, and "Down by the Old Mill Stream" and "Let Me Call You Sweetheart" in 1910. Between 1900 and 1910 almost each of a hundred songs sold more than a million copies and each of forty-odd had amassed a sale in excess of two hundred and fifty thousand copies. More than two billion copies of sheet music in all passed from counter to customer in 1910 alone!

The song industry, then, had by the turn of the century become a business in which publishers and songwriters could make fortunes. It cost a publisher about twenty-five hundred dollars to issue a number with an initial run of ten thousand copies, promotion and overhead expenses included. Since sheet music sold for fifty cents a copy in the early 1900's, a publisher could realize a profit of as much as one hundred thousand dollars from a million-copy sale. Songwriter-composers (who, for the most part, were now getting a five percent royalty instead of selling their work outright for a cash consideration) could share another one hundred thousand dollars.

The sheet-music market spread rapidly, from music stores to department stores. Siegel-Cooper's on Eighteenth Street and Sixth Avenue became the first department store to institute a sheet-music counter. This was in or about 1895 and, soon after that, competitive department stores including Macy's followed suit. In 1907 a fierce price war erupted between Siegel-Cooper's and Macy's, which had violent repercussions in Tin Pan Alley. During this competitive battle Macy's reduced the price on a piece of sheet music from fifty cents to six cents; Siegel-Cooper's did likewise. These moves threatened to throw the music-publishing business into confusion, possibly into disaster. Consequently, several Tin Pan Alley publishers formed an agency, the American Music Stores, Inc., to maintain the existing price structure in sheet music. This organization signed contracts with fifty department stores throughout the United States that guaranteed to maintain a fixed price. But Macy's and Siegel-Cooper's refused to join. To the horror of all other stores selling music, they insisted on retaining the six-cent price level.

The publishers were now driven to work out a carefully prepared maneuver to bring both stores into line. Secretly, they made arrangements with Rothenberg's, a store on Fourteenth Street, to sell a piece of sheet music for a penny, even though it cost the publisher twenty-three cents. The publishers agreed to foot the loss, and to provide Rothenberg's with all the stock it might need; they also guaranteed to keep the price war going for twenty weeks. On October 11, 1907, the bargain price was announced in the *Evening Journal*. The next morning enormous crowds swarmed into and overran Rothenberg's, creating havoc. At the same time the publishers arranged for fifty stooges to invade both Macy's and Siegel-Cooper's and cause pandemonium through their loud and angry insistence that these stores also sell sheet music for a penny apiece. In the hubbub, fixtures were smashed and the stock from other counters was thrown pell-mell over the floor.

The war lasted one day. Late that afternoon representatives from both Macy's and Siegel-Cooper's called the American Music Stores, Inc., to sign agreements protecting the existing price structure, and, the next day, the penny sale at Rothenberg's was called off. Once again the public in New York City had to dig into its pockets and pay fifty cents for every song it wanted to buy.

To feed the now huge market for songs, publishers began manufacturing them assembly-belt-style. "We are dropping the home-made," wrote Mark Sullivan about the industrial changes in the twentieth century, "and taking the machine-made." This was also true for the music business. Songs less and less rarely came into being as the result of inspiration or from the stimulation of a chance remark, a news item, or a witnessed episode. Now it was the product of a calculated effort to meet a specific need. To help increase their list, publishers hired a staff that included arrangers to put melodies on paper and harmonize them for illiterate composers, piano demonstrators to exhibit songs to potential clients, staff writers to manufacture songs on order. Every important news item, invention, or new fashion sent the wheels whirring in Tin Pan Alley. Came the development of telephonic communication and Tin Pan Alley released a barrage of telephone songs, beginning with Charles K. Harris' "Hello, Central, Give Me Heaven" in 1901. "Daisy Bell" stimulated other bicycle songs to comment on the vogue for cycling that started in 1903. In that same year of 1903 the first aerial flight at Kitty Hawk led to the writing of dozens of songs about air travel, among which were "Come Take a Trip in My Airship," "Come, Josephine, in My Flying Machine," "Up in a Balloon," and "Up, Up, Up in My Aeroplane." When the automobile began to crowd the highways, songwriters started to crowd the racks with such automobile songs as "In My Merry Oldsmobile," "The Little Ford Rambled Along," "The Lady Chauffeur," and "He'd Have to Get Under— Get Out and Get Under." The opening of the St. Louis Exposition in 1904 led Andrew Sterling to write the lyrics of "Meet Me in St. Louis," which Kerry Mills set to music and published.

With baseball a national pastime, particularly after the first World Series in 1903, Tin Pan Alley gave birth to Albert von Tilzer's "Take Me Out to the Ball Game." Did Paderewski make front-page news as a piano virtuoso? Tin Pan Alley responded with "Since Sister Nell Heard Paderewski Play." Did the "Merry Widow Waltz" become a national disease in 1907? Like a reflex action, Tin Pan Alley came forth with "I Want to Be a Merry Widow," "I'm Looking for the Man Who Wrote the Merry Widow," and "Since Mariuch Learned the Merry Widow Waltz."

This being an age of specialization, Tin Pan Alley kept an alert eye on, and a cocked ear out for, the kind of song that at any given day was catching the public fancy. Imitation became the high flattery that composers in Tin Pan Alley now paid to a song grown popular. Should a song with "good-by" in its title hit the jackpot, as Theodore F. Morse's Spanish-American ballad "Good-by, Dolly Gray" had done, Tin Pan Alley echoed and reechoed with good-by songs: "Good-by, My Lady Love," "Good-by, Liza Jane," "Good-by, Rose," "Good-by, Good Luck, God Bless You." When the name "Mary" was successfully sentimentalized by George M. Cohan in his two songs, an epidemic of Mary songs erupted: "I Love the Name of Mary," "When Mary Smiles," "Marie from Sunny Italy," "When Sweet Marie Was Sweet Sixteen" (the last was trying to touch two bases at once by using the name of Mary in a title and by flirting with the theme of Thornton's still-popular ballad "When You Were Sweet Sixteen"). In 1903, "Hiawatha" by Neil Moret became popular. Forthwith, songs on American-Indian subjects, such as "Navajo," "Cheyenne," "Anona," and "Tammany," became the rage in Tin Pan Alley. The paradox about this last development lies in the fact that though "Hiawatha" had an American-Indian title, its subject matter was far removed from the American Indian; it had been inspired not by the Longfellow poem but by a little town named Hiawatha in Kansas!

Then there was an outpouring of sentimental ballads, and dialect songs (Yiddish and Italian now, as well as Irish and German), "coon songs," nonsense songs. Specimens of these types were being ground out like sausages by the machinery of Tin Pan Alley.

One of the reasons the song business was doing so well on Twenty-eighth Street was that publishers there were continually uncovering new and novel ways of plugging songs. Through plugging, publishers were widening and extending their market.

In the 1900's the song plugger no longer was satisfied to get his numbers heard merely in theaters, restaurants, and night spots. The plugger now invaded territory never before penetrated by the song industry. He would go by truck to the busy sections of the town (preferably at lunchtime when the streets were crowded) and use the back of his vehicle, first as a stage on which to perform songs, then as an improvised shop from which to sell the sheet music. The plugger used the six-day bike race at Madison Square Garden, where each plugger got several hours to feature his numbers. Some song pluggers tried out material on the Coney Island boardwalk; some managed to place it on brass-band programs in the parks or in amusement centers; some even succeeded in getting it heard at the Polo Grounds between innings.

When amateur nights first started gaining a foothold in burlesque, and then became a part of nickelodeons and vaudeville, publishers would hire young talented performers to enter the contests with the song the publisher wanted to popularize. Song pluggers would go to local department and five-and-ten-cent stores to sing the current hits for shoppers at the sheet-music counters. One of the first to do so and to realize the potential of this form of plugging in terms of sheet-music sales was Jean Schwartz, who invaded the sheet-music counter at Siegel-Cooper's in 1897 to promote the songs of Shapiro-Bernstein. (Undoubtedly, Schwartz's experiences in promoting songs for live audiences at Siegel-Cooper's was a valuable background for his own songwriting career that blossomed in the first years of the new century with "Mister Dooley" and the hit, "Bedelia," which was introduced by Blanche Ring in *The Jersey Lily* in 1903, after which it sold about three million copies.)

Parades, election campaigns, picnics, river excursion boats, circuses—these were some of the other places where the song plugger could introduce songs.

Most of these media helped song sales no end. One—the publication of words and music of a song in the Sunday supplement of a New York newspaper—had less happy results. Such a feature helped promote newspaper circulation, but it also cut into the sale of sheet music. One of the rare instances in which a newspaper made a song into a hit was with H. W. Petrie's "Asleep in the Deep," which became successful only after words and music had been reprinted as a special supplement in one of New York's dailies. Otherwise, newspapers did little to help a song along on the way to success. This was proved with finality in a deal promoted by William Randolph Hearst with Shapiro-Bernstein. Hearst was of the opinion that through the power of his papers he could make any song he wished into a nationwide hit. He entered into a one-year agreement with Shapiro-Bernstein to use six of its songs. At the end of the period the largest sheet-music sale enjoyed by any of these songs was only fifty thousand—at a time when a sale of two hundred and fifty thousand copies did not make much of an impression. "Songs must be heard by the people who pay to buy them," was Bernstein's sad comment.

Most of the song-plugging in Union Square had been done by the publishers themselves. On Twenty-eighth Street the leading pluggers were employees who were specialists in the art and technique of getting songs played in many different places—such people as Johnny Nestor, Joseph Santley, Ben Bloom, Jimmie Flynn, Harry Tenney, Harry Bishop, Sammy Levy, and Mose Gumble.

Mose Gumble, a bald-headed singer, was typical of this group. He made the rounds of places where people gathered, all the way from Coney Island in Brooklyn to 125th Street in Manhattan, singing the songs he wanted to promote. He enjoyed a huge acquaintanceship in the trade, cajoling actors with his charm and glib tongue into using his numbers. As a fifteen-dollar-a-week staff pianist for Shapiro-Bernstein, Gumble demonstrated songs for such stars as George M. Cohan, Nora Bayes, and Weber and Fields. From demonstrations he graduated into plugging.

He would sometimes board a horse-car on Broadway and shout his songs to the throngs in the street. But, initially, at any rate, his favorite stamping ground was Coney Island. From evening to the following day he toured the Coney Island dance halls, restaurants, and other night spots, placing his numbers. Many a time he slept on the beach to be on time for the next morning's rehearsals, and thus put himself in a better position to convince a singer to use one of the pieces he was plugging. Single-handedly he was responsible for starting Jean Schwartz's "Bedelia" on its three-million-copy sale. From then on he was one of the most influential pluggers on Twenty-eighth Street. He went to work for Remick (which also employed young Ben Bloom), remaining there for about two decades. One of Gumble's major coups with Remick was to lift Egbert van Alstyne's "In the Shade of the Old Apple Tree" off the ground and send it soaring as one of the biggest songs of 1905. It was Gumble who got Eva Tanguay to use "I Don't Care," a stroke that not only made it into a big song hit but also made her into a vaudeville star. In the 1910's, Gumble helped launch such big-time favorites as "Oh, You Beautiful Doll," and "I'm Forever Blowing Bubbles." Just before his life came to a sudden end aboard the Twentieth-Century Limited, in 1947, he had been active and successful in plugging Tin Pan Alley's old songs. As a member of the Music Publishers Holding Corporation, he was unusually effective in getting motion-picture producers and stars of stage, screen and radio to revive the old song favorites within new contexts.

Song pluggers like Joseph Santley and Johnny Nestor made the nickelodeon the principal scene of their operations. The movies, or "flickers," were born in West Orange, New Jersey, in 1893, when Thomas Edison invented the "black Maria." He then opened the Thomas Edison New Kinegraphic Theater, the first movie-making studio in cinema history. Later on, in 1896, the movies entered the vaudeville houses. At that time the main appeal of the "flickers" lay in the novelty of seeing pictures move: May Irwin in a protracted kiss; the Empire State Express rushing headlong from the screen and seemingly into the audience; Fred Ott doing a sneezing routine. The flickers amused audiences, delighted them, or terrified them. But nobody was bored. Then, in 1903, *The Great Train Robbery* established the movies as a major source of entertainment. Nickelodeons now blossomed all over the country; by 1907 there were four hundred in operation.

These nickelodeons soon offered pluggers a new place in which to introduce song slides, by this time a basic form of nickelodeon entertainment. But this was not the only way these theaters were exploited by Tin Pan Alley. After all, silent pictures were accompanied by piano music—hours upon hours of music-making. What better way to hammer a new song into the consciousness of a helpless audience than by having a movie pianist play it continuously? The song pluggers also worked out a deal with nickelodeons whereby they could appear in person and entertain audiences with live performances at the beginning of a show or during intermission. The nickelodeon, consequently, soon became such a happy hunting ground for pluggers that it was not unusual to find one of them working eight such theaters an evening and many more during the weekend. Sammy Smither (one-time baseball player turned plugger) once boasted he could plug a song fifty times in a single evening.

The advance of science that had been responsible for the birth of motion pictures was the song plugger's ally in still another area—recorded music. Thomas A. Edison filed a patent application for a reproducing machine on December 15, 1877. By 1890 the Edison phonograph, and the cylinder disk, had ceased to be a novelty and had become a valuable means of projecting musical sound. Apparently, the Joseph W. Stern company sensed that the musical industry could make good use of that new gadget, the phonograph, for in 1897 it opened the Universal Phonograph Company on East Twentieth Street as a recording studio. There they made records of "coon songs" sung by May Irwin and the favorites of such singers as Meyer Cohen and Lottie Gilson. The Universal Phonograph Company had a short lease on life: the impact of the recording business on Tin Pan Alley was not to be felt for some time to come. But already in the early 1900's the song plugger used recorded music to good advantage in penny arcades—first by means of the mechanical piano, then through cylindrical disks. Placing recorded songs in arcades—the sheet-music cover prominently displayed—became still one more valuable plugging method.

But in the 1900's as in the 1890's one method of plugging took precedence over all others—placing songs inside the theater. The vaudeville circuit that now spanned the country and the rapidly expanding musical theater in New York were still the arenas in which the song plugger operated most fruitfully.

In vaudeville the singing stooge had by now become an accepted part of the program. But in 1909 still another gimmick had been introduced in vaudeville and nickelodeons—the songfest. The plugger would distribute song sheets to the audience and have them join him in a community sing. Here, too, specialists took the lead. Arthur Elwell traveled the Pantages circuit for one hundred and seventy-four consecutive weeks, his job consisting exclusively of arranging songfests in vaudeville houses; Edward Roesch played the Sullivan and Considine circuit for one hundred and ten weeks.

The Broadway musical theater was offering the song

plugger ever-richer opportunities to bring songs to audiences. The revue, the musical comedy, and the extravaganza now called on Tin Pan Alley to provide not only complete scores for productions but also hundreds upon hundreds of individual songs. Interpolating individual numbers by various composers into a production—whose basic score might be somebody else's work—was a general practice in the 1900's and 1910's. At that time, songs, dances, humor, and routines did not have to bear a basic relationship to the text. The loosely constructed plot was just a convenient hook on which to hang the elements that went into the making of musical comedy. When a producer or writer came upon a good comedy bit, or a snag that seemed to have audience appeal, he did not hesitate to fit it into his show whether it belonged or not. This was frequently done even while the musical was already running, there being no such thing as a "frozen" production in those days. This custom of interpolation, however devastating it might have been to the integration of a production, was a boon to Tin Pan Alley. It offered virtually limitless opportunities to place songs by unknown composers in important musicals.

More than one hundred songs by young Jerome Kern were placed in some thirty different Broadway musicals between 1905 and 1912 before he was assigned to do a full-length score on his own. Gus Edwards, Jean Schwartz, Ted Snyder were some of Tin Pan Alley's writers who made significant contributions to the theater through single numbers. John H. Flynn's "Sweet Annie Moore" became a hit in *The Casino Girl* in 1900, most of whose numbers were the work of the successful operetta composer Ludwig Englander. Jean Schwartz's first song success, "Mr. Dooley," was slipped into Gustave Kerker's operetta *The Chinese Honeymoon* in 1902, and Charles Zimmerman's "Hurrah for Baffin's Bay" into A. Baldwin Sloane's *The*

*Wizard of Oz* in 1903—both of these songs became hits there. Jerome Kern's first American hit tune was an interpolation—"How'd You Like to Spoon with Me?", fitted into Ivan Caryll's *The Earl and the Girl*. Gus Edwards' "Tammany" was inserted into *Fantana* in 1906, and "Under the Bamboo Tree" by Bob Cole got into *Sally in Our Alley* in 1902. One of the most frequently sung Irish ditties of the time became popular only after Nora Bayes put it across in *The Jolly Bachelors* in 1910—"Has Anybody Here Seen Kelly?"

To get a musical-comedy star or vaudeville headliner to use a song was, then, the surest way a plugger knew to launch a song successfully and keep it alive for years. Initially, song pluggers resorted to little bribes and favors to win the interest of performers. But as more and more pluggers began to compete with one another, the stakes kept growing. Large cash payments, diamond rings, a share in the song's royalties, were soon the lures used to attract a big name in show business to a song. Other means were also uncovered. Sometimes the plugger provided and paid for a regular claque to assure a successful presentation; sometimes pluggers bought for the performer special sets and costumes with which to embellish his act. The price kept growing all the time. Before long, performers were beginning to get a regular weekly stipend from a publisher wishing to tie him up exclusively for his publications. Some performers got a hundred dollars a week or more throughout the year. Though lesser entertainers were paid much less, very often the income they received from the publisher exceeded the amount the theater paid them. By 1905, Tin Pan Alley was paying out a half-million dollars a year to stage stars. This was "payola," pure, simple, direct, and undisguised—even though the word for this practice was not coined till many years later.

Edward B. Marks was one of the few publishers who at first tried to resist this dangerous trend. But when fewer and fewer of the songs of Joseph W. Stern & Company were getting played and sung, Marks had to admit defeat. He instructed his office manager to engage in the prevailing payoff racket. The manager returned to him with sad tidings. So many acts and players were by now signed up by competitive publishing firms that he could not make a single worthwhile deal. "Boss," he remarked ruefully, "I can't *give* your money away."

By 1910 it had become clear to Tin Pan Alley that the racket was getting out of hand. Those who did not have an "in" with performers, because they weren't buying their way or paying a high enough price, were just not getting their songs placed where it counted most. Those who did have an "in" were beginning to realize that money distributed so lavishly week after week was out of all proportion to the value received. These publishers were not selling enough additional sheet music to take care of this expense. However, they were holding a tiger by his tail, unable to let go. The publisher knew that if he even tried to stop making payments for performances he would find that he had left the field wide open to his competitors and had closed it completely to himself.

This racket worked badly not only for the publishers but, curiously enough, for the performers themselves even though they benefited from it financially. As a result of "payola" the quality of performances in vaudeville and musicals—and that of material being used—suffered serious deterioration. A performer was partial to the song and publisher that brought him the highest revenue, even if this particular number did not suit his style or fit into his act. As a corollary, he often had to turn down another number, from a competitive publisher, that would have served his talent far better.

John J. O'Connor, a writer who had become business manager of *Variety*—the Bible of show business—was one of those who saw the whole ugly picture with all its shadows. He decided to do something about it. He created a new organization, the Music Publishers Protective Association, in which publishers could work as a unit to protect their interests and ban handouts. Feist, Remick, T. B. Harms, all declined to become members of his organization, insisting that they did not want to rock a boat that was sailing smoothly, that it was wiser to continue along the same lines that had brought them such unprecedented prosperity, even though they realized that there was no appreciable ratio between the amount spent on "payola" and sheet-music sales. The Music Publishers Protective Association (M.P.P.A.) would have been stillborn had not O'Connor devised a brilliant plan by which to wear down resistance. In 1916 he invited J. J. Murdock, assistant to theater owner E. F. Albee, to attend a vaudeville show at one of the theaters under Murdock's control, the Alhambra in uptown New York. The overture, the music for the acrobatic act, the principal ballad of the Irish tenor, the entrance number for the dramatic sketch, all used the same popular tune—the plugger of that song having done a thorough job in lining up all the acts on this one show. O'Connor saw the point Murdock was trying to make, recognized immediately how deeply this disease had been allowed to fester in the theater. The very next day he issued a directive to all the theaters in his circuit that performers were only to use music owned by publishers who were members of M.P.P.A. Feist, Remick, Harms rushed to become members, followed by the other outfits in Tin Pan Alley. The first thing the organization agreed upon was to outlaw any form of payment by its members to performing artists.

"Payola" stopped dead in its tracks—but only temporarily. It did not take long for now one publisher, now another, to devise devious ways of influencing performers to use their songs. The most effective way, and the hardest to pin down as a violation of the rules, was to give a star a share in the song's royalties by creating the fiction that the performer had collaborated in the writing of either the lyrics or the music. A plugger would bring a manuscript to a star like, say, Jolson or Nora Bayes, to seek advice and criticism. The star might change a word here, or suggest an effect in the melody there. For these changes, which the plugger insisted improved the song no end, the performer had become a collaborator. The fact that the performer thus profited from the future success of the song made him more partial to including it in an act or a show, and keeping it there as long as the sale of the sheet music was swelling his or her income.

# 10

## *"We could make such beautiful music together"*

On Twenty-eighth Street new faces kept cropping up all the time, both among the publishers and among the songwriters, and frequently publisher and songwriter were one and the same man.

The most significant of these newcomers was Harry von Tilzer. As a songwriter he carried the traditions of the sentimental ballad into the twentieth century. As a publisher he dominated Tin Pan Alley from the moment he opened his own office. It is poetic justice to find that the name of Tin Pan Alley was coined at his place on Twenty-eighth Street—if, indeed, he himself had not done the coining. During the years that the song industry was centralized on that street, Harry von Tilzer was regarded as "Mr. Tin Pan Alley."

He was born Harry Gumm, in Detroit in 1872. At fourteen he ran away from home to join a circus troupe with which he performed a tumbling act. After that he wrote songs, played the piano, and at times filled juvenile roles with a traveling repertory company. Since he realized that show business required a name somewhat more romantic and memorable than Harry Gumm, he began calling himself Harry von Tilzer. "Tilzer" was the maiden name of his mother; the "von" he appended as an afterthought to give himself greater distinction.

While playing with a burlesque company in Chicago, Harry von Tilzer met Lottie Gilson. She convinced him to come to New York and try to make his way not as a performer but as a songwriter. She had been particularly impressed by Von Tilzer's first song to reach sheet music, "I Love You Both," which Willis Woodward published in 1892.

Von Tilzer made his way to New York later in 1892 by working as a groom for a trainload of horses. He arrived in the city with just one dollar and sixty-five cents in his pocket. He rented a room in Brooklyn, and soon after that he began to support himself by working as a pianist and entertainer in various saloons. Willis Woodward introduced him to Tony Pastor who interpolated some of Von Tilzer's songs into acts at the Music Hall. In 1896, Harry von Tilzer performed in one of those acts—a German comedy routine that he worked out with George Sidney. A year after that, Von Tilzer had a modest hit song in "De Swellest Gal in Town," which Joseph W. Stern issued and which was introduced by the minstrel George H. Primrose.

In 1898, Von Tilzer was sharing a top-floor furnished room on East Fifteenth Street with Andrew B. Sterling, a budding lyricist. Late one night they worked out the ballad "My Old New Hampshire Home." They had to write this song by the glow of a lamplight in the street outside, their own gaslight having been turned off to keep the landlord away. The next day they went all over Union Square trying to market their song. There were no takers. Then a friend suggested they take it to Orphean, a little printing shop operated by William C. Dunn. Dunn liked "My Old New Hampshire Home" and bought it for fifteen dollars.

In 1899, Von Tilzer and Sterling sold Dunn a second number, this time the novelty "coon song," "I'd Leave My Happy Home for You" (whose use of "oo—oo" in its refrain was the first of its kind in Tin Pan Alley). Annette Flagler introduced it, but it was Blanche Ring who made it popular and who was made popular by it. "I'd Leave My Happy Home for You" sold more than a million copies. Meanwhile, the sales of "My Old New Hampshire Home," which had become a favorite with vaudevillians were also gaining momentum, in time the sheet-music sale exceeded two million copies.

With two such valuable properties as "I'd Leave My Happy Home for You" and "My Old New Hampshire Home," William C. Dunn was able to sell his music-publishing properties to two newcomers to Tin Pan Alley —Lew Bernstein and Maurice Shapiro. Bernstein and Shapiro then did the unprecedented. They voluntarily paid Von Tilzer four thousand dollars as an advance on royalties for "My Old New Hampshire Home," even though they owned the song outright and were not expected to make any further compensation. They did something else at the same time. They convinced Von Tilzer to leave acting to others and to devote himself exclusively to songwriting; as an inducement, they gave him a partnership in their new business.

Shapiro, Bernstein, and Von Tilzer ushered in their new publishing arrangement—and a new century—with one of the most successful sentimental ballads ever issued in Tin

Pan Alley—"A Bird in a Gilded Cage," words by Arthur J. Lamb and music by Von Tilzer. It has been said that Von Tilzer agreed to write the music for Lamb's lyrics only if it was made perfectly clear that the unhappy girl in the song was a millionaire's wife, not his mistress. If this is so, then the fully substantiated story about the first time Von Tilzer tried out his song anywhere comes as the cream of paradoxes. For Harry von Tilzer tested his song in a brothel. When he saw the tearful reaction of some of the girls, he remarked: "Now I know I have a hit—if even *these* ladies can weep over my song."

When, in about a year, "A Bird in a Gilded Cage" sold more than two million copies, Harry von Tilzer decided to part company with Shapiro and Bernstein and set off by himself as a publisher. He opened an office on Twenty-eighth Street in 1902. Before the year ended, he had written and published three songs, the combined sales of which hovered somewhere around the five-million mark. A sentimental sequel to "A Bird in a Gilded Cage" pointed up the moral that gold and diamonds cannot buy a happy heart; this song, titled "The Mansion of Aching Hearts," was a ballad with which the boy Irving Berlin used to encourage passers-by to throw pennies at him when he invaded the Bowery as a street singer. "Down Where the Wurzburger Flows" was a drinking song Von Tilzer had intended for a Broadway musical. It was placed eventually, with a vaudeville newcomer by the name of Nora Bayes, who tried it out at the Orpheum Theater in Brooklyn. When she sang it for the first time, she broke down midway in the song. Von Tilzer, seated in a box, rose and sang the rest of the chorus. This improvisation made such an impact on the audience that the management of the Orpheum Theater urged Von Tilzer to return the rest of the week and plug his song from the box seat. Nora Bayes kept

the song in her vaudeville act for a number of years, long
after Von Tilzer had withdrawn his help. The audience
(which she invited to sing the refrain with her) liked her
rendition so well that she became known as "the Wurzburger girl." Until 1909, when she made her *Ziegfeld Follies* debut with "Shine On, Harvest Moon," Von Tilzer's
"Down Where the Wurzburger Flows" was Nora Bayes's
theme song.

When Von Tilzer again served as his own plugger—
this time with "Please Go 'Way and Let Me Sleep"—he introduced some novel histrionics. While the minstrel Arthur
Deming sang it, Von Tilzer (seated in the audience) pre-
tended to be fast asleep; in fact, he accompanied the song
with loud snores. After Deming seemingly upbraided Von
Tilzer for disturbing his performance, the composer-
publisher rose lazily from his seat, and chanted the chorus
in which he emphasized the line "please go 'way and let me
sleep." This novel routine attracted a good deal of publicity and helped to spur the song's sales.

The idea of "On a Sunday Afternoon"—another of Von
Tilzer's triumphs during his initial year as publisher—came
to him one day when, at the beach, he lay lazily in the
sun. Suddenly a line occurred to him: "People work hard
on Monday, but one day that's fun day is Sunday." He
turned the line and his ideas over to Andrew B. Sterling,
who prepared the lyric for him.

The next Von Tilzer song to reach and exceed a million-
copy sale was "Wait 'Til the Sun Shines, Nellie" in 1905.
Some say this ballad originated when Von Tilzer overheard
a chance remark one rainy day as he passed a theater. Others maintain Von Tilzer got his idea by reading a newspaper account about a pauperized family, one of whose
members made the consoling remark to the others that "the
sun will shine again for us after the storm." Winona Win-

ter (the daughter of songwriter Banks Winter) introduced this Von Tilzer ballad in vaudeville and it soon became a favorite of headliners and male quartets.

It would be impossible to compute the number of songs Harry von Tilzer wrote. He himself put the figure at eight thousand, with one-fourth of them published. Perhaps almost as remarkable as the volume of his production—and the many times with which he reached a million-copy sale —was his versatility. For Von Tilzer was one of those rare composers in Tin Pan Alley at the turn of the century who could strum on many strings. Two of the decade's best "coon songs" were "Alexander, Don't You Love Your Baby No More?" in 1904 and "What You Goin' to Do When the Rent Comes 'Round?" in 1905. The name "Alexander" had long been used with comic effect by the minstrels McIntyre and Heath. When Harry von Tilzer saw that audiences were convulsed with laughter each time the minstrels drawled out the name, he decided to use it in a song. Harry von Tilzer's "Alexander" undoubtedly nudged at Irving Berlin's memory when some years later he was composing "Alexander's Ragtime Band."

In 1909, Harry von Tilzer created "The Cubanola Glide" —this was the first popular song hit about dancing (it helped to start a cycle of such songs in Tin Pan Alley) and one of the early classics of ragtime. Harriet Raymond introduced it, and Sophie Tucker helped make it famous. In 1914, Von Tilzer created a song hit of far different character—an effective "mother" song, in "I Want a Girl."

He was, then, one of the most versatile and most successful song composers of his time. But his significance in Tin Pan Alley did not end there. As a publisher his influence was felt in several important directions. Early in the 1900's he lifted the boy Irving Berlin from the Bowery streets and brought him into Tin Pan Alley by hiring him as a song plugger at Tony Pastor's Music Hall. Von Tilzer also became, in 1909, the publisher of one of Irving Berlin's first songs—he wrote both the words and music—"Just Like a Rose." A number of years later Harry von Tilzer was responsible for George Gershwin's first published song, "When You Want 'Em You Can't Get 'Em."

Von Tilzer also added a footnote to Tin Pan Alley history. He was the first publisher to use a photograph of himself on his publications—the high stiff collar he always favored serving as an easily recognizable trademark for all his publications.

There was more than one Von Tilzer in Tin Pan Alley. Harry's successes as composer and publisher stimulated his brothers to emulation. Julie von Tilzer became the president of the Harry von Tilzer Company after he had worked for a while as a manager of Remick's. Will von Tilzer wrote lyrics and was for a time head of the Broadway Music Company. Jack von Tilzer, the youngest in the family, was director of York Music Company, the music-publishing company that Albert von Tilzer founded.

Albert—outside of Harry, of course—was the most important of the Von Tilzers. Six years younger than his distinguished brother, Albert learned to play the piano by ear, then took some lessons in harmony. When Harry von Tilzer was taken into partnership with Shapiro and Bernstein, Albert worked as piano demonstrator and arranger in that firm's Chicago branch until 1900, when he came to New York City. While working as a shoe salesman in a Brooklyn department store, he published his first piece of music, "The Absent-minded Beggar." In 1903 the firm of Harry von Tilzer published a song for which Albert had produced both the words and the music—"That's What the Daisy Said." Later the same year Albert von Tilzer formed his own company, the York, which, in 1904, released his first song hit, "Teasing." One of his classics, "Take Me Out to the Ball Game," came out in 1908.

Nora Bayes helped make it famous before it became the un-official national anthem of baseball. (Curiously enough, Albert had written this paean to our national pastime twenty years or so *before* he even saw his first baseball game!) Its popularity brought Albert von Tilzer a singing engagement on the Orpheum vaudeville circuit. Another of his song classics was "Put Your Arms Around Me, Honey," published in 1910 and revived many years later for Judy Garland in the motion picture *In the Good Old Summertime*.

In 1916, Albert von Tilzer wrote and published "Oh, How She Could Yacki, Hacki, Wicki, Woo," one of many similar Hawaiian-type numbers then flooding the market, and the song with which Eddie Cantor made his sensational Broadway debut.

The ever-swelling ranks of songwriters-become-publishers on Twenty-eighth Street found an important recruit in Gus Edwards. He was born in Germany in 1879, where his name had been Gustav Edward Simon. When he was eight, his family moved to the United States, settling in the Williamsburg section of Brooklyn. The boy Gus was crazy about the theater. While working in his uncle's cigar store, he spent all his free time—and all his pocket money —at the Union Square shows. Lottie Gilson soon came to know him, and, impressed by the earnestness of his manner and his sensitive soprano voice, hired him as her singing stooge. She placed him in the balcony of Hurtig and Seamon's to follow her in singing refrains of popular songs.

Small, round-faced, eager-eyed—with a soaring voice whose vibrato was perfectly suited for the rendition of popular ballads—little Gus Edwards had no difficulty finding jobs in the theater. He worked with Imogene Comer, Helene Mora, Maggie Cline, Polly Moran, and Emma Carus—always as a boy stooge. At other times, he sang pop tunes in saloons, on ferry boats, at club meetings. Sometimes Witmark hired him for five dollars a week to plug its songs. For a while he sold sheet music in the lobby of the Circle Theater in New York City's Columbus Circle. Many years later he bought this same theater and renamed it the Gus Edwards Music Hall.

In 1896, Edwards was performing in a Brooklyn saloon when he attracted the interest of James Hyde, a vaudeville booking agent. Hyde conceived an act in which Edwards, with four other boys, appeared as newsboys. They were dressed in ragged clothes, had their faces smudged, and carried a bundle of newspapers under their arms. "The Newsboy Quintet," as this act was named, toured the vaudeville circuit in a presentation of current hit songs. George M. Cohan, who sometimes appeared on the same bill, went out of his way to coach Edwards in song delivery; at the same time he gave him valuable hints about songwriting. Paul Dresser also took an interest in him; since Edwards did not own a piano, Dresser arranged for him to use the one at the offices of Howley and Haviland.

In 1898, Edwards wrote his first popular song, "All I Want Is My Black Baby Back." Not knowing how to write down melodies, he asked Charles Frohman to do this for him. The song became a part of the Newsboy Quintet act.

During the Spanish-American War, when he was entertaining American soldiers at Camp Black, Edwards met Will Cobb, a young man with a gift for writing verses. They collaborated on "I Couldn't Stand to See My Baby Lose," which May Irwin introduced in vaudeville in 1899. That same year Edwards and Cobb had a hit with "I Can't Tell You Why I Love You, but I Do," published by Howley and Haviland. Before long, Edwards and Cobb had so many successful songs on the lists that they came to be known in Tin Pan Alley as "Words and Music."

In 1905, Gus Edwards became one of the ace composers of the firm of M. Witmark and Sons by producing three hits, all of them with lyrics by Vincent Bryan: "He's Me Pal," "In My Merry Oldsmobile," and "Tammany." "In My Merry Oldsmobile" was one of the first successful songs about the automobile. It was written to celebrate the successful completion of the first cross-country trip ever attempted by an automobile, a feat then accomplished by two Oldsmobiles. "Tammany," while supposedly a take-off on the Indian-type songs then so popular, was actually written for a party held at the National Democratic Club in New York, at which, even though it touched upon some of the less creditable practices of the Democratic Party, it proved to be a big hit. Soon after that, Lee Harrison sang it in the musical comedy *Fantana*, and Jefferson de Angelis made it extremely popular in vaudeville. Eventually it became the official song of New York City's Tammany Hall.

Weary of seeing the Witmarks reap such a financial harvest from his creative fruits, Edwards decided to open a publishing venture of his own. Late in 1905 he found an office on Twenty-eighth Street. One of the first songs, published, which he wrote with Cobb, was "I Just Can't Make My Eyes Behave," which Edwards convinced Ziegfeld to let Anna Held sing in *A Parisian Model*. Song and singer became so inextricably associated with one another that it became inconceivable to think of the number being sung without a provocative French accent. In 1906, Edwards and Cobb wrote the first number published by the new house of Edwards to realize a million-copy sale—"Sunbonnet Sue."

Having thus become a success as a composer and as a publisher, Edwards was ready in 1907 to conquer still another world, that of vaudeville. He wrote, directed, and starred in a revue which he initially called "School Boys

and Girls." His role was that of a schoolteacher in a room
filled with kids. They were allowed to sing, dance and
mime—in short to bring to the vaudeville stage the welcome infiltration of the fresh, spontaneous gift of youngsters. "School Days," a song Edwards wrote for this revue,
became the greatest success of his whole songwriting career, with three million copies sold.

Gus Edwards' kid act became a headliner in vaudeville
that enjoyed a continuous booking on the circuit. Year
after year Edwards searched for new talent; year after
year he came up with remarkable youngsters who, after
making their stage debuts in his act, went on to achieve the
heights of success. The names of those who at one time or
another were parts of his act read like a *Who's Who* of the
American musical theater: Eddie Cantor, Georgie Jessel,
Groucho Marx, Lila Lee, and Georgie Price. Edwards was
so indefatigable in his search for new faces and fresh talent
that before long the remark circulated freely along Broadway: "Pull your kids in, here comes Gus Edwards."

Of the songs that Edwards wrote for and popularized in
his acts after 1907, the most important were "By the Light
of the Silvery Moon" (which Georgie Price introduced in
1909), "If I Were a Millionaire" in 1910, and "Jimmy
Valentine" in 1912. In 1940, the story of Gus Edwards'
career was dramatized in the motion picture *The Star
Maker*, in which Bing Crosby played the title role.

Then there was Ted Snyder.

In the early 1900's there was a small publishing firm in
Tin Pan Alley called Rose and Snyder. The "Snyder" of
this combination was a talented young composer who had
been a café pianist, then a song plugger. Henry Waterson,
a diamond merchant interested in going into the music-
publishing business, kept his eye on Snyder for some time.
Then in 1907 he offered to back him in a publishing ven-

ture. Ted Snyder formed the Seminary Music Company in 1908 (its name was soon changed to the Ted Snyder Company), and one of its first issues was the Ted Snyder song "If You Cared for Me." A year later the firm published Snyder's "Beautiful Eyes," which was interpolated into the stage musical *Mr. Hamlet of Broadway*. After that, Snyder published a number of substantial hits (which he helped to write), among which were "That Beautiful Rag," "That Mysterious Rag," "How'd You Like to Be My Daddy?" (which Al Jolson sang in *Sinbad*). "Who's Sorry Now?," written with Bert Kalmar and Harry Ruby in 1923, became a standard.

But despite the tremendous success of "Who's Sorry Now?" Ted Snyder's greatest contribution to Tin Pan Alley was not any one of his songs. His major contribution was the prominent role he played in the early songwriting history of Irving Berlin.

Like his parents and seven brothers and a sister, Irving Berlin (born Israel Baline) was a fugitive from a Russian pogrom. The family fled to America in 1892, when Israel, or Irving, was just four, and found a home in the Lower East Side of New York. There, where they had expected to encounter only milk and honey, they found overcrowded tenements, slums, poverty, long and hard work. Four of the children had to find jobs in sweatshops or sell papers in order to help support the family. The father—a part-time cantor in a synagogue and a part-time *shochet* in a kosher slaughter house—hardly earned enough to support his large brood.

When his father died, Irving, now aged eight, ran away from home. Since he had the gift of song, he made his way as best he could by singing. For a while he worked for Blind Sol, a singing beggar, whom he led into cafés and through the streets. Then he gave song renditions of his own. After leaving Blind Sol's employ, he

found many opportunities to sing Tin Pan Alley's sentimental ballads in night spots and saloons on the Bowery
or in Chinatown. He also worked for a while as Harry
von Tilzer's song plugger at Tony Pastor's Music Hall.

In 1906 he found a job as a singing waiter in Pelham's
Café in Chinatown. He served at the tables and cleaned up
the café when it closed down for the night. But his main
function was to entertain the guests with renditions of popular songs. It was there and then that he wrote his first published song.

Around the corner from Pelham's was Callahan's,
which could boast that one of its waiters had written the
lyrics for "My Mariuccia, Take a Steamboat" (music by
Al Piantadosi, published by Shapiro-Bernstein). The proprietor of Pelham's, was convinced that what could be
done at Callahan's could be done better at Pelham's. On
his encouragement, the saloon pianist Nick Michaelson
wrote a melody, and Israel Baline, who had proved himself adept in making up parodies, was asked to do the lyrics. In obvious imitation of their rivals around the corner,
Michaelson and Baline called their song "Marie from
Sunny Italy"—and the clientele of Pelham's loved it. Then
in 1907 the song was published by Joseph W. Stern & Company. It was on this effort, for which Baline had contributed
only the words, that the assumed name of Irving Berlin
makes its first appearance. On a green and white cover on
which was pictured a gondola and a photograph of Lillian
Russell, the name Irving Berlin stood out bold and clear in
large type. Berlin's total income from his first song was
thirty cents in royalties.

In 1908, Berlin left Pelham's to become a singing waiter
at Jimmy Kelly's saloon in Union Square. A vaudevillian
asked Berlin to write a topical poem he could use in his act.
In those days Dorando, a marathon runner, was in the
news, and Berlin used him as the inspiration for "Dorando."

Since the vaudevillian did not use the poem, Berlin tried selling it as a song lyric. He found an interested taker in Ted Snyder, propietor of the recently established Seminary Music Company, who offered to buy it for twenty-five dollars on the assumption that the words had a melody. To insure his sale, Berlin hurriedly dictated a tune to an arranger in Snyder's office. "Dorando" thus became the first Irving Berlin number for which he wrote the melody as well as the lyrics; it was also the song that brought him together with Ted Snyder.

Max Winslow, one of the employees at the Seminary Music Company, was immediately impressed with young Berlin's talent and got him a permanent job as lyricist there. Between then and 1913 Berlin wrote lyrics, which Snyder set to music, for many songs Snyder's publishing house issued. These included "Next to Your Mother, Who Do You Love?", "Call Me Up Some Rainy Afternoon," "Kiss Me, My Honey, Kiss Me," "That Beautiful Rag," "Sweet Italian Love," and "My Wife's Gone to the Country." "That Beautiful Rag" and "Sweet Italian Love" were interpolated in 1910 in a Broadway revue, *Up and Down Broadway* (Jean Schwartz had provided the basic score for it), in which both Berlin and Snyder appeared as performing artists. "My Wife's Gone to the Country" was a hit that sold a half-million copies.

In addition to his collaborations with Snyder, Berlin wrote both the music and lyrics for "That Mesmerizing Mendelssohn Tune" (a rag treatment of Mendelssohn's "Spring Song"), which gave Ted Snyder's company another respectable hit. And Berlin did the music for a delightful takeoff on opera, "Sadie Salome, Go Home" for which Edgar Leslie wrote the lyrics. Berlin's songs were doing so well that Ted Snyder decided to take him into the firm as a full-fledged partner. As of 1912, the firm was called Waterson, Snyder and Berlin. Now that Berlin was beginning to write music as well as lyrics—and now that he was a publisher to boot—a great new epoch was about to unfold for Tin Pan Alley.

Hand in hand with the appearances of new publishers came vital changes in some of the older establishments along Twenty-eighth Street. In 1904, F. B. Haviland, for example, had left the firm of Howley, Haviland and Dresser (which he had helped to form) to go into partnership with Theodore F. Morse to start the F. B. Haviland Company. As the composer of "Good-by, Dolly Gray," "Hurrah for Baffin's Bay," and "Dear Old Girl," Morse was no unknown quantity in 1904. As Haviland's publishing partner after that, he rose to new and greater success as a songwriter. In his very first year with the F. B. Haviland Company he contributed to its catalogue no less than six hits: "Blue Bell" (still another of those "good-by" songs that were then in such style), "I've Got a Feelin' for You," "A Little Boy Called Taps," "Nan! Nan! Nan!" "Please Come and Play in My Back Yard," and "Where the Southern Roses Grow." Succeeding years brought forth still more Morse song hits. But the curious thing about Morse's songwriting career is that few today remember him by any of his original melodies, while everybody knows one of his adaptations: the lyrics of "Hail, Hail, the Gang's All Here," was written by Morse to a theme by Sir Arthur Sullivan from the Gilbert and Sullivan operetta *The Pirates of Penzance*.

Another paradox about Morse's career touches upon his long and fertile period of collaboration with his wife, Theodora Terris, who provided lyrics for so many of his songs. Yet when Theodora Terris became famous, at last, it was not as Morse's collaborator at all—it was many years later with "Three O'Clock in the Morning" and "Siboney."

T. B. Harms was another firm that underwent reorganization early in the 1900's. In 1904, Alex and Tom Harms left the organization to be replaced by Max Dreyfus. Dreyfus had once been the demonstration pianist and song plugger for Howley, Haviland and Dresser. Then he joined T. B. Harms as arranger. There he demonstrated extraordinary acumen in lifting songs out of Broadway shows and making them triumphs in Tin Pan Alley and inversely by placing the Harms songs strategically in Broadway musical shows. He soon became a power at Harms, his decisions respected and followed. A creative publisher who knew how to recognize latent talent and to nurse it to fulfillment, Dreyfus rose to the top echelon of command in Harms, at last displacing the owners and taking over the direction completely. From then on his creativity as a publisher made him one of the most influential figures in Tin Pan Alley.

He had a particularly sensitive gift for sniffing out potential genius in young, untried, unknown composers. Hardly had Dreyfus acquired control of Harms when this uncommon flair was successfully put to the test. A neatly dressed young man, who peered soberly through his eyeglasses and gave the appearance of a college professor, came to him for a job. He had a quiet air, a dignified manner, a self-assurance, all of which sold themselves to Dreyfus at once. Dreyfus still recalls that first meeting. "He said he wanted to imbibe the atmosphere of music. I decided to take him on, and to start him off by giving him the toughest job I had—selling music." The salary was twelve dollars a week, and the assignment was to sell sheet music up Hudson Valley and to plug songs at Macy's and other department stores. He was also asked to do arrangements. "He was good," Dreyfus recalled. "He was full of youthful spirit, and with it a certain charm. He sold music."

This young man was Jerome Kern. Though only nineteen at the time, he was no novice either to songwriting or to Tin Pan Alley. He was born in New York City in 1885 to comparatively well-to-do parents. His mother gave him his first piano instruction when he was five, and he continued music study with other private teachers while attending public school. At high school in Newark he was identified by his teachers as "the little genius," because he played the piano and organ at assemblies and wrote the music for school productions. When he graduated from high school, he went to the New York College of Music for advanced music instruction. During this period he wrote the piano piece *At the Casino,* which was published by the Lyceum Music Company (a subsidiary of Joseph W. Stern) in 1902. This was Kern's first foot into Tin Pan Alley, but he withdrew it quickly. After spending a year at the New York College of Music, he went to Europe. In London he got a job writing songs for stage productions. The first to get a hearing was "My Little Canoe," which Billie Burke sang in *The School Girl* in 1903. Then, with young P. G. Wodehouse writing the lyrics, Kern completed a topical number that became one of London's big hits in 1903. This was the song "Mr. Chamberlain"—the Mr. Chamberlain in the song being one of the most famous politicians of that day, the father of Neville Chamberlain.

Kern came back to New York in 1904 and once again stepped into Tin Pan Alley. Edward Marks paid him seven dollars a week in the office of Lyceum to make out bills and invoices. Kern then went to work for Shapiro-Bernstein as a song plugger—and got a raise of two dollars a week. For Shapiro-Bernstein he demonstrated songs at five-and-ten-cent stores and occasionally at Wanamaker's in Philadelphia.

All this while he was writing songs and more songs. In 1904 he adapted for Broadway the score of the London musical *Mr. Wix of Wickham.* The show was a disaster. But Kern's score—including four of his own numbers—made the critics take notice. "Who is this Jerome Kern," inquired the critic Alan Dale, "whose music towers above the average primitive hurdy-gurdy accomplishments of present-day musical comedy?"

It was at this point in his career that Kern went to Dreyfus for a job. Dreyfus took full measure of the young man, recognized his potential, and left no stone unturned to develop his talent. Dreyfus found him jobs as piano accompanist for vaudevillians and as rehearsal pianist for Broadway musicals. Dreyfus also accepted a few of Kern's numbers for the Harms catalogue. One of these was "How'd You Like to Spoon With Me?" which found a place in the Ivan Caryll operetta *The Earl and the Girl*, in 1905. Georgia Caine and Victor Morley introduced it in the show, followed by six girls on flower-decorated swings, singing as they floated from the stage into the audience. It became the big song of the production. "The most successful number ever introduced here," was the way the New York *Dramatic Mirror* described it. "Demanded again and again." Jerome Kern had his first American hit song.

With Dreyfus as his ally, Kern was now able to place one song after another in various Broadway musicals. At long last, in 1912, he was assigned to do a full score of his own. The result of his labors was *The Red Petticoat*—a failure.

Kern's first successful Broadway musical came two years after that: this was *The Girl from Utah*, starring Julia Sanderson. It is here that we encounter the first of Kern's song classics, "They Didn't Believe Me," a number that put him in a class all by himself both on Broadway and in Tin Pan Alley. "The way in which the melody of the refrain expands opulently for eight bars in simple quarter notes," as I have written in *The World of Jerome Kern*, "the way in which a poignant climax is achieved through a subtle change of key—this is sheer Jerome Kern magic. Equally remarkable is the way in which, in the recapitulation of the opening section, Kern suddenly introduces a new four-bar thought before proceeding with his original intentions." These subtleties notwithstanding, "They Didn't Believe Me" was one of the leading hit songs of 1914, selling about two million copies.

From here on, Kern went straight toward greatness and for fabulous successes. He soon became such a significant contributor to the Harms catalogue that Max Dreyfus gave him a partnership in the firm.

# 11

## "Sing an old-fashioned song"

The sentimental ballad that told a long tale of woe in the style of "After the Ball" was on its way out. In fact, in the early 1900's, Charlie Case, a popular vaudevillian, used to bring down the house with his deadpan deliveries of parodies of such ballads, reducing them to the ridiculous. When the public started to laugh at the genre that recently made it cry, the story-ballad was doomed. The simpler and less pretentious type of ballad—like "Daisy Bell" or "The Band Played On" of an earlier period—was now moving over into the limelight in Tin Pan Alley.

This simple kind of ballad found its master on Twenty-eighth Street in Ernest R. Ball. His songs were about every-day emotional experiences projected sincerely and honestly.

Born in Cleveland in 1878, Ball attended the conservatory there before coming to New York in 1890. For a while he worked as a pianist at the Union Square Theater. Then in 1903 he was hired as a piano demonstrator by Isidore Witmark for twenty dollars a week. While holding this job, Ball started writing ballads. The first to attract some interest was "In the Shadow of the Pyramids," but this was so primarily because May Irwin sang it so effectively in vaudeville. Its sheet-music sale, however, was virtually nonexistent.

Other song failures followed. A change of luck came in 1905 with "Will You Love Me in December As You Do in May?" Its lyrics were by a dapper young New Yorker of Irish extraction who delighted people with his spicy wit and debonair manner. He was James J. Walker, later to become a state senator and the mayor of New York City. As a boy, Walker's ambition had been to write songs. In this he was encouraged and guided by Paul Dresser. Walker was only seventeen when his first lyric, "Good-by, Eyes of Blue," with music by Harry Armstrong was published—a song inspired by the Spanish-American War. Witmark issued it, then gave Walker a contract as staff lyricist. Under this arrangement Walker wrote, once again with Armstrong "I Like Your Way."

Walker later reminisced: "When I jotted down the words [to "Will You Love Me in December As You Do in May?"] I knew I had something around which a capable composer could build a singable melody." The composer he wanted for his lyric was Ernest R. Ball, whom he met often at Witmark's. Ball tells the rest of the story. The lines, said Ball, were "scribbled on a piece of paper. I read them over. . . . I put the bit of paper in my pocket and, for the next two months, carried the scribbled lines around with me. . . . Bit by bit, I worked out a tune that somehow seemed to fit and, finally, I wrote the music to the words."

"I'll never forget," Walker continued, "the night when Ernie ran his magical fingers over the keyboard. . . . He finally swept both hands over the keys in the broad chords of the finished melody and I knew that a hit was born. I clasped Ernie about his shoulders and kissed his cheek."

The song did become a hit, a big one. "I awoke one morning," says Ball, "to find I had written a piece that was sung from one end of the country to another." Ball and Walker each earned more than ten thousand dollars in royalties within a year's time—a sum that represented to each a fortune. Petite and winsome Janet Allen, a member of the vaudeville team of Allen and McShane, introduced it and helped to send it off toward its nationwide popularity. In 1912, when Janet became Jimmy Walker's first wife, "Will You Love Me in December" was played as their wedding march.

Walker wrote about a half-dozen more lyrics after 1905, none of which even came close to the success of his December-May song. Then he deserted Tin Pan Alley for politics. But for Ernest R. Ball, "Will You Love Me in December" was the beginning of a triumphant career as a composer of simple, straightforward ballads. "Then and there, I determined I would write honestly and sincerely of the things I knew about and what folks generally knew about and were interested in." In 1906 he wrote "Love Me and the World Is Mine," with lyrics by David Reed. At first the song did not do well. It attracted no interest when introduced at Proctor's Fifth Avenue Theater. Then such vaudeville headliners as Maude Lambert (Ball's second wife) and Trudy Shattuck sang it on the circuit across the country, and with such impact that the sheet-music sales suddenly swooped beyond the million mark in less than a year.

A twenty-dollar-a-week employee in early 1905, Ball

soon found himself in the financial stratosphere. The Witmarks could recognize a gilt-edged investment when they saw one. They gave Ball a twenty-year contract as staff composer with a handsome yearly guarantee. This was the first time that any Tin Pan Alley publisher gave a composer such a long-term contract, and it was unusual when such a contract was so generous. (The agreement was renewed for an additional ten years just before Ball's death.) As Ball produced one big hit after another, these guarantees—generous though they were—were completely outdistanced by the royalties. Between 1907 and 1910, Ball wrote "When Sweet Marie Was Sweet Sixteen," "As Long as the World Rolls On," "In the Garden of My Heart," and "My Heart Has Learned to Love You." In 1911 he did "Till the Sands of the Desert Grow Cold." Between 1910 and 1912 came the Irish gems, which soon became a permanent part of the repertory of every Irish tenor, in vaudeville or on the concert stage, with John McCormack or with Morton Downey. First there was "Mother Machree" (lyrics by Rida Johnson Young), which Ball wrote in collaboration with Chauncey Olcott; Olcott introduced it in the musical *Barry of Ballymore*, in 1910. In 1912, Ball wrote a second Irish classic—"When Irish Eyes Are Smiling," with lyrics by Chauncey Olcott; and George Graff, Jr., introduced it in *Isle of Dreams*. In 1914 came "A Little Bit of Heaven, Sure They Call It Ireland."

Ball continued to pile success upon success with such other song classics as "Good-by, Good Luck, God Bless You." It was estimated that through the years his ballads sold over twenty-five million copies.

Beginning with 1905, Ball made numerous appearances in vaudeville, frequently costarring with his wife Maude Lambert. He had featured a potpourri of his song hits in a vaudeville house in Santa Ana on the night, May 3, 1927, that he suffered a fatal heart attack in his dressing room. "Ernie Ball," said John McCormack when he heard the news, "is not dead. He will live forever in his songs."

Harry Armstrong, who had started Jimmy Walker on his lyric-writing career, was the creator of what is perhaps the most celebrated of the simpler form of sentimental ballads to come out of Tin Pan Alley in the early 1900's— "Sweet Adeline." Then it was a classic of barbershop quartets; now it is still the song most often associated with the blissful state of inebriation. It is also one of the most successful examples of the "echo type" song so popular a half-century ago—the echo effect here used for the words "Sweet Adeline" and "My Adeline."

Armstrong had come from Boston, where he had been employed in a jewelry shop. His spare hours there were devoted to singing in barbershop quartets, and in writing melodies suitable for such performances. One of these tunes, sketched out in 1896 without any accompanying lyrics, was later to become "Sweet Adeline"—but only after he had changed his address from Boston to New York.

After coming to New York he played the piano in various honky-tonks, music halls, and restaurants, in Coney Island, Union Square, and further uptown. While trying to peddle some of his songs on Twenty-eighth Street, he found a job at Witmark's for eighteen dollars a week. Although it was considerably less than he was earning at that time as pianist at the Old Bohemia; he was more than willing to make the necessary financial sacrifice to further his songwriting career. Meeting the lyricist Richard H. Gerard (his real name was Richard Gerard Husch), Armstrong asked him to provide words for a melody completed some years earlier in Boston. Gerard complied with a lyric entitled "You're the Flower of My Heart, Sweet Rosalie." When this song was turned down by one publisher after another, Gerard suggested a change of title; he insisted that the name "Rosalie" lacked commercial appeal. Coming upon a poster advertising the farewell tour of Adelina Patti, the celebrated prima donna, Gerard decided to change the name of his heroine to Adeline. As "Sweet Adeline" the song was accepted by Witmark, and issued in 1903 with a none-too-modest legend scrawled across the printed copy: "one of the most charming ballads ever written." The song did not move for a while; piles of the music lay untouched in the stockroom for more than a year. Then, one day, Harry Ernest, manager of The Quaker City Four, a vaudeville act, dropped in at Witmark's in search of some new songs. When he came upon "Sweet Adeline" he remarked: "That's what we've been looking for." When The Quaker City Four introduced the song at Hammerstein's Victoria the following week, it was a huge success.

By 1906 the ballad had become so famous that John F. "Honey" Fitzgerald used it as his campaign song when he was running for mayor in Boston. He used it again so effectively for the same purpose in 1910 and 1914 that the song henceforth was as much his musical identification as "The Sidewalks of New York" was Alfred E. Smith's. In 1929, "Sweet Adeline" was used as the name of an Oscar Hammerstein-Jerome Kern Broadway musical, starring Helen Morgan. As far as Tin Pan Alley was concerned, another point of interest in this production was that the cast included one of the greatest of all the ballad-writers of the Alley, James Thornton, appearing as himself.

Year in, year out, the simplified ballad continued to roll up fabulous sales until, finally, it pushed the story-ballad out of the song picture. In 1902 a million-copy sale was realized by "In the Good Old Summertime" by George "Honey" Evans. Evans, of course, was the popular minstrel, one of the last of the immortal blackface performers in minstrel shows. He got his nickname of "Honey" from his own hit song of 1894, which he introduced in one of his performances, "I'll Be True to My Honey Boy."

One day in 1902 Evans visited Brighton Beach, in Brooklyn, with Ren Shields, the lyricist, and Blanche Ring, the musical-comedy star. They were dining at the Brighton Beach Hotel when Evans commented: "Give me the good old summertime—anytime." Blanche Ring recognized that this chance remark had the germ of a good song idea. At her suggestion, Ren Shields wrote the words and Evans the music. Blanche Ring herself introduced it in *The Defender* at the Herald Square Theater. When she sang it for the first time, Evans stood in the wings and—unseen by the audience—harmonized with her in the chorus. Though the song was well liked by the audiences at the Herald Square Theater, publishers were reluctant to take it on. They insisted that the song could have audience appeal only three months a year, that the rest of the time it would be scrupulously avoided by performers. Howley, Haviland and Dresser, however, finally took a chance with it and saw its popularity extend through all the four seasons. It remained a vaudeville favorite for many years. Meanwhile, in 1903 Shields and Evans with "In the Merry Month of June." tried once again to break the calendar jinx but this effort met with far less success.

A sale of several million copies was Remick's reward in 1905 for publishing "In the Shade of the Old Apple Tree," with words by Harry Williams, music by Egbert van Alstyne. Van Alstyne and Williams had toured as a vaudeville team before they settled in New York in 1900. Then Van Alstyne worked as a Tin Pan Alley song plugger. His first hit song was the Indian novelty number "Navajo," published by Shapiro-Bernstein in 1903 and successfully interpolated by Marie Cahill in the Broadway musical *Nancy*

*Brown.* "Back, Back, Back to Baltimore," published in 1904, was a Negro comedy number that had only a modest appeal in vaudeville and in minstrel shows. But "In the Shade of the Old Apple Tree" placed Van Alstyne permanently into the big time as a composer. He often said that the inspiration for his song came in Central Park, in New York—a curious fact, indeed, since there are no apple trees in Central Park. Perhaps it was the very absence of apple trees there that stirred Van Alstyne's nostalgia for those he had known as a boy in his own home town.

Van Alstyne's significance in Tin Pan Alley, established so solidly with his apple-tree song, was increased during the following years with a string of hits that included "Pretty Baby" (written in collaboration with Tony Jackson), "When I Was Twenty-one and You Were Sweet Sixteen," and "Your Eyes Have Told Me So."

In 1909, not one but three ballads either reached or passed the million-copy sale. "Put On Your Old Gray Bonnet" was written by Percy Wenrich to Stanley Murphy's words, and was published by Remick. It has since become a favorite at community sings. Wenrich had been a song plugger plying his trade in a Milwaukee department store before he came to New York. Then, in 1908, he wrote and had published "Up in a Balloon," to Ren Shields' lyrics. After writing "Put On Your Old Gray Bonnet," he sang it to Remick at his office late one Friday afternoon. Remick was dubious about the appeal of the song but he did not make a final decision. He said he'd like to take the manuscript with him to Atlantic City, where he was spending the weekend. When he returned to New York the following Monday, he told Wenrich he was going to publish the song. "I can't carry a tune, but yours kept running through my head all weekend. Any song that even *I* can't forget, *must* become a hit." Among Wenrich's later successful ballads were "Moonlight Bay" in 1912 and "When You Wore a Tulip" in 1914.

During 1909, Joe E. Howard's all-time favorite, "I Wonder Who's Kissing Her Now" was issued by Charles K. Harris. Howard maintained that the idea for the song came to him when he overheard a chance remark made by a college student in Chicago. Howard himself introduced the song in *The Prince of Tonight*, one of the musicals he was then putting on so successfully in the Windy City. After that Harris published the song and it realized a three-million-copy sale. From 1909, until Howard's death, a half-century later, he always featured this song whenever he made appearances, whether on the stage, over the radio, or on television. When his screen biography was filmed in 1947 (starring Mark Stephens and June Haver), it was named after the title of his most celebrated ballad, which of course was featured in it prominently. It therefore came as a shock when, in the last years of Howard's life, the decision of the courts established the fact that Joe E. Howard had been palming off somebody else's creation as his own all that time. In a later chapter we will have occasion to discuss this lawsuit and its revelations.

"Meet Me Tonight in Dreamland," also published in 1909, was a success almost as great as "I Wonder Who's Kissing Her Now." Leo Friedman wrote the music, and Beth Slater Whitson provided the lyrics. When Will Rossiter published it in Chicago, it was the first time his house ever enjoyed a two-million-copy success. Rossiter, who had a lifelong prejudice against paying royalties, had bought the song for a pittance. When, therefore, Will Rossiter's brother, Harry, went into the publishing business for himself in 1910, and stood ready to pay royalties, Whitson and Friedman had no hesitancy in turning over to him their new opus, "Let Me Call You Sweetheart." Published in

1910, it eventually accumulated a sheet-music sale approaching five million copies. "Meet Me Tonight in Dreamland" was revived in 1949 for Judy Garland in the motion picture *In the Good Old Summertime*.

One of the publications of 1910 deserves attention not only because of its huge sales in records and sheet music but also because, through the years, it was associated inextricably with one of the great show-women of all time—Sophie Tucker. The song was Shelton Brooks's "Some of These Days."

Sophie Tucker's uncommon gift for belting out a song and electrifying audiences with her dynamic delivery made her, like Jolson, an incomparable salesman for Tin Pan Alley's products. Like Jolson, she frequently had merely to sing a number in order to make it popular; and like Jolson, the number of songs she helped make successful is legion.

She had come to New York in 1906 on the advice of the comedian Willie Howard. Doggedly she made the rounds of publishers in Tin Pan Alley looking for new numbers she could use as a springboard for a career in show business. That career began at an amateur night in a theater on 125th Street and Third Avenue. After that she got a job singing in an Eighth Street café in exchange for her meals. With that as a background, she got a booking on a small-time, out-of-town vaudeville circuit for twenty-five dollars a week. At the insistence of a booking agent—who told her frankly she was too big and ugly to appear in whiteface—she blackened her face with burnt cork and was featured as a "world-renowned coon singer." Before the year of 1906 had ended she was appearing in a New York City theater on 116th Street. One year after that she was singing "Rosie, My Dusky Georgia Rose" and other "coon songs" (still in blackface) at Tony Pastor's Music Hall.

She was a member of a burlesque company (that also included Fanny Brice) when a trunk with her makeup and costumes got lost. For the first time in several years, she had to appear in whiteface. Singing "That Lovin' Rag," she created a furor that convinced her that she had no further need of burnt cork. "I don't need blackface," she remarked. "I can hold an audience without it. I've got them eating right out of my hand. I'm through with blackface. I'll never black again." After this, except for her sad misadventure with Ziegfeld's *Follies of 1909*, Sophie Tucker was headed straight for stardom—in vaudeville if not on Broadway. Touring on the William Morris circuit on which she was first billed as a "coon shouter" and then as "the Mary Garden of ragtime," she sang "Carrie," "Yiddishe Rag," "The Cubanola Glide," and "I Just Can't Make My Eyes Behave"; before many months passed, she was one of vaudeville's top headliners.

It was at this juncture in her career that she came upon "Some of These Days." Shelton Brooks, a Negro singer famous for his impersonation of the outstanding Negro entertainer Bert Williams, came to her one day pleading that she listen to a song he had just written. At first, Sophie Tucker was reluctant to waste time on an unknown composer, but her maid and friend, Mollie Elkins, prevailed on her to change her mind. She listened to "Some of These Days" and knew at once this was a winner. She introduced the song in 1910 at the White City Park in Chicago. From then on she and the song became inseparable. As she wrote in her autobiography many years later: "I could have kicked myself for almost losing it. A song like that. It had everything. Hasn't it proved it? I've been singing it for thirty years, made it my theme. I've turned it inside out, singing it every way imaginable, as a dramatic song, as a novelty number, as a sentimental ballad, and always audiences have loved it and asked for it." As "the queen of jazz," and after 1927 as "the last of the red-hot mamas," she carried the song to the height of success, and the song in turn lifted her to the pinnacle of fame in vaudeville, night clubs, movies, radio, and television. Today it is almost inconceivable to think of the song in any rendition but Sophie Tucker's. And when she put down on paper the story of her life, she inevitably called it *Some of These Days*.

A half-dozen years after she had introduced "Some of These Days," Sophie Tucker once again brought to the public a new Shelton Brooks song and helped it on its way to inevitable success—the ragtime classic, "The Darktown Strutters' Ball."

Ragtime, as we shall presently observe, crowned Irving Berlin king. But, in 1912, Berlin tapped a new creative vein by writing words and music for a poignant ballad that was to be his first classic in that style. He named the song "When I Lost You." Since Berlin was to become one of the foremost creators of ballads in Tin Pan Alley, the publication of the first of these has particular historic importance.

Like so many of Irving Berlin's later ballads, this one was autobiographical. It had been inspired by a major personal tragedy. In 1912, Berlin married Dorothy Goetz; on their honeymoon in Cuba, Dorothy contracted typhoid, and died soon after the couple returned to New York City. Berlin's first sentimental ballad, then, was an epitaph for his beloved young wife.

# 12

## "Oh, that beautiful rag"

In counterpoint to the soft sweet ballads, there were the vigorous accents of more robust types of songs. We already have had the occasion to speak about "coon songs" and cakewalks with their emphasis on syncopation. Now in the early 1900's something new was being heard in Tin Pan Alley—a nervous, febrile strain that came to be known as ragtime. Already in the 1890's, ragtime had begun to penetrate into the song industry, even if only hesitantly. By the early 1900's, its advance was growing bolder, just as its voice was growing louder and more insistent. And by the 1910's, ragtime had become one of the most highly favored song styles being exploited by the Tin Pan Alley tunesmith—and for the very good reason that by then the entire country had gone ragtime-crazy. As Gaby Deslys sang so infectiously in the finale of Irving Berlin's musical comedy in 1915, *Stop, Look and Listen,* "Everything in America Is Ragtime."

Down in Union Square before 1900, ragtime was occasionally heard at Tony Pastor's Music Hall; and from time to time the publishers in Union Square issued ragtime pieces. This music, of course, must not be confused with the improvisations and blues that, in New Orleans, became the language of real jazz. The ragtime in Union Square, however, was of Negro derivation just as the jazz of New Orleans was; as someone once said, ragtime talked about the six days of the week that the Negro spiritual ignored. As first heard in the publishing cubicles of Union Square and on the stage of Pastor's Music Hall, ragtime was nothing more than the persistent use of syncopation. (Syncopation is the placing of a strong beat where a weak beat is usually placed.) Commercial ragtime used a steady 2/4 and 4/4 rhythm in the bass while the treble deployed marked syncopations. Here is how Sigmund Spaeth in his *History of Popular Music in America* explained the technique: "The simple trick of putting an artificial accent on the offbeat, anticipating or delaying the real emphasis, came up from the South where the Negroes had been using it for years. . . . Ragtime concentrated on this typical distortion of rhythm, literally tearing the melody to tatters." "Coon songs" made effective use of syncopation, but the "coon song" was not ragtime because it did not employ syncopation consistently throughout the number.

Piano rags had been played in saloons and brothels long before anybody thought of putting them down on paper. The first to write down a rag was Scott Joplin, a Negro pianist from Missouri. When he was working as a ragtime pianist at the Maple Leaf Club, he attracted a local publisher, John Stilwell Stark, who offered to publish some of his rags. *Oriental Rag* in 1899 was not only Joplin's first published piece of music but also the first piano rag ever printed. Later the same year Stark issued Joplin's *Maple Leaf Rag*—to this day a classic in piano ragtime. Among Joplin's later pieces were *Sunflower Rag, Sugar Cane Rag, Pineapple Rag,* and *Gladiolus Rag.* Joplin also prepared a primer on ragtime, and completed a ragtime opera, *Treemonisha,* whose text described the joy of Negroes at Emancipation, and whose music was based entirely on ragtime. The *Jazz Record Book* notes: "His work is the best tribute to the ragtime era."

Ben Harney was the man responsible for popularizing piano rags in New York; he was also the first white man to consign piano rags to paper. He started out as a ragtime pianist in saloons in Kansas City and St. Louis. Then he became a member of a minstrel company with which he sang songs and did a "stick dance specialty." His initiation as a popular composer came with "coon songs." The first two, and the best, came in 1896: "You've Been a Good Old Wagon but You Done Broke Down" and "Mister Johnson, Turn Me Loose." Frank Harding published them but failed to sell many copies. Then Ben Harney started to popularize both songs in his minstrel shows, and May Irwin interpolated "Mister Johnson" in *Courted at Court.* Sensing a mounting interest in both numbers, M. Witmark and Sons bought the publication rights from Frank Harding and reissued them. These two numbers now became so successful that other publishers were tempted into issuing syncopated numbers and "coon songs" of their own.

From "coon songs" Ben Harney progressed to piano rags. After coming to New York, just before the end of the nineteenth century, he played his rags at Tony Pastor's Music Hall, where both he and his music became a rage. Some of his rags consisted of original pieces; most were syncopated versions of hymns and semiclassical compositions. His vaudeville act, however, consisted of much more than just piano music. He used a Negro stooge named Strap Hill in the audience. Strap Hill would sing the verse of a song. Then Harney would follow by giving a faithful imitation of his stooge. Strap Hill would finally mount the stage to do some "coon shouting" to Ben Harney's ragtime piano. Harney's act also included his ragtime singing and "coon shouting" of his own songs. "He had the huskiest voice most people had ever heard in a human being," said Isidore Witmark, "and this quality made his voice just right for ragtime singing." One of the newer songs popularized by Harney was his own "Cakewalk in the Sky," the first number in which the words as well as the music were in ragtime, the rhythm of the words following the rhythm of the melody.

Piano rags soon became sufficiently popular to be attacked. *Musical Courier,* in an editorial in 1899, exclaimed: "A wave of vulgar, filthy and suggestive music has inundated the land. The pabulum of theater and summer hotel orchestras is 'coon music.' Nothing but ragtime prevails, and the cakewalk with its obscene posturings, its lewd gestures. . . . Our children, our young men and women, are continually exposed to the contiguity, to the monotonous attrition of this vulgarizing music. It is artistically and morally depressing and should be suppressed by press and pulpit. The 'coon song' must go."

Supporters of ragtime were also vocal. Rupert Hughes wrote in *The Musical Record* of April 1, 1899: "If ragtime were called *tempo di raga* . . . it might win honors more speedily. . . . Ragtime will find its way gradually into the works of some great genius and will thereafter be canonized." Emma Nevada, the prima donna, told an interviewer for the Boston *Herald* in 1901 that she favored ragtime and prophesied that "they will not squelch the new fad."

\*

Attacked on the one hand, lauded on the other, ragtime music continued to flourish. While initially it was an instrumental style, ragtime soon invaded popular-song writing. Syncopated effects—previously used sparingly in "coon songs" and cakewalks—abounded in Joe E. Howard's first great song success, "Hello, My Baby," in 1899. Some authorities consider this the first important ragtime tune ever written. Three years after that came another ragtime song, one still in high favor—Hugh Cannon's "Bill Bailey, Won't You Please Come Home?" Hugh Cannon's weakness for liquor and narcotics eventually brought him into a poorhouse in Wayne County in Michigan, in which he spent his last miserable days as a human wreck. But while he was still flourishing as a ragtime pianist and composer, he had an inordinate capacity for making friends in all walks of life. One of them was the big Negro Bill Bailey. Late one night, Bailey was locked out of his house by his irate wife. Cannon provided Bailey with the price of a hotel room, and advised him to stay away from home not one night but several nights. "She'll be begging you to please come home," Cannon advised him. We do not know if Cannon's strategy worked. We do know, however, that the episode was responsible for one of the best ragtime songs ever created— the crowning success of Hugh Cannon's musical life. This number is still popular enough to be sung today with uncommon effect by such top performers as Ella Fitzgerald and Jimmy Durante's long-time singing partner Eddie Jackson. The first person to present "Bill Bailey" in public was John Queen, in a musical pastiche, *Town Topics*, presented in Newburgh, New York. "Bill Bailey" soon became so popular that a rash of Bill Bailey songs, by composers other than Cannon flooded the market. Some of them related the later experiences of the hapless hero: "I Wonder Why Bill Bailey Don't Come Home," for example, and "Since Bill Bailey Came Back Home."

If "Bill Bailey" was the king of the early ragtime songs, then the crown prince was "Under the Bamboo Tree," which also appeared in 1902. Bob Cole, a member of the vaudeville team of Cole and Johnson, wrote it to provide his act with some fresh material. Originally he named the song after the opening phrase of the chorus "If you lak-a me." When Joseph W. Stern & Company accepted it for publication, Stern suggested a change of title to "Under the Bamboo Tree." Marie Cahill heard the song at a backstage party one day, and insisted on doing it in her show *Sally in Our Alley*. She was a sensation.

There were still other important ragtime songs in the first decade of the 20th century: in 1904, "Me an' the Minstrel Band," which the minstrel George Walker introduced; in or about 1907, "Let It Alone" (described on the sheet music as a "ragtime philosophical song") and "Somebody Lied," featured by Bert Williams; in 1908, "You're in the Right Church, but the Wrong Pew," which Bert Williams made a triumph in *My Landlady*, and "That Lovin' Rag," which Sophie Tucker sang in burlesque; and in 1909, two other Sophie Tucker favorites, "The Cubanola Glide" and "Carrie."

Lewis F. Muir was probably the most original and the most significant of these early creators of ragtime songs. His experiences as a ragtime pianist in the honky-tonks of St. Louis during the Exposition helped him out when he started to write such tunes of his own. Soon after he came to New York in 1910, he wrote "Play That Barber Shop Chord" (based on one of his earlier piano tunes, "Play that Fandango Rag"). Bert Williams scored such a success with it at Hammerstein's Victoria in 1910 that he used it again for his debut with the *Ziegfeld Follies* later the same year. In 1911, Muir wrote "When Ragtime Rosie Ragged the Rosary." Reviewing this song for the New York *Clipper*, L. Wolfe Gilbert (a vaudevillian turned lyricist) denounced it in no uncertain terms. This low opinion of Muir's rag, however, did not deter Gilbert from inviting Muir to write the music for some of his own lyrics. One was inspired by a scene Gilbert witnessed on a levee in Baton Rouge, Louisiana, where Negroes were unloading freight from a Mississippi river boat, The Robert E. Lee. Muir's music with Gilbert's words—written in 1912—became one of the greatest of all ragtime songs to emerge from Tin Pan Alley: "Waiting for the Robert E. Lee."

In those days, Muir habitually visited the publishing offices of F. A. Mills in Tin Pan Alley. He liked to play his ragtime tunes there for Irving Berlin, E. Ray Goetz, and any other professionals who happened to be around. It was there that he played his "Waiting for the Robert E. Lee" for the first time, hoping to interest Mills into publishing it. Mills at first said the song was not much to his liking, but he had a sudden change of heart. When Gilbert dropped in later to pick up the manuscript, Mills told him he was publishing the number after all.

Tubby Garron, a song plugger, brought the song to Jolson, who introduced it with great success at a Sunday-evening concert at the Winter Garden in 1912. The boy Eddie Cantor sang it the same year in vaudeville in the Gus Edwards' revue *Kid Kabaret*. Ruth Roye and Belle Baker were two other vaudevillians to use it in their acts, with extraordinary effectiveness and success.

Like Irving Berlin, Muir was a one-key pianist; also, like Berlin, he had a special mechanism installed into his piano, making it possible for him to play any piece of music in the key of his preference. Since "Waiting for the Robert E. Lee" was in two keys (the verse in C, the chorus in F), anybody who sang the tune to Muir's accompaniment had to hold the last note of the verse until Muir had a chance to manipulate the handle under the piano so that the keyboard might slip into the key of F.

Among Muir's later ragtime songs were "The Natchez and the Robert E. Lee" (an unsuccessful sequel to "Waiting for the Robert E. Lee"), "Here Comes My Daddy Now," "Mississippi River Steamboat," "Ragtime Cowboy Joe," and "Hitchy-Koo." Muir's fame as a ragtime composer and performer brought him an invitation to play his tunes at the Oxford Theater in London just before World War I. At the same time he was contracted to write some ragtime music for a London revue for which (incongruously enough) some of the music was being written by Ruggiero Leoncavallo, the composer of the opera *Pagliacci*.

Irving Berlin's "Alexander's Ragtime Band" became the most popular and the most profitable "ragtime" song ever written; and the irony of it all is that it is *not* a ragtime song.

Syncopation had intrigued Berlin since 1909 when he gave a rag treatment to Mendelssohn's "Spring Song" in "That Mesmerizing Mendelssohn Tune." During that same year he wrote words and music of "Stop That Rag," which Stella Mayhew sang in *The Jolly Bachelors*, and "Yiddle on Your Fiddle, Play Some Ragtime." In 1910 came "The Opera Rag," which May Irwin introduced in *Getting a Polish*, "Grizzly Bear," which he wrote in collaboration with George Botsford, and "Oh That Beautiful Rag," a minor hit in *Up and Down Broadway*. Then, in 1911, Berlin gave the world an outstanding ragtime number in "Ragtime Violin."

In 1911, Berlin became a member of the Friars Club in New York. On that occasion he was invited to appear as a performer in its annual *Frolics*. For this affair Berlin wanted to write a special song. The year before, he had written a ragtime song that he titled "Alexander and His Clarinet." Dissatisfied, he had put it aside. Now, needing something for the *Friars Frolics*, he salvaged the lyrics and rewrote them to fit the tune of an instrumental number he had recently concocted. The new opus was called "Alexander's Ragtime Band." Berlin submitted it to Jesse Lasky (the same man who later became the powerful motion-picture executive) for a vaudeville show he was then producing on Broadway. Lasky turned it down. Soon after that the Columbia Burlesque House used it in one of its productions, but nobody seemed to take note of it.

It was Emma Carus, in a vaudeville theater in Chicago, who turned the tide for "Alexander." Her dynamic shouting style suited the song perfectly, and she brought down the house. "If we were John D. Rockefeller," wrote an unidentified Chicago critic, "or the Bank of England, we should engage the Coliseum and get together a sextet including [Enrico] Caruso. . . . After the sextet sang it [Alexander's Ragtime Band] about ten times, we should, as a finale, have Sousa's band march about the building tearing the melody to pieces with all kinds of variations."

In a few months' time the sheet music sold more than one million copies. Within a year "Alexander's Ragtime Band" was the most widely sung, played, danced-to "ragtime" song ever written. The country, now long conscious of the allure of ragtime, went mad over syncopation.

But "Alexander's Ragtime Band" is not a ragtime song at all—except for the use of the word in the title and the single use of syncopation on the word "just" in the chorus. It is essentially march music, with interpolations of bugle calls and a quotation from Stephen Foster's "Swanee River." But its fabulous success—and the mistaken notion that it was pure ragtime—brought syncopation to its highest peak of popularity, to a point where ragtime songs usurped the imperial position formerly occupied in Tin Pan Alley by ballads.

Though "Alexander's Ragtime Band" was not ragtime, other Berlin numbers were identifiably so. The best included "Everybody's Doin' It," "That Mysterious Rag," and "The Ragtime Jockey Man"—the last two were brought into the Broadway revue *The Passing Show of 1912*. In 1913, Berlin's now-great fame as a ragtime composer brought him an engagement at the Hippodrome Theater in London, where he was billed as "the ragtime king." For this appearance he produced the "International Rag." At the London Hippodrome, Berlin always ended his act by asking the audience to call out the Irving Berlin ragtime tunes it would like to hear. The audience would shout the titles of every ragtime number it had ever heard of, in the mistaken belief that Berlin had written them all.

As the ragtime hysteria mounted, so did the chorus of denunciations in press and pulpit. "Ragtime is tonal drunkenness," said the *Musical Courier* in 1917.

"Ragtime," said Ivan Narodny in a letter to the New York *Evening Sun*, "suggests the odor of the saloon, the smell of the backyard, and subways. Its style is decadent. It is music meant for . . . tired and . . . bored minds. It is essentially obvious, vulgar, and yet shockingly strong, for the reason that it ends fortissimo."

Daniel Gregory Mason—distinguished composer, musicologist and professor—called ragtime "not a new flavor, but a kind of curry or catsup, strong enough to make the stale old dishes palatable to unfastidious appetites."

But there were also affirmative opinions. "To me," said Hiram K. Motherwell in the *Seven Arts Monthly* in July, 1917, "ragtime brings a type of musical experience which I can find in no other music. I like to think that it is the perfect expression of the American city, with its restless bustle and motion, its multitude of unrelated details, with its underlying rhythmic progress toward a vague Somewhere."

A prophetic (as well as appreciative) voice was sounded from across the seas, in the letter columns of the London *Times* in 1913. "From nowhere but the United States could such music spring. It is the music of the hustler and of the feverishly active speculator. . . . We look to the future for an American composer—not, indeed, to the Parkers and the MacDowells of the present who are taking over a foreign art, ready-made, imitating it with more or less success, and with a complete absence of vital force, but to someone as yet unknown, perhaps unborn, who will sing the songs of his own nation in his own time and of his own character."

# 13

## "Shall we dance?"

The passion for ragtime that seized America was followed by one for social dancing. This was not a coincidence, it was cause and effect. Before 1910 social dances, such as the polka, the whirling waltz, and the schottische, taxed the endurance and agility even of the young. Rest periods of ten or fifteen minutes were necessary between dances to allow the participants to catch their breath and revive their energy. Even then, many had to sit out some of the numbers. Older people seldom ventured out on the dance floor, and even younger married folk rarely indulged in dancing.

But ragtime changed all that. The 2/4 and 4/4 rhythm encouraged the creation of simpler kinds of dances. Call it what you will—a turkey trot, or a grizzly bear, or a bunny hug, or a camel walk, or a lame duck, whether the movements involved rocking, or swaying, or sliding—the new dances brought in by ragtime required little more than walking around the dance floor with a partner in an embrace. These dances were easy to learn, simple to perform, and made no exacting demands on the stamina or the heart. With syncopated rhythms stirring the senses and making feet restless, the disease of dancing was easily contracted and, once contracted, became chronic. The ragtime song of Tin Pan Alley was changing the social habits of America.

The early experiences of Sigmund Romberg in the United States help to illuminate what was happening in dance-crazy America in the early 1910's. Romberg, coming to the United States when he was twenty-two, had some vague notions about making a living through music, though precisely how had not yet been crystallized in his mind. In his native Hungary—and later on in Vienna where he spent his early manhood—he had received a thorough musical education; he had also absorbed in Vienna the traditions of waltz music and the operetta.

Soon after his arrival in New York City, Romberg found a job as house pianist in a café on Second Avenue. Somewhat later he was hired to play dinner music at the Pabst-Harlem Restaurant. Finally, in 1912, the management of Bustanoby's, one of New York's prime eating places, hired him to lead a salon orchestra.

One evening at Bustanoby's, Romberg experimentally introduced several ragtime tunes on his salon program. To his amazement he saw first one couple, then another, rise from their tables and begin to dance—something then unheard of in restaurants. Before long, so many people were dancing that tables had to be removed to make additional room.

Romberg continued to play ragtime, and the clientele at Bustanoby's continued to dance. It was not long before people were coming to Bustanoby's more to dance than to eat. Salon music now had to give way to dance music. Business soared. Romberg's salary jumped from fifty dollars a week to a hundred and fifty.

L. Wolfe Gilbert, the lyricist then working for Edward B. Marks, used to come to Bustanoby's to hear Romberg's music. One day he urged Romberg to compose American dance tunes of his own. Romberg complied by writing first the turkey trot "Leg o' Mutton," next the one-step "Some Smoke," and after that the waltz "Poem"—all of which Joseph W. Stern & Company published in 1913. The dance craze that Romberg had so innocently encouraged had, in turn, transformed him from a dance-orchestra conductor into a popular composer. Romberg was on his way toward becoming one of the most successful composers of American popular music—and operetta music particularly —of his time.

One after another of the famous New York restaurants began to imitate Bustanoby's by introducing dancing at mealtime—places such as Louis Martin's Café de l'Opéra on Broadway, Reisenweber's on Columbus Circle, and Murray's on Forty-second Street. Restaurants with good dance bands and dance floors began to attract far more patrons than those specializing in gourmet meals and rare vintage wines. The era of great dining, which had characterized the 1890's and the first part of the 1900's, was making way for the era of great dancing. Some of the older establishments, disgusted with this development, preferred to go out of business rather than allow culinary art to be relegated to such a secondary role.

Even tearooms and Chinese eating places had to introduce dancing both afternoons and evenings. Such swank spots as Sherry's and hotels such as the McAlpin and even the Waldorf-Astoria, succumbed, after offering resistance for a while, to the vogue for dancing.

Businessmen would slip away from their offices for a half-hour or so in the afternoon to dance with hostesses hired by restaurants, tearooms, and hotels for this purpose. Wives deserted their homes for a turn or two with the male counterparts of these hostesses—*maîtres de danse*. Even factory workers began to sneak in some dancing during the lunch hour.

To cater to this expanding and demanding public need for dancing, Lee Shubert opened up the first American night club, the Palais de Danse, near Broadway. William Morris followed Shubert's lead with the Jardin de Danse atop Loew's New York Theater. Other night clubs and dancing halls appeared all over New York City. To avoid the curfew law, these places described themselves as "dance clubs," since it was not illegal for a club to keep open all night. Consequently, it was possible to do a "dance crawl" across the town through the night, from one restaurant or night club to the next. Indeed, it became *the* thing to do.

"Rag" dancing contests were instituted in ballrooms and vaudeville theaters in 1913. One of the most successful was staged by William Morris in his Jardin de Danse. Gimbel's department store opened an afternoon *thé dansant*, for which an admission charge of seventy-five cents was made. The Arena Skating Rink announced that, after 11 P.M., skating would make way for ballroom dancing. A group of society women, headed by Mrs. W. K. Vanderbilt, opened a charity cafeteria lunch-dansant atop the Strand Theater— admission was fifty cents, lunch cost an additional twenty-five cents. In Cincinnati, in 1914, dancing was allowed in the public parks! In 1915, Florenz Ziegfeld created a new era in entertainment by opening the *Midnight Frolic* atop the New Amsterdam Theater. Eating and dancing were now combined with a lavish floor show to create what in essence was the city's first cabaret. Morris Gest had a venture of his own atop the Century Theater soon after that, and by 1917 Broadway boasted still another fine cabaret in the Palais Royal.

Fashions in dance steps came and went. The turkey trot (and its variants) were succeeded by the Castle walk; the Castle walk by the tango; the tango by the fox trot. And all the while the dancing fever kept climbing. Dance schools as well as dance halls were beginning to flourish, and dancing teachers giving lessons to the social élite, including John D. Rockefeller, were getting wealthy. Newspapers and magazines tried to build circulation by printing diagrams of the latest dance steps. For a long time the *Ladies' Home Journal*, edited by Edward W. Bok, refused to fall in line, but, eventually, it, too, had to cater to the dance craze.

Ministers, reformers, do-gooders, and some newspaper editorialists looked askance at the sight of a whole nation spinning around so helplessly and deliriously on dance floors in a close embrace. Even the Pope spoke with disapproval. When the tango was at the height of its initial popularity, in 1914, it was condemned as immoral, regarded as the shocking public exhibition of an activity that belonged in the privacy of a boudoir, described as an excuse for promiscuous hugging.

"The very air of these places is heavy with unleashed passions," remarked one newspaper writer. Another journalist spoke of public dancing as "lascivious orgies." William Inglis, in *Harper's*, insisted that what went on every day in respectable restaurants surpassed even the excesses of drunken sailors on holiday. The tango was officially barred from the Yale prom of 1914. Mrs. Stuyvesant Fish, eager to allow her guests to dance the tango at one of her functions, yet critical of some of the abandoned poses it encouraged, had a new type of tango devised expressly for use at her party, a dance in which the couples never touched each other. When Henry Blossom (Victor Herbert's librettist) and Mrs. Ethel Fitch Conger (daughter of playwright Clyde Fitch) broke their ankles tangoing, the newspapers insisted even more strenuously that the new dance was not only immoral but dangerous as well.

The dance craze was nurtured and sustained by the flood of dance tunes that poured out of Tin Pan Alley. Irving Berlin's "Everybody's Doin' It" was inspired by the turkey trot, and his "Grizzly Bear" by the dance of that name. For the tango, J. Rosamond Johnson wrote "Tango Dreams," described as "Brazilian," and J. Tim Brymn, "La Rumba," identified as "Argentine." For the waltz—E. T. Paull created "The Hesitation Waltz"; C. D. Mesquita, "Esmeralda"; and J. R. Europe and F. T. Dabney, "The Castle Classic Waltz." The last two composers, as collaborators, also created numbers for the Castle walk and the Castle lame duck. "The Gaby Glide" was written by Louis A. Hirsch for a new dance routine introduced by Gaby Deslys in the Broadway musical *Vera Violetta*.

On the stage the dance craze was glorified, as in "The Spirit of the Tango" in the *Ziegfeld Follies of 1914* and in "The Floradora Glide" and "The White House Glide" in *The Passing Show of 1913*. The dance craze was also material for ridicule. Leon Errol did a hilarious "turkish trot" routine in the *Ziegfeld Follies of 1913*, while Ina Claire did an unforgettable takeoff of Irene Castle in the *Follies* edition of 1916. In "The Puritan Prance," Sophie Tucker did a burlesque of the bunny hug and the grizzly bear.

Many a stage performer was lifted to stardom by this dance craze. Bessie Clayton did the turkey trot in *The Passing Show of 1913* and overnight became the talk of the theater world. The teams of Maurice Mouvet-Florence

Walton and Joan Sawyer-Lew Quinn danced their way to public adulation in vaudeville and revues. Gaby Deslys, Mae Murray, and Clifton Webb were others to achieve their first major successes through dancing.

But one pair of dancers stood apart from all the others, to become the idols of the dancing age—Vernon and Irene Castle. After their marriage in 1911, each played bit parts on Broadway. Then as a dancing couple they scored a major success at the Café de Paris, the smartest supper club in the French capital. Returning home as dance celebrities in 1913 they were starred in the Broadway musical *The Sunshine Girl*. The beginning of the Castle rage in America can be said to have started when, in this show, Vernon and Irene Castle did a turkey trot and Vernon Castle and Julia Sanderson did a tango. Both dances brought down the house. From then on, the Castles did more than any others to intensify the dancing madness. They set the styles, which the dancing public were to adopt, by inventing and popularizing dances such as the Castle walk, the Castle classic waltz, the Castle lame duck, the maxixe, the hesitation waltz. They earned as much as thirty thousand dollars a week doing one-night stands. On one such tour they visited thirty-two cities in twenty-eight days, ending up at Madison Square Garden. Wherever they appeared, they conducted a dance contest at the end of their formal program.

They were not only vaudeville headliners but also stars of Broadway musical comedy. In 1914, *Watch Your Step* was written and produced as a vehicle for them. This musical—produced by Charles Dillingham and described in the program as "a syncopated musical show"—was the first for which Irving Berlin wrote an entire score, a score that included "The Syncopated Walk" for the Castles and a ballad still popular enough forty years later to sell a million records for Bing Crosby and his son Gary, "Play a Simple

Melody." The Castles held the stage—and the fascinated interest of their audiences—with their tangos, fox trots and one-steps.

One unidentified critic reported: "*Watch Your Step* has all the allurements of the [dancing] craze that has kept a majority of the populace high-stepping in ballrooms and restaurants for the last two or three years. If there were ever a doubt that the tango and the fox trot would resist becoming a musical-comedy theme it was dispelled by Mr. Dillingham's stroke of genius in making the Castles his two stars."

The Castles founded the Castle School of Dancing, at which William Randolph Hearst, the Rockefellers, and others in the upper social strata paid $100 an hour for private lessons. The Castles also opened a dance palace favored by the élite—The Castle House, where in one room a Negro band played ragtime, while in another a string orchestra performed for those preferring to dance tangos or the maxixe. The Castles also opened their own night clubs: the Castle Sans Souci on Forty-second Street and Seventh Avenue, where Jim Europe's band performed, and Castles in the Air atop the Forty-fourth Street Theater.

Gilbert Seldes wrote that the Castles, "determined the course dancing should take. . . . They were decisive characters . . . for they understood, absorbed, and transformed everything known of dancing up to that time and made it something beautiful and new. . . . There were no steps, no tricks, no stunts. There was only dancing, and it was all that one ever dreamed of flight, with wings poised, and swooping gently to rest."

As the symbols of their times, the Castles affected not only the dance but also social habits. Women began to imitate Irene Castle when she replaced the old-time hobble skirt for a simple flowing gown that gave her freedom of movement in her dancing; when she chose Dutch bonnets;

when she wore jodhpurs for horseback riding; and, most radical of all, when she bobbed her hair. Small, slight, petite, she made permanent the trend Anna Held before her had started—toward the new American concept of female beauty. Now more than ever the boyish, sylphlike figure became the ideal female form. "If any one person is responsible for the appearance of the modern young lady of fashion whom we admire so much today," said Cecil Beaton, "it is certainly Mrs. Vernon Castle."

# 14

## *"I gotta right to sing the blues"*

Ragtime was one of two significant contributions made by Negro folk music to Tin Pan Alley. The "blues" were another.

Blues were born out of the sorrow songs Negroes used to improvise to lament their sad lot in an unhappy world. In New Orleans, such legendary jazz musicians as Buddy Bolden are reported to have improvised remarkable blues melodies. But, as a commercial product manufactured in Tin Pan Alley for general consumption, the blues were born with W. C. Handy's "The Memphis Blues," the first blues song to be published.

In the blues the lyric usually consisted of three-line stanzas in iambic pentameter, the second line repeating the first. Musically, a twelve-bar melody is made up of three four-bar phrases. As the blues evolved and became crystallized, certain stylistic features distinguished it from all other kinds of Negro songs. Most significant was the "blue note," a flatting of the third and seventh steps in the diatonic scale. Another was the "break," consisting of a pause in the melody to permit the singer to utter some such exclamation as "Oh Lawdy" or "Oh baby." (In New Orleans, the "break" offered the instrumentalist an opportunity to improvise variations and figurations on the basic melody.)

When W. C. Handy published his autobiography, he called it *The Father of the Blues*. To the end of his life he persisted in the fiction that the blues were something he had invented; he harbored a permanent hurt when jazz writers traced the blues back to New Orleans and further back than that to the folk songs of the Negro. Actually, Handy's blues were a commercial item rather then one that realized the authentic New Orleans product. Handy's contribution lies in the fact that he brought a form of the blues to a mass public, performing the same service that Scott Joplin and Ben Harney had done for ragtime. Another way in which Handy is important is that he was the creator of "St. Louis Blues," the most celebrated and one of the most distinguished examples of blues music ever published.

W. C. Handy was the son of a Negro minister who regarded secular music of any kind as sacrilegious. "Son," the father told the boy, "I'd rather see you in a hearse than see you become a musician." Born in Florence, Alabama, in 1873, Handy somehow managed to buy a trumpet for a dollar and to learn how to play it. Without his father being aware of it, Handy made appearances as a trumpet player, first with a brass band, then with a minstrel show.

But he was officially being educated to be a teacher. When he was graduated from Teachers Agricultural and

Mechanical College in Huntsville, Alabama, in 1892, he entered the schoolroom. But he disliked teaching, and abandoned it promptly, after which he took a job in a steel foundry and followed various musical pursuits. Then, in 1893, he found a job playing the cornet at the world fair in Chicago, and three years later, he was hired as cornetist, arranger, and performer with the Mahara Minstrels. In 1903 he organized a band for popular concerts. This was the first of several that he founded through the years, with which he gave concerts of popular music throughout the South for a quarter of a century.

In his autobiography, Handy singled out two episodes that brought him to the blues. One was the experience of hearing a Negro chant a "sorrow song" at a deserted railway station. This was Handy's first contact with this form of music. The other episode was a concert of jazz music given by a Negro band. "That night," Handy confessed, "a composer was born, an American composer. Those country black boys had taught me something that could not possibly have been gained from books, something that would, however, cause books to be written."

Not until 1909 did Handy write his first blues; the motivation was a mayoralty campaign in Memphis, Tennessee. Handy favored Edward H. Crump, a candidate who was running on a reform ticket. To gain the Negro support for Crump, Handy wrote a campaign song in a musical style to which his people could respond instinctively and enthusiastically. The song "Mr. Crump" became so popular that it may have been the factor that elected Handy's favored candidate.

Handy later rewrote the song as a piano composition, now calling it "The Memphis Blues," and published it, in 1912, at his own expense. In 1913, the Theron A. Bennett Company of New York City purchased all the rights for fifty dollars. With new lyrics by George A. Norton Bennett, "The Memphis Blues" was republished in New York and became a tremendous success. The blues had come into Tin Pan Alley.

In an attempt to capitalize on the growing fame of "The Memphis Blues"—which had brought him so little financially—Handy set out to write a second blues. Rummaging through the storehouse of his memories for some suitable subject, he saw the mental image of himself "unshaven, wanting even a decent meal, and standing before the lighted saloon in St. Louis, without a shirt under my frayed coat." He also recalled "a curious and dramatic little fragment that till now seemed to have little or no importance. While occupied with my own memories during the sojourn, I had seen a woman whose pain seemed even greater. She had tried to take the edge off her grief by heavy drinking, but it hadn't worked. Stumbling along the poorly lighted street, she muttered as she walked: 'My man's got a heart like a rock cast in the sea.' . . . By the time I had finished all this heavy thinking and remembering, I figured it was time to get something down on paper, so I wrote 'I hate to see de evenin' sun go down.' If you ever had to sleep on the cobblestones down by the river in St. Louis, you'll understand the complaint."

Handy called his new piece "St. Louis Blues." Forming a publishing partnership with Harry Pace (the Pace and Handy Music Company in Memphis, Tennessee) Handy issued his new blues in 1914. The song did not at first catch on. Before it did, Handy had completed and published several more blues, including "Beale Street" (later renamed "Beale Street Blues") and "The Joe Turner Blues."

"St. Louis Blues" started to stir into life soon after Handy had transferred his publishing unit to Tin Pan Alley in New York. Sophie Tucker began to sing it in vaudeville. Then the Victor Company made an instrumental recording that did so well that competing companies issued versions of their own; piano-roll companies followed suit.

Through the years few single pieces of music—popular or serious—have sold more records than "St. Louis Blues" has. The sheet music did almost as well. Toward the end of his life (Handy died in New York City in 1958), the composer was still drawing annual royalties of twenty-five thousand dollars a year from this one number. "St. Louis Blues" was used in a Broadway revue, a movie short, and in *Is Everybody Happy?*, a full-length talking picture in 1929. When Handy's life story was filmed in 1958, starring Nat King Cole, it was called *St. Louis Blues*.

"St. Louis Blues" has been transcribed for every possible musical instrument and combination of instruments. In short, it has become a classic, recognized as such throughout the civilized world. During the visit of Prime Minister Ramsay MacDonald of England to the United States, the "St. Louis Blues" was used to welcome him. Queen Elizabeth of England (mother of Elizabeth II) said it was one of her favorites. When Ethiopia was invaded by Italy, the Ethiopians used "St. Louis Blues" as their war song.

Though Handy wrote some notable blues after 1914 (among which are "The John Henry Blues," "Careless Love Blues," and "East of St. Louis Blues"), it is through "St. Louis Blues" that he is most frequently remembered and honored. Because of this blues melody, a public park in Memphis bears the name of Handy, and, at the 1939 New York World Fair, he was named one of the leading contributors to American culture.

What Handy had started, other composers continued: making the blues a useful formula for song production in Tin Pan Alley. So many blues were being written on Twenty-eighth Street and its environs that by 1917 one of the songs to come out of the Alley was called "Everybody's Crazy 'bout the Blues."

In 1915 there was the "Honolulu Blues"; in 1916, "I've Got the Army Blues"; and in 1918 "Dallas Blues," "Livery Stable Blues," and "Barnyard Blues." With Prohibition, Albert von Tilzer wrote the "Alcoholic Blues." In 1921, Leo Feist published the "Wang, Wang Blues" and the "Wabash Blues," two outstanding hits that year. In 1923, George Gershwin wrote the "Yankee Doodle Blues." Gershwin was inspired by the blues to write in 1922 a one-act Negro opera, *Blue Monday*, for the *George White Scandals*, (it was later retitled *135th Street*); and the blues were the source and inspiration of the instrumental work that made Gershwin world-famous, the *Rhapsody in Blue*.

In 1926, the blues was apotheosized in a production number in the *Scandals*, the core of which was "The Birth of the Blues" by De Sylva, Brown, and Henderson. In this scene the blues was represented as being in conflict with the musical classics. Harry Richman sang the De Sylva, Brown, and Henderson number. "The Memphis Blues" and "St. Louis Blues" were then briefly represented. The climax was reached with a compromise between the blues and the classics, realized through an excerpt from Gershwin's *Rhapsody in Blue*.

In 1930, "Bye, Bye, Blues" served as the signature for Bert Lown and his Hotel Biltmore Orchestra. Harold Arlen, who was to write a number of blues classics in a style all his own, created his only authentic blues in 1932. It was called "I Gotta Right to Sing the Blues," and Lillian Shade introduced it in the Earl Carroll *Vanities*.

# 15

## *"I've heard that song before"*

No growth comes without attendant pains. As Tin Pan Alley outgrew the infancy of Union Square into the manhood of Twenty-eighth Street, it was subjected to its own healthy dose of growing pains—in the form of altercations and litigations of all sorts. Most of the legal problems besetting the song industry involved plagiarism and the violation of copyrights—and sometimes with unexpected, even astonishing results.

On one occasion a hit song threw a publishing house out of business. This was Muir's "Play that Barbershop Chord." When the J. Fred Helf Company published it in 1910, the name of the lyricist (Ballard MacDonald) was omitted from the sheet music and replaced by William Tracey, whom the publisher had called in to revise MacDonald's lyrics. The Edward B. Marks Company, who at the time had MacDonald under contract, instituted suit against Helf. MacDonald was awarded damages of thirty-seven thousand five hundred dollars, which compelled Helf to close shop.

Not a publishing house but a record company was ruined by a plagiarism suit involving "Avalon," the song Jolson helped make famous and Remick published in 1920. The melody of "Avalon," by Vincent Rose, sounded so much like the aria "E lucevan le stelle," from Giacomo Puccini's opera *Tosca*, that Puccini's publisher, Ricordi, instituted suit against Remick. The defense tried to prove that the *Tosca* melody had often been used before Puccini's time. The plaintiff had a trio play "Avalon" at the same time that a gramophone record presented the *Tosca* aria. Though "Avalon" was in a major key—and the opera aria in the minor—and despite a flat or two difference, the two numbers sounded virtually the same. Puccini and his publishers were awarded damages of twenty-five thousand dollars and all future royalties from "Avalon" were confiscated and turned over to Ricordi. One of the smaller record companies, convinced that "Avalon" had the makings of a big hit, had staked all its assets on the recording, promotion, and release of this song. On the basis of the court action, the record company had to go out of business.

There was one suit in which Witmark was penalized for seemingly violating its own copyright. In the early 1890's a publishing outfit in Chicago did a landslide business on its song sheets, which reprinted lyrics without bothering to get permission from the copyright owners. This outfit worked *sub rosa*; it did not even identify itself on its publications. Witmark was one of the publishers whose lyrics were thus being outrageously exploited without compensation. Deciding to do something about it, a Witmark executive called upon Sol Bloom, himself a one-time music publisher (and later a distinguished member of the United

States Congress) to study the situation. An astute and resourceful young man, Bloom went to Chicago, and there, by means of some slick detective operations, located the illicit publishers. He then managed to convince them that he was the head of a combine ready to place an order for twenty-five thousand song sheets. When the printing job was done, Bloom had the sheriff pounce upon and seize the shipment. Damages to the publishers would have amounted to a dollar a song sheet, or twenty-five thousand dollars in all. But when the case came to trial, the expected did not take place. Isidore Witmark, who went to Chicago for the trial, tells the story in his autobiography: "The lawyer for the other side . . . was Arndt, a big, blustering fellow, leaning on a pair of crutches for effect. . . . Arndt hobbled painfully on his crutches up and down before the jury box, immediately gaining the sympathy of the jurors. He made a speech as far distant from copyright as the North Pole is from the South, emphasizing all his points in farm language, talking more about straying cows than copyrights (the jury was made up of farmers and small-storekeepers) and managing somehow to put the shoe on the other foot. He ended his long harangue by accusing Sol Bloom of being the culprit! He told these men, in language they understood, that Sol had deliberately ordered the copies in a diabolical scheme to make an innocent man do wrong. The jury brought in a verdict for the defendant, and the judge even thought that there might be a case of conspiracy against the plaintiff. The twenty-five thousand song sheets which were to bring to Sol Bloom's employers twenty-five thousand dollars or more were solemnly burned in the furnace of their office building. The Witmarks, to all intents and purposes, had violated their own copyright!" Actually the Witmarks had the winning cards in the end, because unauthorized song sheets disappeared from then on.

Then there was the case of the composer who could have successfully contested a plagiarism suit instituted against her if she had been willing to confess that she, in turn, had borrowed her melody from an earlier song. The music that started this whole controversy was "Starlight," with words by Joe Young and music by Bernice Petkere. After its successful publication, an amateur California songwriter emerged with evidence (including a copyright stamp and a dated manuscript) of having written an unpublished song that resembled "Starlight" in details. During the ensuing court action, Sigmund Spaeth, the "tune detective," pointed out that there just was no basis for this action by revealing that both songs had a common ancestor in "Violets" by Ellen Wright, which, published in 1900, was already in public domain. Indeed, "Violets" and the two later songs in question were just about identical. If Petkere were ready to concede that she had known "Violets" and had lifted its melody, the suit would have been dismissed. But Petkere was insistent that she had never heard the earlier number. By doing so, she lost her case and, on a decision by Judge Alfred Coxe, had to pay damages of ten thousand dollars.

Not cash but acknowledgment went as damages to a composer who proved decisively in court that he was the composer of "I Wonder Who's Kissing Her Now," the song long attributed to Joe E. Howard. Through the years "I Wonder Who's Kissing Her Now" had been bringing Howard both immense prestige and profits. Then the startling revelation emerged, after a bitterly contested legal battle, that Joe E. Howard had not written the ballad after all—it was the work of one Harold Orlob.

And this is what had happened. In 1909, Orlob had been employed by Howard as an arranger. On this job he wrote the melody of "I Wonder Who's Kissing Her Now" to lyrics by Will M. Hough and Frank R. Adams, to be used by Joe E. Howard in his Chicago production of the musical *The Prince of Tonight*. Because Orlob was a paid employee who had composed the melody as a job assignment, Howard regarded it as his property—lock, stock, and barrel. He saw nothing wrong in using his own name as composer when Charles K. Harris published the song. In fact, this kind of expropriation was done so frequently then that Orlob did nothing to claim authorship; he maintained silence during all the years that the song was selling millions of copies of sheet music. But when the motion-picture biography of Joe E. Howard was being released, using as its title *I Wonder Who's Kissing Her Now*, Orlob sued to establish his rights as the author. He did not ask for any financial redress. A compromise was effected whereby Orlob was given collaboration status in partnership with Howard, in return for which Howard was not required to compensate him.

The proof was incontestable that the melody of Joseph Santley's hit song, "There's Yes, Yes in Your Eyes"—published by Remick in 1924—was lifted from the earlier song, "With You the World Don't Seem the Same," by an obscure composer named Wolf. Both melodies were alike. Nor could Santley maintain he had never heard the Wolf song since he had plugged it when he worked for the publisher George Head. Nevertheless, Judge Bondy gave the plaintiff modest damages of two hundred and fifty dollars, maintaining that the first published song had never made any money and that Remick deserved to profit from being able to market the second song so successfully.

A similar situation involved two other composers, Al Piantadosi and Cohalin. Cohalin had written "How Much I Really Cared," which he could prove had been performed publicly in the spring of 1914. Later the same year Piantadosi composed his great hit, "I Didn't Raise My Boy to Be a

Soldier," whose melody was so similar to that composed by Cohalin, that the latter sought redress in court. When it was shown that Piantadosi had worked for the publishing house that had issued "How Much I Really Cared"—and therefore had had access to it—the court ruled in favor of Cohalin.

The charge of plagiarism that Fred Fisher, composer of "Dardanella," brought against Jerome Kern, composer of "Ka-lu-a," was somewhat more difficult to substantiate. Fisher sued on the grounds that the bass accompaniment, *not* the melody, was the same in both numbers; that, because the success of "Dardanella" had depended so greatly on its recurring bass rhythm, Kern's use of the same device in "Ka-lu-a" was an invasion of his private domain. "Dardanella" was one of the fabulous song hits of the 1910's. It started out as a piano rag by Johnny S. Black called "Turkish Tom Tom." Adapting it into a popular song, with lyrics, Fisher (who was also a publisher) issued it in 1919 and saw it sell upward of five million copies of sheet music and two million records. Two years later, Kern wrote "Ka-lu-a" and used it in his musical comedy *Good Morning, Dearie*. Feeling that Kern had stolen his own way of using a recurring bass rhythm, Fisher sued on the grounds of plagiarism. Artur Bodanzky (conductor of the Metropolitan Opera), Leopold Stokowski (conductor of the Philadelphia Orchestra), and Victor Herbert all testified that this rhythmic concept was not original with Fisher. Realizing he had no case, Fisher offered to settle with Kern for a token payment—a suit of clothes. Infuriated that he had thus been accused of pilfering somebody else's musical ideas, Kern refused to accept the settlement. Judge Learned Hand ruled damages to Fisher of two hundred and fifty dollars, adding that the whole suit had been just "a trivial pother of scarcely more than irritation and a waste of time for everyone concerned." In all probability, the only reason Kern had to pay anything at all was that he had proved so hostile and acrimonious on the witness stand that he had prejudiced the court against him.

The irony of this case was that Fisher himself had previously been the defendant in a lawsuit involving "Dardanella." Felix Bernard, a vaudevillian, maintained that he had written the melody long before Johnny Black had conceived his ragtime number. Bernard added that he had sold all his rights to Fisher for a hundred dollars and, in view of the song's fabulous success, had been duped into accepting a pittance. But Bernard had no legal ground to stand on, having sold his rights long before "Dardanella" had proved its commercial value; he lost his suit.

When the blues began to flood the song market, Leo Feist sued Roger Graham, a minor competitor, maintaining that the "Livery Stable Blues," which Graham had published, was stolen from the Feist publication "The Barnyard Blues." He did not prove his case and consequently received no damages. But the suit is remembered because of an amusing remark made by one of the witnesss, supposedly a blues expert. The court wanted to know for its own information just what the blues were. The expert hardly clarified the issue. His answer was: "Why, your Honor, the blues are blues, that's what the blues are!"

The long arm of the law, however, could not touch those Tin Pan Alley troubadours wise enough to lift their musical material from copyright-free sources—the classics, for example.

In 1955, when the celebrated composer for the screen Dimitri Tiomkin received an Academy Award for his score to *The High and the Mighty*, he sent his colleagues into an uproar of laughter—and made news in the papers the next day—by confessing how much he owed, not to his wife or producers or coworkers, but to Brahms, Beethoven, Wagner, and so forth. Without their help, he added, he could not possibly have achieved the success he had in Hollywood.

There is a good deal of truth in this jest. Through the years, Tin Pan Alley's composers have been heavily indebted to the masters of music—though it is hardly likely they would have confessed it with Tiomkin's charm and disarming frankness. Harry Carroll comes to mind. One-time Tin Pan Alley arranger, Carroll produced his first song hit in 1912—"On the Mississippi," which he wrote in collaboration with Arthur Fields; the song was heard in the Broadway revue, *The Whirl of Society*. During the next few years, Carroll topped this effort with greater successes, particularly with "The Trail of the Lonesome Pine" and "By the Beautiful Sea." Here, as elsewhere, Carroll proved he had a gift for fashioning an ear-caressing tune. Yet when he achieved the greatest triumph of his songwriting career he did it with a melody he had unashamedly lifted from one of the classics. The song was "I'm Always Chasing Rainbows," with lyrics by Joseph McCarthy, and the melody of its chorus was one that Chopin had created in his *Fantaisie-Impromptu in C-sharp Minor*. Introduced in the Broadway musical, *Oh, Look!* "I'm Always Chasing Rainbows" sold more than a million copies of sheet music and almost as many records. It pointed up for Tin Pan Alley, as nothing had done up to this time, that stealing from the classics could be a highly profitable practice.

But tapping the classics for melodic material was not new in 1918, though it had never before brought quite such lavish rewards. In fact, it had existed as long as Tin Pan Alley had. Percy Gaunt's "The Bowery" carries recollections of the Neapolitan folk song "La Spagnola"; Joseph J. Sullivan's "Where Did You Get That Hat?" utilizes a leitmotif from Wagner's *Lohengrin;* Monroe Rosenfeld's "Johnny, Get Your Gun" is close to the American folk tune, "The Arkansas Traveler"; Victor Schertzinger's "Marcheta" was derived from Nicolai's *Overture to The Merry Wives of Windsor*.

In 1906, the lyricist Vincent Bryan was quoted in the New York *Herald* as saying: "Filching is the only thing that counts in the songwriting business. All you need to compose a song that will sell is a good memory." Still another lyricist, Will D. Cobb, once remarked wryly: "It's a wise song that knows its own father."

In 1903, Herbert H. Taylor published the following amusing recipe for the popular mystery known to the world as a popular song:

As for the music, you'll manage that easily,
Get a few songs that were written before.
Swipe 'em and change 'em and have 'em sung breezily,
Get an arranger, you'll want nothing more.

Harry Carroll's success with "I'm Always Chasing Rainbows," however, was the impetus that moved other Tin Pan Alley composers to seek out the classics for suitable melodies. One master after another was now being greedily ransacked. Beethoven's *Minuet in G* was used for "If You See the Girl" and, later, for "When It's Apple Blossom Time in Normandy." Tchaikovsky's *Troika* was borrowed for "Horses"; and Chopin's *Minute Waltz* provided the main theme for "Castle of Dreams" in the Broadway musical *Irene*. Rachmaninoff's *Prelude in C-sharp Minor* lent a helping hand to "Rose of No Man's Land," as Fibich's *Poème* did to "My Moonlight Madonna." Sigmund Romberg found the release for "Lover Come Back to Me" in Tchaikovsky's *June Barcarolle*, and the main melody for "Song of Love" in Schubert's *Unfinished Symphony*.

The dramatic contrast between the earnings of those who

stole and those who were stolen from was perhaps most strongly stressed by Romberg's "Song of Love." It is estimated that Romberg's royalties from this one number alone were in excess of a hundred thousand dollars. His total income from the operetta *Blossom Time*—all of its melodies were taken from Schubert—probably reached a million dollars. Yet, it is generally believed that, all that Franz Schubert earned from a lifetime of productivity—not only from his songs but also from symphonies, Masses, operas, quartets, and sonatas—was just five hundred dollars.

The practice of tune lifting was accelerated and intensified as the years went on. Between 1930 and 1945 there was hardly a great composer of the past, or near past, who was safe from this predatory practice. Chopin's *Polonaise in A-flat Major* made radio's Hit Parade (which featured the ten most popular songs of the week) nineteen consecutive weeks in 1946, sold almost a million and a half copies of sheet music, and more than a million disks in Perry Como's recording—but, of course, not as a polonaise; it had become "Till the End of Time," introduced in the motion picture about Chopin *A Song to Remember*. There was one period, between 1939 and 1941, when Tchaikovsky's music was heard more often on the Hit Parade than that of any Tin Pan Alley composer—not excepting Irving Berlin and Richard Rodgers. *Piano Concerto No. 1* became "Concerto for Two" and "Tonight We Love"; the *Fifth Symphony* became "Moon Love"; *Romeo and Juliet* became "Our Love"; and these are just a few of the many Tchaikovsky themes that were made into hit songs. A popular song of this period even tried to capitalize on this phenomenon: "Everybody's Making Money but Tchaikovsky."

Not even the more esoteric pieces of music were exempt. For, out of Mozart came "In an Eighteenth-Century Drawing Room"; out of Ravel, "The Lamp Is Low"; out of Debussy, "My Reverie"; and out of Rachmaninoff's *Second Piano Concerto*, "Full Moon and Empty Arms."

One of the most highly publicized court actions involving Tin Pan Alley in the early 1900's touched upon libel as well as plagiarism. The plaintiff was Victor Herbert, then already America's foremost operetta composer, whose songs published by Witmark became classics almost as soon as they were released.

It was toward this figure renowned in both popular and serious music that Marc A. Blumenberg, editor of *Musical Courier*, directed a scurrilous editorial attack. What had prompted it is no longer clear. Some in the know maintained that Blumenberg bitterly resented seeing a popular Broadway composer become permanent conductor of the Pittsburgh Symphony. A few hinted that Blumenberg had been outraged because Herbert refused to place any advertisements in the *Musical Courier*. Whatever the reason, Blumenberg apparently set out to destroy Herbert's reputation. In the July 17, 1901, issue of *Musical Courier* he wrote: "All of Victor Herbert's 'written to order' comic operas were pure and simple plagiarisms. . . . Everything written by Herbert is copied; there is not one original strain in anything he has done."

Victor Herbert was usually an amiable, genial, happy-go-lucky, live-and-let-live type of man. But when aroused, he was a tiger. This editorial aroused him. He sued *Musical Courier* for libel asking fifty thousand dollars in damages.

The trial began on October 22, 1902, to become (as Herbert's biographer, Edward N. Waters, described it) "one of the most remarkable cases in musical jurisprudence." On the witness stand Blumenberg tried to prove his case by pointing out similarities between the classics and various pieces by Herbert. He found, for example, a parallel between Fauré's song, "The Palms" and something in the Herbert operetta *The Singing Girl* and between the opening of Beethoven's *Ninth Symphony* and a passage in *The Wizard of the Nile*. "Authorities" were summoned to substantiate Blumenberg's accusations. Under the withering cross-examination of Herbert's lawyer Nathan Burkan, their testimony was quickly reduced to absurdity.

Herbert's principal witness was Walter Damrosch, one of America's most highly revered conductors and musical personalities. Damrosch insisted that the similarities existing between some of the classics and some of Herbert's music were no more flagrant than those found among the classics themselves. He maintained that he could find "hundreds of resemblances" in different classical compositions, and he emphasized that in no way could these similarities be regarded as plagiarism.

In his column in the New York *Tribune* the eminent music critic Henry E. Krehbiel became particularly upset at Blumenberg's attempt to see borrowings in Herbert from Beethoven's *Ninth Symphony*. "It was a silly device, and so bunglingly done that it was easy for Mr. Walter Damrosch to testify that the alleged quotation from Herbert was not within a mile of the *Ninth Symphony*."

Blumenberg's lawyer Gilbert Ray Hawes saw that the case was going badly for his client. He therefore tried in his summation to soften the imminent blow by insisting that Blumenberg had no intention of accusing Herbert of "theft" but only of "reminiscences." "We have the kindest and best feelings toward Mr. Herbert personally," he said. Then he sought refuge in the "privileged" nature of editorials, insisting that Blumenberg's editorial was a justifiable form of public criticism within a reputable journal.

If Hawes had any hope or expectation that his summation would sway the jury, it was forthwith shattered by the charge of Judge Truax. He warned the jury that, far from being privileged, Blumenberg's editorial had been libelous;

that Herbert was entitled to compensation even though his income or his career had not suffered as a result of the editorial. "I know of no law," Judge Truax said, "that gives the publisher of a paper a right to say an untruthful thing about a private individual or a public individual."

The jury came in with a verdict after two hours of deliberation. It awarded Herbert damages of fifteen thousand dollars. Though in later appeals, the judgment was reduced to five thousand dollars, Herbert's victory had proved decisive, and the cause of irresponsible criticism and journalism had suffered a humiliating defeat.

Herbert's victory in court had the incidental effect of bringing to American popular music and to the popular-music composer a touch of dignity and self-respect—perhaps for the first time.

# 16

## *"Pennies from heaven"*

The law courts helped Tin Pan Alley iron out problems other than those involving plagiarism and libel. The development of mechanical instruments—the player piano, at first, and then the phonograph—involved the Alley in new issues and complications that necessitated legal solutions.

In 1906 manufacturers of phonograph records and piano rolls insisted that the copyright law did not apply to them; consequently, they claimed to have the right to use the music of Tin Pan Alley without compensation. The Aeolian Company, then one of the leading manufacturers of player pianos and piano rolls, now made a deal with Tin Pan Alley. It stood ready to defray all expenses for any litigations entered into by publishers to prove that any use of printed sheet music was protected by copyright law. In return,

Aeolian wanted an exclusive contract for the right to use music on their rolls should the suits prove successful. The battle of "canned music"—the term coined at about this time by John Philip Sousa (but since applied to all mechanized music)—was on. The fight went through all the stages of the law courts, right up to the Supreme Court, which finally decided against the publishers. Manufacturers of mechanized music now enjoyed a field day, helping themselves without payment to whatever music they wished.

The publishers were defeated—but only temporarily. Headed by the Witmarks, and with Nathan Burkan as their legal representative, the publishing interests invaded Washington, D. C. Their aim was to do whatever necessary to convince legislators to draw up and pass a new copyright law. In their statement to members of Congress they said: "When the copyright bill was framed years ago, the sound-producing instruments, such as the phonograph . . . and the automatic piano were unheard of or unthought of; naturally, no specific provision for the protection of the composer against them was made into law. Thousands of records and perforated rolls are turned out, and before long the country is surfeited with the 'composition canned for the home,' and ere long the talking machines are grinding the melody out by the yard in every gaudy penny theater in the country. When the composer's work reaches this stage, it is killed, as far as the publishing profits are concerned, for as soon as a musical composition becomes too popular the public ceases to buy it. Hence the composer not only loses his royalties due him from the talking and playing machines, but from the aforesaid short life of music sales as well."

With Victor Herbert as an eloquent spokesman for publishers and composers, a good deal of interest was aroused in Washington for the new legislation. In 1909 a new copyright bill was finally signed into law by President Theodore Roosevelt, his last official act during that Congressional session. It provided for the payment of a two-cent royalty for each side of a phonograph disk and on each piano roll for each piece of music used. The publishers, though victorious, were not satisfied. They had expected a far better deal than a two-cent royalty, which they regarded as a pittance hardly able to add appreciably to the income of either the publisher or the songwriter. What they could not realize at that time was that mechanical music was eventually to grow to Gargantuan size, and that what they believed would be a mere trickle in royalties was destined some day to grow into a giant flood.

This payment of a two-cent royalty on each song reproduced mechanically was, however, only the detail of a much larger picture to develop later on in the courts. Using popular music mechanically was, after all, only one of many ways in which the work of composers, lyricists, and publishers was being used without compensation. With the rise and spread of dance orchestras, popular music was being played throughout the country to the financial advantage of restaurants, night clubs, cabarets, dance schools, dance halls, and every other possible place of public entertainment. Yet the ones responsible for the writing and the publishing of this music gained absolutely nothing from this wide circulation, except promotion. Promotion was, of course, the lifeblood of the song industry, as every publisher knew. But publishers also felt that they and their songwriters deserved some sort of payment whenever a piece of music was being performed.

One day in 1913, in New York City, this problem was first discussed by three men: Raymond Hubbell, composer of operettas, musical comedies, and songs for the *Ziegfeld Follies;* the lawyer Nathan Burkan; and George Maxwell, American representative of Ricordi, the powerful

Italian music-publishing house. Maxwell pointed out that in Europe, ever since 1871, it had become a normal and expected procedure for the publisher to be paid a fee or royalty for the public performance of any musical composition through the agency of SACEM (Société des Auteurs, Compositeurs et Éditeurs de Musique). Nathan Burkan commented that, according to provisions of the 1909 copyright law it was possible to demand such payments in the United States even though this was not being done. The three men decided to sound out Victor Herbert for his ideas on this controversial problem. Because Herbert was then in Philadelphia, Hubbell decided to go there to see if Herbert would join them in the formation of some sort of protective society for writers and composers.

Herbert, of course, was sold the idea without difficulty. A dynamo when he went into action, Herbert helped lay plans for a detailed analysis and discussion of this problem with many of his colleagues. Arrangements were then made for thirty-six prominent composers, authors, and publishers to gather in a private dining room at Luchow's Restaurant in Union Square in October of 1913. When the day for the meeting arrived, only nine men showed up: Herbert, Burkan, Hubbell, Maxwell, Louis A. Hirsch (composer of scores for *The Passing Shows* and other musicals), Glen MacDonough (Herbert's librettist for some of his operettas), Jay Witmark, and Silvio Hein (musical-comedy composer). Intense disappointment was felt by those present that the others had not bothered to come. Nevertheless, those attending proceeded to lay the foundations for an organization; and they committed themselves to do what they could to recruit the support and enthusiasm of their colleagues. Another meeting was set for February 13, 1914, at the Hotel Claridge on Forty-third Street.

That day, twenty-two publishers and one hundred and seventy writers came to the Hotel Claridge. They formalized the basic plans for the American Society of Composers, Authors and Publishers, and became its charter members. Originally, the plan had been to baptize the new organization "American Society of Authors, Composers and Publishers"—placing the word "author" ahead of "composer," as was then traditional on sheet-music publications. But George Maxwell pointed out that by putting "composer" first, it was possible to use the combined initials of the society into the well-sounding word "Ascap," a useful abbreviation and cable address. American Society of Composers, Authors and Publishers was what it was named—and "ASCAP" the way most people henceforth identified it.

At that meeting, the first officers elected included George Maxwell as president; Victor Herbert, vice president; Glen MacDonough, secretary; and John Golden, treasurer. Victor Herbert, who refused to assume the presidency, compromised by accepting the lesser post.

Now Nathan Burkan felt that the time was ripe to test the validity of the 1909 copyright law as it pertained to live performances, and, at the same time to ascertain if ASCAP was a feasible, functional organization. Victor Herbert's music was chosen to spearhead the legal attack. Shanley's Restaurant between Forty-second and Forty-third streets on Broadway was sued on the grounds that its orchestra played excerpts from Victor Herbert's *Sweethearts* on the evening of April 1, 1915, without authorization.

The long-repeated and often reprinted story that Herbert had heard *Sweethearts* at Shanley's in 1913—and that this incident was the inspiration for the test case against Shanley's, and, coincidentally, was responsible for the formation of ASCAP—is sheer fiction. Shanley's had been singled out by Burkan after careful calculation and consideration because it was so well-known and because it had an orchestra playing salon and popular music for the din-ers; any similar restaurant would have done just as well. The legal action made it clear that the performance of *Sweethearts* under question took place in 1915, *not* in 1913, and that the one who heard the music was a theater manager, who stood ready to provide a sworn affidavit to that effect, *not* Victor Herbert.

The case was tried before Judge Learned Hand beginning on May 1, 1915. Judge Hand finally pronounced a decision against the plaintiff. He maintained that music performed in a public restaurant was not done for profit because no admission had been charged. The Court of Appeals then confirmed the Hand decision; a death blow was now seemingly struck both at the specific suit and at ASCAP. Burkan, however, continued the fight up to the U. S. Supreme Court. On January 22, 1917, Justice Oliver Wendell Holmes announced that the high tribunal had reversed the decisions of the two lower courts.

In this epoch-making decision, Justice Holmes said in part: "If the rights . . . are infringed only by a performance where money is taken in at the door, they are imperfectly protected. Performances not different in kind from those of the defendants could be given that might compete with and even destroy the success of the monopoly that the law intends the plaintiffs to have. It is enough to say that there is no need to construe the statute so narrowly. The defendants' performances are not eleemosynary. They are part of a total for which the public pays, and the fact the price of the whole is attributed to a particular item which those present are expected to order is not important. It is true that the music is not the sole object, but neither is the food, which probably could be got cheaper elsewhere. The object is a repast in surroundings that to people having limited powers of conversation or disliking the rival noise give a luxurious pleasure not to be had from eating a silent meal. If music did not pay, it would be given up. If it pays, it pays out of the public's pocket. Whether it pays or not, the purpose of employing it is profit, and that is enough."

This decision strengthened and made permanent the foundation stones on which ASCAP could now be built. But it took years of hard and patient work, of costly litigation, of frustrations and despair before that complete structure could be made functional and profitable. The law might be on the side of ASCAP. But getting compliance with the law was something else again. Many more court battles had to be waged to bring about the submission of restaurants, cabarets, dance halls, theaters, and so forth. All these had been using music free of charge so long that the thought of having to make a payment was a plague to be scrupulously avoided. Many of these public places insisted that if they were required to pay for the use of music they would cut down the size of the orchestra, perhaps eliminate the orchestra altogether. This threat, which endangered the jobs of so many musicians, led the president of the musicians' federation to order its union members to boycott all ASCAP music. Panicked, some of the publishers disassociated themselves hurriedly from ASCAP and went out of their way to advertise that their music was all "tax free."

The war raged on for several years. Members of ASCAP put forth Herculean efforts to carry on the fight, receiving no wages for their work. Slowly, first one, then another organization started to make peace with ASCAP. The numbers grew first by arithmetical then by algebraic progressions. In time, six thousand hotels, restaurants, cabarets, and theaters signed up with ASCAP. They paid a fee for the use of the copyrighted music of ASCAP members through special licenses. The year of 1921 was the first in which ASCAP members (now numbering 163) were able to divide a kitty—eighty thousand dollars. In 1922 the intake of ASCAP passed a hundred thousand dollars, and in 1923 it reached almost two hundred thousand dollars. In 1924, the motion picture industry, which had previously brought suit against ASCAP for being a monopoly in restraint of trade (insisting that when people came to a movie they came to see a picture and not to hear music), lost its case and became licensees. It was not long after this that the radio industry tried to get Congress to pass new legislation that would allow it to play music free of charge as a public service. It insisted that ASCAP was nothing but a racket. Nothing came of their lobbying; but it took another half-dozen years or so before radio stations around the country could be persuaded to pay a percentage of their gross income for using ASCAP music.

By the time Tin Pan Alley was coming to the dusk of its life—in the early 1930's—ASCAP was drawing an immense annual revenue for several thousand of its publishing, composer, and lyricist members. Its gross income had risen to several million dollars a year. In 1937 this figure was almost doubled. Sixty-two percent of the income came from six hundred and fifty-seven radio stations; twenty-one percent from theaters and movie houses, and the remainder from hotels, dance halls, night clubs, and so forth. Almost thirty thousand establishments were licensed to use copyrighted music every day.

As a nonprofit organization, ASCAP divides all income (once deductions are made for running expenses) equally between publishers on the one hand and composers and lyricists on the other. In the early 1930's, ASCAP used an arbitrary rating system for composers and lyricists. The top men—composers like Irving Berlin and George Gershwin, lyricists like Lorenz Hart and Oscar Hammerstein II—were assigned a rating of "AA." Their annual return amounted to about twenty-five thousand dollars a year (fifty thousand dollars if, like Irving Berlin, composer and lyricist were one and the same man). Lesser composers and lyricists were put in a lower category with a consequent lower annual draw.

In time, however, ASCAP changed its system to a more equitable method whereby a composer and lyricist could get a top rating only on the basis of the number of performances of his works during the year through various media. A complex method had to be worked out to compute the number of performance-hours for each ASCAP song each day through every possible medium of public consumption. Thus a composer or lyricist who had succeeded in producing a library of standards could still get top rating, even though he had stopped producing hits, or had stopped writing altogether, or even though he was dead.

The subsequent history of ASCAP—the never-ending trials and tribulations—does not come within the scope of this volume, since Tin Pan Alley had perished by then. It need only be pointed out, however briefly, that through the years, since the middle 1930's, ASCAP has been accused of being a monoply now by one faction, now by another, which has hoped to achieve its dissolution under the antitrust law. The matter had to be fought out again and again, and probably will continue to be fought through for many years to come. All this notwithstanding, ASCAP has continued to grow stronger and to become ever more firmly entrenched. Even the emergence of a powerful rival did not seriously endanger its existence. The rival was BMI (Broadcast Music Incorporated), which was created in 1941, and promoted thereafter by radio interests to provide a continuing source of music for broadcasting. The appearance of BMI was the result of a bitter struggle between radio and ASCAP. When, in 1940, a five-year contract expired, ASCAP demanded from radio an annual fee of nine million dollars (twice the figure it had previously been receiving). Radio executives considered the demand outrageous and refused to sign a new agreement. ASCAP then withdrew all the music of its members from the air waves. Since virtually almost all popular music in copyright was then under ASCAP jurisdiction, radio music for many months consisted entirely of songs in the public domain—Stephen Foster's "Jeanie With the Light Brown Hair" was heard practically every hour on the hour—and those by young and inexperienced creators who were rapidly affiliating themselves with the new organization in order to get a hearing. The dispute dragged on until the fall of 1941, when a compromise was reached whereby ASCAP reduced its fee to three million dollars a year on a five-year contract. This compromise represented a setback for ASCAP on two counts. It would receive an annual return of only one third the sum it had originally demanded; and, more significant still, it had acquired a powerful rival group that, in a decade's time, would begin drawing about six million dollars a year in licenses, and would gather under its wing a number of highly gifted young composers and lyricists and a carload of new song hits.

But despite such a retreat—and despite temporary setbacks in earning power—ASCAP continued to be a giant force working for the financial interests of publishers and songwriters. Before the 1940's ended, ASCAP was earning close to ten million dollars a year, and by the end of the 1950's this figure had almost doubled.

ASCAP lived to celebrate its fiftieth anniversary on February 13, 1964, and to disclose that it was stronger than it had ever been. In 1962 it had grossed over thirty-five million dollars in representing seven thousand composers and lyricists and more than two thousand music publishers. Each of the top beneficiaries—Irving Berlin, Richard Rodgers and Cole Porter—was receiving an annual royalty of more than seventy-five thousand dollars. Each of the composers and lyricists just below them in status—Harold Arlen, Johnny Mercer, Harry Warren, Oscar Hammerstein II, Lorenz Hart, George Gershwin, Ira Gershwin, Jerome Kern—was receiving between fifty and seventy-five thousand dollars a year. Forty thousand licensees were now paying an annual fee for the right to use the music of ASCAP members.

The ASCAP all-time hit parade publicized during the golden anniversary celebration is also, basically, the all-time hit parade of Tin Pan Alley: "Alexander's Ragtime Band," "April Showers," "Begin the Beguine," "Darktown Strutters' Ball," "God Bless America," "Happy Days Are Here Again," "I Wonder Who's Kissing Her Now," "Night and Day," "Over the Rainbow," "Rudolph the Red-nosed Reindeer," "September Song," "Star Dust," "Tea for Two," "The Birth of the Blues," "White Christmas," and "You Made Me Love You."

# 17

*"A pocketful of miracles"*

Many successful popular composers of the 1910's had learned their craft and art in Tin Pan Alley from the ground up. Some had been piano demonstrators, some song pluggers, some sheet-music salesmen, some arrangers. Their apprenticeship enabled them to learn not only the basic tools of melody writing but also how and why an audience reacts favorably to a song—in short, what makes a song click. How well this apprenticeship served these men when they stopped selling or arranging songs and began to write them was proved by the high percentage of hits that came from these Tin Pan Alley graduates year after year. In the same way that, in the early 1900's, Irving Berlin, Ted Snyder, Gus Edwards, Jean Schwartz, Egbert van Alstyne, Karl Hoschna, Gustave Kerker, and John Stromberg (among many others) rose to fame as composers after having held miscellaneous jobs in Tin Pan Alley, so in the 1910's new composers who had served their apprenticeships in the cubicles of publishing houses began to emerge.

There was, for example, Walter Donaldson.

For a number of years Donaldson had been a piano demonstrator. Then he wrote his first song hit, "Back Home in Tennessee," which he produced without ever having visited that state. With lyrics by William Jerome, "Back Home in Tennessee"—published by Waterson, Snyder and Berlin in 1915—became one of the major hits of the year; and it was to become the song most often recruited to identify that state. During World War I, Donaldson's most successful song was an appealing comedy number that both Sophie Tucker and Eddie Cantor helped make popular— "How You Gonna Keep 'Em Down on the Farm?" After the war Donaldson returned to publishing in a more influential position than before by affiliating himself with the then newly established firm of Irving Berlin, Inc. As his own publisher, Donaldson now created those giant successes that were to make him a dominating figure in Tin Pan Alley. The first of these was "My Mammy" in 1920, which Al Jolson sang in *Sinbad;* he made this so famous that from then on all interpreters of mother songs came to be known as "mammy singers" while Jolson himself became the king of such interpreters. "My Mammy" played a significant part not only in Jolson's first screen success, *The Jazz Singer*, which made him the star of stars in the early history of talking pictures, but also in *The Jolson Story* in which he made his screen comeback.

Having written "Back Home in Tennessee" without having glimpsed that state even once, Donaldson proceeded in 1922, without ever having been in the Carolinas, to write "Carolina in the Morning." This song was introduced by Willie and Eugene Howard in *The Passing Show of 1922.* In 1925, "Yes Sir, That's My Baby" became the year's pet song and pet catch phrase after being popularized by the irresistible and irrepressible Eddie Cantor (in whose living room Gus Kahn, the lyricist, first got the idea for the words). Two years after that Donaldson (a bachelor) sang the praises of marital bliss in perhaps his most famous song of all, "My Blue Heaven" (lyrics by George Whiting). Eddie Cantor interpolated it into the *Ziegfeld Follies of 1927*, altering a line to include his own daughters within the boundaries of his personal blue heaven. Tommy Lyman then made it his radio theme song, and Gene Austin (comparatively unknown at the time) made a recording that sold several million disks and made him just about the hottest property in the record industry. "My Blue Heaven" was now well on its way toward being one of the greatest song successes of the decade. One year after that, in 1928, Donaldson prepared the score for the Eddie Cantor musical produced by Ziegfeld, *Whoopee*, in which Eddie Cantor sang "Makin' Whoopee," a Cantor *spécialité* from then on. A second Cantor favorite from *Whoopee*—"My Baby Just Cares for Me"—was written by Donaldson for the screen adaptation of that musical.

Then there was Harry Ruby.

Ruby's rich and varied background for writing song hits came from working as staff pianist and song plugger for Gus Edwards and later as a song plugger for Harry von Tilzer. Like his fellow pluggers, Ruby used to tour department and five-and-ten-cent stores, rathskellers, and restaurants, exhibiting the songs of the firm he was representing. In this he was sometimes assisted by a youngster named Walter Winchell, whose piping sweet voice brought him sporadic assignments to help out the pluggers. On several occasions Ruby was recruited to play the piano in movie houses for song slides. He even became a stage performer—a member of "The Messenger Boys Trio" featured in vaudeville, and of Edwards and Ruby, a duo that sang in nickelodeons. (The Edwards in that was not songwriter and publisher Gus Edwards; it was the stage name of Harry Cohn, who was to become a czar in the motion-picture industry.) Thus through the years Ruby was fortunately enabled to study audiences from several different perspectives.

Finding a collaborator in Bert Kalmar, a vaudevillian who wrote lyrics, Ruby began composing songs. Realizing that Hawaiian songs were very much in vogue, he wrote in 1917 "When Those Sweet Hawaiian Babies Roll Their Eyes." Recognizing that postwar America needed a good humorous number, he came up with "What'll We Do on Saturday Nights When the Town Goes Dry?" (His inspiration, of course, was the Volstead Act.) He wrote several other comedy hit tunes around the same time, including "And He'd Say Oo-la-la-wee-wee" and "So-Long, Oo-Long," and "The Vamp from East Broadway," the last of which Fanny Brice introduced in the *Ziegfeld Follies of 1920*.

In 1923 (with the help of Ted Snyder and Bert Kalmar) Ruby wrote one of his most celebrated standards, "Who's Sorry Now?" It sold more than a million copies of sheet music in its own day. A generation later it came back to sell more than a million disks for the singer Connie Francis, whose poignant delivery of it on M.G.M. records made her at once a recording star of the first magnitude.

After 1923, Harry Ruby wrote scores for Broadway musical comedies, and after 1930 for the movies. His maiden effort for the talking screen, in fact, was one of the great successes of his career—"Three Little Words," which was introduced by Bing Crosby in the Amos n' Andy movie *Check and Double Check*, and soon after that promoted by

Rudy Vallee over radio and on records. *Three Little Words* was the title used in 1950 when the Kalmar-Ruby story was filmed.

The composers Fred Ahlert and Milton Ager started out as arrangers for Waterson, Berlin and Snyder. It took a number of years of durance vile in Tin Pan Alley—and writing a number of songs that made no impression anywhere—before Ahlert had his first hit. This happened in 1920 with "My Mammy's Arms." Eight years later Ahlert wrote the song with which his name is most often associated—"I'll Get By." It sold a million records and a million copies of sheet music before 1930; and in 1944, when it was revived in the motion picture *Follow the Boys*, it again became a major song hit.

Milton Ager came to success even while he was still employed as arranger. In 1918, in collaboration with George W. Meyer, he wrote "Everything Is Peaches Down in Georgia," which was introduced by Al Jolson at a Sunday evening concert at the Winter Garden. This was the song that made it possible for Ager to give up arranging and concentrate on composing. "I'm Nobody's Baby" in 1921 (written with Lester Santly), "I Wonder What's Become of Sally" in 1924, and "Ain't She Sweet?" in 1927, which Lillian Roth helped to make popular on the vaudeville circuit, placed Ager permanently in the winning circle. Ager's most frequently heard number, "Happy Days Are Here Again" was written in 1929 for the motion picture *Chasing Rainbows*. George Olsen's band used to play it at the Pennsylvania Hotel to a Depression-weary public that enjoyed and reacted enthusiastically to its rousing optimism. Then a bright song plugger promoted it for the Democratic presidential convention in Chicago in 1932. It made such an impression there that it was forthwith adopted as the theme song of Franklin Delano Roosevelt—not only for the 1932 campaign, but for the next three as well. The song has been played at every presidential convention held by the Democratic party since Roosevelt's time.

George W. Meyer, with whom Ager had written his first hit, "Everything Is Peaches Down in Georgia," had been employed as song plugger for several different firms in the early 1900's. He became a full-time composer when "Lonesome," which he wrote with Kerry Mills, was published in 1909 and sold about a million copies. His big hits came just before World War I: "When You're a Long, Long Way from Home" in 1914; "There's a Little Lane Without a Turning" in 1915; and in 1916 the song that Al Jolson made popular in *Robinson Crusoe Jr.*, "Where Did Robinson Crusoe Go with Friday on Saturday Night?" But all this was just the prologue, so to speak, for the main act—the song "For Me and My Gal," which, after its release in 1917, sold about three million copies of sheet music. Al Jolson, Belle Baker, Sophie Tucker, and Eddie Cantor were some of the stars who sang it on the stage all over the country. In 1942, "For Me and My Gal" was used as the title for a highly successful movie starring Judy Garland; and so effectively was the song revived there by Judy Garland that it went on once again to become a leader in sheet-music and record sales.

J. Fred Coots became a song plugger in Chicago after he heard one demonstrating a song. Though he had planned to become a stockbroker, and was already employed as a clerk in a brokerage house, that performance convinced him to change to the music profession. While promoting other people's songs, he started writing some of his own. But it took years before he could make any headway as a composer. Then the first break came—when Sophie Tucker and Van and Schenck started to use some of his musical material in vaudeville. For all that, he was pretty much of an unknown quantity when in 1923 he met Eddie Dowling, then planning to mount a lavish musical comedy on Broadway. Somehow, Coots managed to convince Dowling to let him write the score for that production. Since the show was *Sally, Irene and Mary*—and since it ran on Broadway for about two years—Coots finally had made it big. After that he went on to write a good deal of music for the Broadway theater. But some of his best songs came from numbers written for Tin Pan Alley. One was "I Still Get a Thrill Thinking of You" which Bing Crosby introduced; another, "Love Letters in the Sand," was a major success in 1931, and an even greater triumph a generation later when it was revived on Dot records by Pat Boone.

Con Conrad's experiences in Tin Pan Alley had come not from song-plugging or arranging but from serving in a minor executive post. He had previously worked as an usher and later as a pianist in moving-picture theaters, then as a performer on the vaudeville circuit. His first published song was "Down in Dear Old New Orleans" in 1912, which was interpolated into the *Ziegfeld Follies* of that year.

After a stint in music publishing, and after writing a number of minor successes, Con Conrad, collaborating with J. Russel Robinson, created the song "Margie" that put him in the big time as a composer. It had been inspired by Eddie Cantor's five-year-old daughter, Marjorie; Cantor sang it to nationwide fame. In 1921, Con Conrad managed to get Al Jolson to sing no less than four of his numbers in *Bombo*. After that, and up to the time he went to Hollywood to gather new successes as a composer for the screen, his big hits included "Ma, He's Making Eyes at Me" (introduced in the *Midnight Rounders*), "Barney Google," with lyrics by Billy Rose (which Olsen and Johnson made popular), and "You've Got to See Your Mama Every Night."

*

All these composers were men of talent, with an uncommon gift for creating an easily remembered tune and for knowing how to write the kind of melodies the public wanted to hear.

But one man, risen from the ranks in Tin Pan Alley, was a genius—George Gershwin.

He was only fifteen when, in 1913, he found a job in Tin Pan Alley. Already he was a young musician of the most extraordinary gifts, vision, and ideals. Raised in New York City's East Side—though born in Brooklyn, in 1898—he was a typical American boy who liked to roller skate, play street games with his friends, and argue the strength and weaknesses of his favorite baseball team, the New York Giants.

He hated school, and just about anything else that had the smell of books and culture. His first contacts with music, however, created something of an upheaval in his young life and were responsible for bringing about in him a radical change of interests and values. When he was six he heard Anton Rubinstein's *Melody in F* on an automatic piano in a penny arcade in Union Square. "The peculiar jumps in the music held me rooted," he later recalled. One year later, while roller skating in the Harlem section of New York City (the Gershwin family at the time was living uptown), he heard some real jazz music floating from an open window of a night club. The performers were Jim Europe's band. Gershwin sat on the curb and listened to the sounds of rags and blues and spirituals that seemed to him then like a revelation. After that he made frequent pilgrimages to that street with the hope of hearing some more of this strange and fascinating music.

When George was ten Dvořák's *Humoresque* was played in the school assembly by his schoolmate Max Rosenzweig. (Max later under the name of Rosen became the famous concert violinist.) George was so entranced with this composition and its performance that he set about getting to know the violinist and to become his friend. From Maxie, George discovered for the first time the world of great music and composers. All other activities now palled for George. Whenever he found a piano at a friend's home, he would make straight for the keyboard and try to reproduce the melodies as he had heard Maxie play them. One day he even attempted to concoct a piece of music of his own. When he played it for Maxie, the latter said firmly: "You haven't got it in you to be a composer, Georgie. Take my word for it. I know."

About this time a piano was brought into the Gershwin household so that George's older brother, Ira, might take lessons. George and the instrument became inseparable. He soon started taking lessons from local teachers. Though most of this instruction was singularly inept, Gershwin did manage to acquire the elements of piano playing, harmony, and notation.

Then, in 1912, Gershwin found a teacher able to give him the guidance and inspiration he needed. Through Charles Hambitzer, a remarkable musician, the boy received an introduction to the basic literature for the piano and to the works of such moderns as Debussy and Ravel. Gershwin now made rapid progress. In fact, Hambitzer, in communicating with his own sister, did not hesitate to describe his new pupil as a "genius who will make a mark in music if anybody else will." He then added: "He's crazy about music and can't wait until it's time to take his lessons."

Though young Gershwin responded so sensitively and enthusiastically to the classics, he was passionately interested in American popular music of the Tin Pan Alley variety, and, for an adolescent, had remarkably forceful ideas about American popular music. Nothing Hambitzer could say or do could dilute that enthusiasm. Gershwin told

Hambitzer that he was convinced that American popular music, when good, was important music; that a composer bringing to the Tin Pan Alley popular song the full resources and the advanced techniques of good music could lift it to an exalted station; that this Tin Pan Alley music was basically America's music and that an American composer should fully cultivate it; and that if he, Gershwin, was to have any place at all in music, it would have to be in the popular field.

Many years later, after he had fulfilled his mission as a serious composer of popular music, Gershwin, in *Revolt in Arts* (edited by Oliver M. Saylor), wrote: "Jazz has contributed an enduring value to America in the sense that it has expressed ourselves. It is an original American achievement that will endure, not as jazz perhaps, but which will leave its mark on future music in one way or another." He also wrote: "I regard jazz as an American folk music, a very powerful one which is probably in the blood of the American people more than any other style of folk music. I believe that it can be made the basis of serious symphonic works of lasting value."

As a boy of fourteen and fifteen he regarded two Tin Pan Alley composers as the stars by which he would steer his own course. One was Irving Berlin, whose "Alexander's Ragtime Band" he regarded as a masterwork. The other composer was Jerome Kern. George heard Kern's music for the first time while attending his aunt's wedding in 1914. The band struck up a tune so novel in harmonic and melodic construction that the boy rushed to the stand to find out who had written it. He was told that the song was the Jerome Kern composition "You're Here and I'm Here." At Gershwin's urging, the band played other Kern songs including "They Didn't Believe Me," which held the boy spellbound. From that day on, Gershwin used Kern as his model. "I paid him the tribute of frank imitation, and many things I wrote at this period sounded as though Kern had written them himself."

"The kid has talent," Hambitzer reported in another of his letters, "and I believe I can make something of him. He wants to go in for this modern stuff—jazz and whatnot. But I'm not going to let him for a while, I'll see that he gets a firm foundation in standard music first."

Gershwin was already beginning to write popular songs. The first, "Since I Found You," in 1913, was never published. By late 1913 he had become convinced that the popular song was the medium he wished to work in. It was then that he became determined to find a job in Tin Pan Alley and to learn all he could about the music business and popular music from the inside. Through the song plugger Ben Bloom, a friend of the Gershwin family, George found a job as piano demonstrator under Mose Gumble at Remick's at a salary of fifteen dollars a week. Leaving high school, at which he had been, at best, an indifferent pupil, he became (at fifteen) the youngest piano demonstrator in Tin Pan Alley. It was the first time that Remick had hired for such a job a completely inexperienced hand.

Gershwin from the beginning was a phenomenon in Tin Pan Alley. Here was a piano demonstrator who spent his spare time studying piano with Charles Hambitzer and theory with Edward Kilenyi (for by now Gershwin was beginning to penetrate more deeply into music theory), who was practicing the piano and composing all the time. When his cubicle at Remick's was emptied of potential clients, he was hard at work on piano exercises and working over the musical classics. One day a fellow employee at Remick's found him laboring painstakingly over Bach's *Well-Tempered Clavier*. "Are you studying to be a concert pianist, George?" he inquired. Gershwin's answer was characteristic. "I'm studying," he answered, "to be a great popular composer."

But one particular thing about Gershwin made all those who came into contact with him stop short with amazement—the way he played the piano. His gift for evoking unusual colors, his extraordinary sense of rhythm, his instinct for sensitive phrasing, his unusual harmonies made everybody who heard him exclaim that his playing was unique. Irving Caesar, then just a budding lyricist, often visited Remick's just to hear Gershwin play. "His rhythm," Caesar once told me, "had the impact of a sledgehammer. His harmonies were years ahead of their time. I had never heard such playing of popular music." Harry Ruby, whose path as a song plugger often crossed that of Gershwin when he was out song-plugging for Remick's, never tired of listening to Gershwin talk about music. "I still recall," Ruby says, "George's earnestness, his intense enthusiasm for his work, his passionate interest in every phase of the music business. Sometimes when he spoke of the artistic mission of popular music we thought he was going highfalutin'. The height of artistic achievement to us was a 'pop' song that sold lots and lots of copies, and we just didn't understand what he was talking about." As for young Gershwin's handling of the piano, Ruby (himself a fine pianist) said: "It was far and beyond better than the piano playing of any of us. As I look back upon it I can say it was a completely different musical world from ours, and we did not completely understand it at the time, though we all reacted to it instinctively. I am also sure we were all jealous of him."

While still employed at Remick's, Gershwin completed a number of songs. One of these was "When You Want 'Em You Can't Get 'Em." When he showed it to Mose Gumble, his boss at Remick's, Gumble said: "You're here to play the piano, not to write songs. We've plenty of songwriters here." But Sophie Tucker liked the tune enough to bring it to the attention of Harry von Tilzer, who issued it in 1916 —Gershwin's first published song. It sold so few copies that Gershwin's royalties did not even cover the five dollars advance Von Tilzer had given him.

Sigmund Romberg—now a staff composer for the Shuberts and the creator of successful scores for revues and extravaganzas—also began taking an interest in young Gershwin. He interpolated Gershwin's "The Making of a Girl" into *The Passing Show of 1916*.

Nor was Romberg the only successful popular composer to become aware of Gershwin's rare talent. When Gershwin felt he had outgrown Remick's, after working there for about two years, he went to Irving Berlin for a job. Berlin had been admiring Gershwin's work for some time. When Gershwin now played a Berlin number with his own harmonizations, the older man told him that the song had just been reborn. Berlin stood ready to take Gershwin on as a musical secretary and arranger, at five times the salary Gershwin was getting at Remick's. "The job is yours if you want it," Berlin told him, "but I really hope you don't want it. You have too much talent to be anybody's arranger. Your job is to write songs of your own. You're destined for big things."

Gershwin did follow Berlin's advice and turned down the attractive offer. He found work as a rehearsal pianist for *Miss 1917*, a Broadway musical with a score by Victor Herbert and some interpolated songs by Jerome Kern. This was the first time that Gershwin came into personal contact with Kern. When his chores as pianist were over, Gershwin often played the piano for members of the cast. The first time Kern heard him he became so excited that he went home and insisted that his wife come down the very next day and hear this Gershwin perform. After *Miss 1917* was produced, Kern personally arranged to have Gershwin hired as rehearsal pianist for another Kern musical, *Rock-a-bye, Baby*. During this period the relationship of Gershwin and Kern flowered into friendship.

Harry Askin, company manager for *Miss 1917*, was so taken with Gershwin's abilities that he talked about him to Max Dreyfus. Kern also had warm words to contribute. Dreyfus, therefore, set up a meeting with the young man, even though up to this point he had neither seen nor heard anything Gershwin had written. Gershwin's sincerity and seriousness of purpose impressed the publisher no end. As he put it: "He was the kind of man I like to gamble on, and I decided to gamble." He told Gershwin he was ready to pay him thirty-five dollars a week just for writing songs. Gershwin was to have no office hours or any set duties. All he was required to do was, from time to time, show Dreyfus the songs he was writing. If Dreyfus liked anything he would publish it and pay royalties. And that's how Dreyfus came to publish "Some Wonderful Sort of Someone" in 1918, with which the fruitful composer-publisher relationship was officially started.

Dreyfus now began to put the full weight of his influence to work for the young composer. He got Gershwin an assignment to write the music for the revue *Half Past Eight*. Unfortunately, the show opened and closed out of town—a total bust; Gershwin did not even collect the fee due him. Then Dreyfus interested Nora Bayes in singing "Some Wonderful Sort of Someone" in *Ladies First*. When Nora Bayes needed a piano accompanist for a six-week tour, Dreyfus urged her to take Gershwin on. During this tour she sang some of Gershwin's songs, including "The Real American Folk Song," the first of Gershwin's melodies to which his brother Ira supplied the lyrics.

Gershwin's career now went into high gear. In 1919 he stepped forward with his first Broadway musical-comedy score in one hand and his first hit song in the other. The musical comedy was *La, La, Lucille*, which enjoyed a profitable six-month run on Broadway. The hit song was "Swanee" (not in *La, La, Lucille*), with lyrics by Irving Caesar, which was first heard in a giant stage show at the Capitol Theater when that movie palace opened its doors for the first time on October 24, 1919. Sixty chorus girls, with electric lights glowing on their slippers, danced to its rhythms on a completely darkened stage. Despite such effective treatment, "Swanee" did not seem to make an impression, and the sheet music (sold in the lobby) did not move. Then Al Jolson heard it with delight and sang it at a Sunday-evening concert at the Winter Garden and later in the Winter Garden extravaganza *Sinbad*. Suddenly "Swanee" caught fire. The sheet-music sale passed the million mark in a year's time, and more than two million records were sold. In fact, no song Gershwin wrote after that enjoyed such a financial bonanza.

Gershwin was now ready for his first big Broadway assignment, which came from George White (who was one of the cast of *Miss 1917* to be won over by Gershwin's piano playing). In 1919 George White became the producer of the lavish new revue the *Scandals*, with which he hoped to rival the *Ziegfeld Follies*. In 1920 he contracted Gershwin to write the whole score for the second edition. Gershwin wrote the music for the *Scandals* of that year and for those of the next four years. To the 1922 edition he contributed "I'll Build a Stairway to Paradise," which Carl van Vechten then called "the most perfect piece of jazz ever written." With its subtle enharmonic changes, unconventional harmonies, and daring accentuations, "I'll Build a Stairway to Paradise" was indeed something completely new for Broadway and Tin Pan Alley. It was so new, in fact, that in 1922, because of this and similar efforts, Gershwin was described as "a great composer" with "the spark of musical genius," by Beryl Rubinstein, a distinguished concert pianist, teacher, and composer. To a somewhat startled interviewer, Beryl Rubinstein maintained: "With Gershwin's style and seriousness he is not definitely from the popular-music school but one of the really outstanding figures in the country's musical efforts. . . . I really believe that America will at no distant date honor [him] for his talent . . . and that when we speak of American composers, George Gershwin's name will be prominent on our list." In the literary journal *The Dial*, Gilbert Seldes said of Gershwin's popular songs in 1923: "Delicacy, even dreaminess, is a quality he [Gershwin] alone brings into jazz music. And his sense of variation in rhythm, of an oddly placed accent, of emphasis and color, is impeccable."

By the end of 1924, Gershwin had fulfilled the most exalted hopes of his admirers, not only on Broadway but even in the concert hall. For Broadway he wrote "Somebody Loves Me," a ballad with a personalized lyricism and an equally individual harmony that Winnie Lightner introduced in the *Scandals of 1924*. During the same year he wrote the first of his distinguished musical comedies, *Lady Be Good!* for which his brother Ira wrote all the lyrics. Among its leading songs were such sophisticated items as "Fascinating Rhythm" and "So Am I," once again offering a new concept of rhythm and harmony within the popular-song context.

And, in 1924, Gershwin produced for the concert stage a composition that forthwith established him as the "white hope" of American music, gave him international stature, and made him a wealthy man. The composition was *Rhapsody in Blue*, which was introduced at Aeolian Hall in New York on February 12, with the composer appearing as soloist and Paul Whiteman conducting his orchestra.

And so, by the end of 1924, the one-time piano demonstrator and song plugger of Remick's had set one foot solidly on Broadway and the other in Aeolian Hall. For the remainder of his life, Gershwin would continue to bestride both worlds—the popular and the serious—with the span of a colossus.

# 18

## "I may be gone for a long, long time"

Europe went to war in 1914. By cultural ties and by common institutions, the sympathy of the American people went out to the Allies. But in spite of this, a profound anti-war sentiment drew many Americans in 1914 and 1915 to neutrality, pacificism, isolation, and chauvinism.

Like a sensitive barometer forecasting every subtle change in the weather, Tin Pan Alley often reflected, and at times even anticipated, the changing social and political climate. Two songs came out of the Alley in 1915, which, because they gave voice to the spirit of the times, became nationally popular. One was "America, I Love You," which Americans everywhere sang out loud and clear as an expression of an aroused patriotism. Pacifist Americans who wanted no part of Europe's conflicts sang Al Piantadosi's "I Didn't Raise My Boy to Be a Soldier." Its sheet music portrayed a gray-haired old mother shielding her son while shells were busting all around them.

Many another song of the day catered to the temper of the times: "We'll Never Let Our Old Flag Down," "Under the American Flag," and "Don't Take My Darling Boy Away." When President Wilson announced that America was too "proud to fight," Tin Pan Alley responded with "Our Hats Off to You, Mr. President."

But the European war, which had been expected to end in three or six months, dragged on and on, and Americans began to take sides. German militarism, the arrogance of German statesmen, the unprovoked invasion of Belgium, unrestricted submarine warfare—all helped to arouse in Americans a rapidly developing hostility toward Germany. Then one or two incidents struck home. In 1915 the *Lusitania* was sunk by a German submarine, with the loss of a hundred and twenty-eight lives. And that same year a mysterious explosion of a munitions plant at Black Tom Island in New Jersey was rumored to have been the work of German saboteurs. Thus the war was creeping ever closer to America, and as it did so, the war fever in the United States began to rise. In 1916 a new slogan was circulated: "We are *not* too proud to fight." Sales and performances of pacifist songs vanished. Vaudeville headliners were now bringing down the house with such numbers as "I Did Not Raise My Boy to Be a Coward," "I'd Be Proud to Be the Mother of a Soldier," and "I Didn't Raise My Boy to Be a Soldier, but I'll Send My Girl to Be a Nurse." Hand in hand with this martial spirit came such patriotic ditties as "My Country, I Hear You Calling Me," "Following the Flag You Love," and "Stand By Your Uncle Sam." It was almost as if Tin Pan Alley were prognosticating the imminent active participation by America in the war.

Once America made the plunge into the world conflict,

songs began to depart even more sharply from any suggestion of pacifism. Now the public was responding to:
"I'm Glad I Raised My Boy to Be a Soldier" and "I Didn't
Raise My Boy to Be a Molly-coddle." Variations on a similar theme included "I Didn't Raise My Boy to Be a Soldier but He Will Fight for the U.S.A." and "I Didn't Raise
My Boy to Be a Slacker."

The war, of course, created a major upheaval in the
American way of life, to which Tin Pan Alley reacted in
several different ways. One of the direct results of the out-
break of war was the sudden boom in the sale of sheet music. Many theaters and cabarets closed down because fuel
and power were hard to get or because the draft had
depleted the supply of live entertainment. The dancing
madness had subsided. People were compelled to return to
their own living rooms and to provide their own fun—in
the singing of popular songs.

Besides, it was considered patriotic to sing. Most of the
songs flooding the market had a direct bearing on the war.
Community sings, songfests in the theaters, singing at war
bond rallies—all this became the proper and fitting thing
to do as part of the war effort. It was a way of proclaiming
one's allegiance to country in time of peril; of keeping the
home fires burning; of nurturing civilian morale. Singing
songs was also a safety valve through which the pent-up
emotions of a people stirred by the drama of war and the
impact it was having on their personal lives could be released. George Creel's Committee on Public Information
considered singing so important to the war effort that it
compiled a song book at government expense to be distributed in movie houses and vaudeville theaters; it also
dispatched song leaders to the theaters to encourage audiences to participate in mass singing.

With live acts growing increasingly scarce, amateur song
competitions flourished on the stage—the winners going

off proudly with loving cups in their arms. Something else now came into vogue: competitions in which new war songs were introduced before audiences that would select the winner. To these competitions all the major publishers in Tin Pan Alley provided not only the latest in martial tunes, but also performers, song pluggers, and sometimes even claques.

With everybody singing as never before—with the public eagerly seeking out new songs that echoed and reechoed with its own aroused sentiments and emotions—sheet-music sales soared to astronomical figures. Since the war department had decreed that popular music was essential to a successful war effort, Tin Pan Alley could get all the paper it needed; nothing, then, stood in the way of the rising flood of sheet-music sales. Only one concession was now made by Tin Pan Alley to the paper shortage—the size of sheet music was reduced. This abbreviation, however, proved in the end so practical that it was continued permanently after the war. And this concession merely spelled bigger and better profits for the publishers, since it reduced the cost of production.

Once America was in the war, Tin Pan Alley went into high gear in the production of war songs. "My Boy, He Just Can't Help Being a Soldier" and "America, Here's My Boy" were two of the earliest hits calculated to stir the martial spirit. From then on, and up to the Armistice, there was not a single note, in the whole gamut of emotions seizing and holding Americans, that was not touched upon by popular songs. Every area of war experience was covered; every major war episode was commented upon; anybody and everybody who was directly involved in the war, whatever the capacity, was hymned in songs.

Songs about the Allies? There were "Belgium, Dry Your Eyes," "Joan of Arc," "Belgian Rose," "Lorraine,

My Beautiful Alsace Lorraine," and "Lafayette, We Hear You Calling."

Songs about the various branches of the services? There were "Tell It to the Marines," "Give a Little Credit to the Navy," "Rose of No Man's Land," and "I Don't Want to Get Well" (the last two honored the Red Cross).

There were songs to stir the fighting blood, to inflame the patriotic fires, to send the boys to the trenches with spirit and the will to victory: "We Don't Want the Bacon, What We Want Is a Piece of the Rhine"; "Just Like Washington Crossed the Delaware, General Pershing Will Cross the Rhine"; "Good-by Broadway, Hello France"; "Liberty Bell, It's Time to Ring Again"; "We're Going Over"; and "We'll Knock the Heligo-into Heligo-out of Heligoland."

And there were songs about and for those who stayed behind at home: "Keep the Home Fires Burning"; "There's a Vacant Chair in Every Home Tonight"; "Keep Cool, the Country's Saving Fuel"; "We'll Do Our Share While You're Over There"; and "Cheer Up, Father, Cheer Up, Mother."

There were nostalgic songs, and sentimental songs, and songs about the pain of separation, the poignancy of loneliness, and the cherished dream of reunion: "When the Flowers Bloom in No Man's Land"; "Send Me Away With a Smile"; "I May Be Gone for a Long, Long Time"; "Au Revoir, But Not Good-by, Soldier Boy"; "Bring Back My Daddy to Me"; "Oh How I Wish I Could Sleep Until My Daddy Comes Home"; "Hello Central, Give Me No Man's Land"; "Say a Prayer for the Boys Over There"; and "When the Boys Come Home."

There were songs—hundreds of them—about the Kaiser. Originally, some were mild in their expression of belligerence. But before long the hostility of tone and the violence of mood became intense and passionate. These are samples: "We Want the Kaiser's Helmet Now"; "The Kaiser Will be Wiser When Uncle Sam is Through"; "We're All Going to Call on the Kaiser"; "We're All Going to Hang the Kaiser Under the Linden Tree"; "We're Going to Whip the Kaiser"; "The Crazy Kaiser"; "Hunting the Hun"; "I'll Kill the Kaiser for You"; "The Kaiser Is a Devil"; "Hang the Kaiser to a Sour Apple Tree"; and "I'd Like to See the Kaiser with a Lily in His Hand."

And there were songs that sought out the humor of army life and the absurdities of civilian problems: "Oh, Frenchy"; "Oui, Oui, Marie"; "K-K-K-Katy"; "Would You Rather Be a Colonel with an Eagle on Your Shoulder or a Private with a Chicken on Your Knee"; "If He Can Fight As He Can Love, Good Night Germany"; "They Were All Out of Step but Jim"; "When Yankee Doodle Learns to Parlez-Vous Français."

When the war was at its height, a song contest was held at Keith's Fifth Avenue Theater in New York. Five war songs were picked out by the audience as favorites, sometimes with a push from song plugger and claque. Top honors went to Charles K. Harris' "Break the News to Mother," the sentimental ballad popular during the Spanish-American War, now enjoying a successful revival. After that, in the order of audience preference, came "Joan of Arc," "Somewhere in France Is a Lily," "Send Me Away With a Smile," and "It's a Long Way to Berlin."

But the greatest songs to come out of World War I, and those most often remembered today, are not to be found among the winners of the Keith Theater contest. There is, for example, the ballad "Till We Meet Again," which sold about three and a half million copies of sheet music during the first year of its publication; in all, it is more than probable that about ten million copies have been sold throughout the years.

Its music was by Richard Whiting, a native of Peoria,

Illinois; the lyrics were by Ray Egan. Whiting first became interested in popular music while he was attending the Harvard Military School in Los Angeles. At that time he sold three songs to Remick for fifty dollars apiece. The transaction ended up with the offer of a job as office manager of Remick's branch in Detroit. Whiting's first hit song, "It's Tulip Time in Holland," was published by Remick in 1915. Since nothing he had written up to this point had earned him more than a few dollars in royalties, Whiting was convinced he had made a strategic coup when he had convinced Remick to present him with a Steinway piano in lieu of royalties for "It's Tulip Time." When the song sold about a half-million copies, Whiting's Steinway piano turned out to be the costliest instrument of its kind. Now convinced that he had best return to a royalty arrangement, Whiting completed two songs in 1916 that brought him about thirty thousand dollars: "And They Called it Dixieland" and "Mammy's Little Coal Black Rose." "Where the Black-Eyed Susans Grow" was his big hit song of 1917. But however successful these numbers might have been, they were all dwarfed by the triumph of "Till We Meet Again."

Margaret Whiting—the composer's daughter and a famous singer of pop tunes—once revealed that when Richard Whiting first wrote "Till We Meet Again" he was so dissatisfied with it that he threw the manuscript into his trash basket. His wife, however, had faith in it, retrieved the manuscript and, without her husband's knowledge, sent it off to Remick. While "Till We Meet Again" was being published, and before its release, it was entered into a patriotic song contest in a Detroit movie house, at which it won first prize.

"Till We Meet Again" was the foremost ballad inspired by World War I. But there were others only slightly less successful and popular, and of these the most famous was "There's a Long, Long Trail," with music by Zo Elliott and words by Stoddard King. Actually, this ballad had been written long before America went to war. As students at Yale in 1913, Elliott and Stoddard were asked to do a musical number for a fraternity banquet. The boys decided to do a song with a heart throb, and wrote "There's a Long, Long Trail" by fits and starts while they were cramming for an exam. The fraternity boys did not like the song and would not use it at the banquet; the publishers to whom the song was submitted liked it even less.

That fall, Elliott enrolled in Trinity College, in Cambridge, England. Told about an obscure and financially insecure little publisher on the lookout for song manuscripts, Elliott sent them his ballad. The publishers offered to print it if Elliott were willing to pay the expenses for the initial printing, this money to be refunded from the income from subsequent printings. Before Elliott could even receive his first royalty check, World War I erupted in Europe. Elliott, who at the moment was touring Germany, was able to escape to Switzerland where a sizable sum was awaiting him from the sale of his song, which had been doing extraordinarily well in England. After returning to America, late in 1914, Elliott interested Witmark in taking over the copyright. Nothing much happened to the song until America went to war. The heart-throb ballad was a reflection of what many Americans were then feeling, and the song skyrocketed to a sheet-music sale of over two and a half million copies.

One song above all others is associated with World War I —George M. Cohan's "Over There." He wrote it early one morning at his home in Great Neck, Long Island, after reading in the morning paper that America had just declared war on Germany. "I read those war headlines," he later recalled, "and I got to thinking and humming to myself—and for a minute I thought I was going to dance. I was all finished with both the chorus and the verse by the time I got to town. I also had a title."

"Over There" was first sung at a Red Cross benefit at the Hippodrome Theater in the fall of 1917 by Charles King. Soon after that, at Cohan's request, Nora Bayes put it into her show, and almost caused a stampede. The effect of the bugle-call motive in the main melody, repeated some ten times, was irresistible. So was what Sigmund Spaeth described as "the steady irresistible movement of the bass down the scale, under the sustained bugle notes." An "inevitable impression of marching feet" was thus created, "completing the overwhelming militant effect."

Leo Feist bought the publishing rights from Cohan for twenty-five thousand dollars. Cohan thought he had driven a hard and profitable bargain, but to Feist the deal turned out to be a gilt-edged investment. In four months' time, four hundred thousand copies of sheet music were sold; by the time the war was over, the total sales passed two million, with an additional sale of a million records. Even the great Enrico Caruso made a recording of it in his peculiar English diction, and so did Ernestine Schumann-Heink. President Wilson described it as a "genuine inspiration to all American manhood." Subsequently, "Over There" was admitted to the Hall of Fame to represent American patriotic music; and during World War II, the song was responsible for bringing its composer a Congressional Medal of Honor from President Franklin D. Roosevelt, by a special act of Congress.

In *Show Biz: From Vaude to Video*, Abel Green and Joe Laurie, Jr., contribute an amusing footnote to the history of "Over There." Though there was hardly anyone anywhere in the United States during World War I who did not know the words of this rousing war ballad, George M. Cohan himself forgot the lines when invited to sing his song during a charity performance at Ebling's Casino. While he was fumbling for a line, Irving Berlin and Joe Laurie, Jr., sprang up from the audience to the stage to help him out.

Irving Berlin's "Oh, How I Hate to Get Up in the Morning" is perhaps the most successful comedy song of World War I. It was the result of the composer's own experiences as a rookie in an army camp. Berlin was then stationed at Camp Upton—in Yaphank, Long Island—a temporary station for troops embarking for Europe. A new service center was needed for the camp. To raise the money (about twenty-five thousand dollars), Berlin suggested the production of an all-soldier show. He wrote book, lyrics, and music of *Yip, Yip, Yaphank* and opened it with his soldiers' cast at the Century Theater in New York on July 26, 1918. The revue provided a many-sided picture of army life in song, skit, dance, and production number. It was within such a context that "Oh, How I Hate to Get Up in the Morning" was seen and heard for the first time, to become one of the high spots of the whole show. Berlin himself was the star of this scene. He appeared as a sadly bedraggled rookie who, roused by the bugler's morning blast, stumbles sleepily out of bed for reveille, singing his sad lament.

*Yip, Yip, Yaphank* netted one hundred and twenty-five thousand dollars for Camp Upton's new service center; and "Oh, How I Hate to Get Up in the Morning" became Berlin's biggest hit song of the war period. A generation later, during World War II, Berlin once again wrote and produced an all-soldier show, *This Is the Army*. Wearing his old World War I uniform, Berlin himself here revived "Oh, How I Hate to Get Up in the Morning," bringing back to many in the audience the poignant reminder of the way he had sung it a quarter of a century earlier.

The era of World War I also produced numerous songs

that provided an avenue of escape from the war. Soldiers in uniform and civilians at home needed a respite from the problems that the war was pressing on them all the time. That respite also came from singing—sentimental, nostalgic, ragtime, or comic songs whose lyrics and music allowed the performer and listener to forget at least momentarily that a war was on and that it was exacting a heavy toll.

One of the most popular of these escapist songs was "Smiles," with music by Lee G. Robert and words by J. Will Callahan. They wrote it in 1917, just as America was on the eve of declaring war; its inspiration was a sentence that Roberts heard a speaker deliver at a music-dealers' convention in Chicago, explaining the value of a smile in transacting business. That same day, Roberts wrote his melody and sent it to his friend Callahan, suggesting the subject of the lyric. Every publisher turned it down. The authors then issued it themselves. First a few bands began to feature it, then vaudevillians started to use it in their acts. To a war-weary public the song was a soothing anodyne. Within six months, almost two million copies of sheet music were sold; another million copies went the next two years. Piano rolls and phonograph records were also best sellers.

Many other songs avoided the war and answered the public need to forget the news of the day. Sentimentality and nostalgia were richly tapped with such hit songs as "I'm Sorry I Made You Cry"; with George W. Meyer's "For Me and My Gal"; with Robert A. King's elegant waltz that sold five million copies, "Beautiful Ohio," a number that had started out as an instrumental background for "allez-oop" acts in vaudeville; with Harry Carroll's "I'm Always Chasing Rainbows" introduced in the Broadway musical, *Oh Look!;* with Shelton Brooks' dynamic ragtime tune, "The Darktown Strutters' Ball," which was a Sophie Tucker favorite.

Humorous and nonsense songs also offered a route of escape from war cares: Abe Olman's "Oh, Johnny, Oh, Johnny, Oh," which sold a million copies in 1917 and then returned twenty years later to become an even greater financial success through Bonnie Baker's infectious presentation; Fred Fisher's, "They Go Wild, Simply Wild over Me"; Jean Schwartz's "Why Do They All Take the Night Boat to Albany?"; Anatole Friedland's "Lily of the Valley"; Bob Carleton's "Ja-Da."

A new song craze seized the country as soon as Europe went to war, and grew in dimension after America entered in the conflict; it also took life from the need of people to forget. These songs evoked pictures of far-off Hawaii, a musical flight into a glamorous never-never land untouched by the devastation and heartaches of war. This cycle began in earnest in 1915 with "On the Beach of Waikiki" and "Song of the Islands," both of which had been published in Hawaii but soon grew popular in the States. This trend continued with "Hello, Hawaii, How Are You?" As soon as Tin Pan Alley caught on to the commercial value of Hawaiian-type songs, the dykes were down and the floods were let loose: "Yacka Hula, Hickey Dula"; "Oh, How She Could Yacki, Hacki, Wicki, Woo"; "They're Wearing 'Em Higher in Hawaii"; "Hawaiian Butterfly"; "The Honolulu Hicki Boola Boo"; "I Lost My Heart in Honolulu"; "My Honolulu Ukulele Baby," to mention some examples.

# 19

## "Runnin' wild"

The armistice on November 11, 1918, brought World War I to an end. Released of wartime tensions, Americans could now happily discard military trappings and war problems and resume a normal course of life. As an aftermath to the heartaches and weariness of the preceding months, Americans at first sought out life's simpler pleasures. They had had a stomach full of adventure, excitement, tragedy, loneliness, and deprivations. What they now wanted were peace and serenity, the sight of familiar places and people, the feel of simple sentiments.

War songs were dead. Throughout the country signs were posted backstage warning entertainers to "cut out" from their acts any number that reminded audiences of the war. Realizing that new times were at hand—and that new times required new tunes—Tin Pan Alley reoriented its giant machinery toward the production of songs that concerned themselves with elementals: romance, the love of the boy for the girl next door, family life, the comforts and delights of the old home town.

Published immediately after the war, "In My Sweet Little Alice Blue Gown," which Harry Tierney wrote for the Broadway musical *Irene*, concerned itself with fundamentals. It enjoyed a phenomenal success. Albert von Tilzer's nostalgic "I'll Be with You in Apple Blossom Time," introduced in vaudeville by Nora Bayes, was in a similar homespun style; so was Louis Hirsch's "Love Nest," which glorified marital happiness simply and directly in the musical comedy *Mary* in 1920. ("Love Nest" served a generation later as the radio and television theme music for the comedy team of Burns and Allen.) Songs about the old home town were plentiful and popular: "Tuck Me to Sleep in My Old 'Tucky Home," "Saw Mill River Road," "My Home Town Is a One-Horse Town but It's Big Enough for Me," "Carolina Sunshine," and Walter Donaldson's hit, "Carolina in the Morning."

The end of the war brought overtones of optimism reflected in Jerome Kern's "Look for the Silver Lining"— stunningly introduced by Marilyn Miller in the Ziegfeld production *Sally*—and in Ernest Seitz's "The World Is Waiting for the Sunrise" (its lyrics were the work of Eugene Lockhart, who is better known to movie audiences as Gene Lockhart). The escapism that made a vogue of Hawaiian songs during the war sought out other exotic, far-off places: with Richard A. Whiting's "Japanese Sandman," first made famous by Nora Bayes; "My Isle of Golden Dreams"; "Avalon" (which Al Jolson had made popular before the plagiarism suit destroyed it); and Harry Ruby's "Timbuctoo."

\*

Then a decade turned the corner, offering a new vista, a new ambience, a new social climate. This decade, the second in the twentieth century, is sometimes remembered as the "frenzied twenties" or the "roaring twenties" or the "turbulent twenties." Suddenly, inexplicably—sentimentality, nostalgia, small-town romance, the little home in a far-off picturesque village, story-book escapism—all this was swept rudely away to make room for hard-boiled cynicism, reckless abandon, a devil-may-care attitude toward living that proclaimed the gospel that "today we live, for tomorrow we die." This was the *real* aftermath of World War I. Long pent-up emotions now found full release. Freed of their one-time inhibitions, many Americans emancipated themselves from old conventions and taboos.

Women, risen to equality with men through the power of the vote, flaunted their new freedom as if it were a flying banner for all to see. They bobbed their hair, shortened their skirts, rolled their stockings below the knees, smoked in public, began using cosmetics to excess, reduced their home chores by introducing canned goods into the kitchen. Old values, standards, shibboleths were debunked in such magazines as the *American Mercury*, edited by H. L. Mencken and George Jean Nathan, which claimed "to attempt a realistic presentation of the whole gaudy, gorgeous American scene"; in novels like *Main Street* and *Babbitt* by Sinclair Lewis; in plays like *Gentleman Prefer Blondes,* adapted from Anita Loos's novel. Sophistication became the wisdom of the day, growing fat on irony and the wisecrack; Dorothy Parker was the high priestess of this cult, and the newly founded journal *The New Yorker* its trumpet. Racy new words and expressions invaded the everyday language: "chicks," "sheiks," "flappers," "cake-eaters," "Dumb Doras," "the cat's meow," the "cat's pajamas."

Sex came out of hiding into the full light of day. It dominated the screen with sex symbols like Clara Bow, the "It" girl, and Rudolph Valentino of the throbbing nostrils and bedroom eyes. It was glorified in Atlantic City with the bathing beauty contest and the crowning of the first Miss America in 1921. It dominated the press, particularly through the sensationalism with which tabloids (a child of the 1920's) fattened their circulation figures—extensive pictorial and verbal handling of juicy scandals involving Fatty Arbuckle and Virginia Rapp, Daddy Browning and Peaches, the murder trial of Ruth Snyder-Judd Gray, and the Hall-Mills murder case. The gossip columnist (also an offspring of the 1920's) provided prurient readers with a keyhole glimpse into the extracurricular activities of the famous and the infamous. Petting had become a favorite sport of the young and the not-so-young; "companionate marriage"—a trial marriage without benefit of clergy— was advocated by Judge Benjamin Barr Lindsay; the ex- change of jokes and epithets between the sexes would have brought a blush even to a roué a decade earlier.

There seemed no ceiling to prosperity, either in the land boom in Florida, or on Wall Street, or in Hollywood, where profits and salaries assumed astronomical figures. Movies were bigger, better, and more spectacular than ever. There were eighteen thousand theaters in the country where the public made gods and goddesses of such screen idols as Gloria Swanson, John Barrymore, Norma Tal- madge, and Richard Barthelmess. There were idols in the sports world as well—Babe Ruth, Jack Dempsey, Bobby Jones, Red Grange.

Stunts and fads and vogues took deep root: flagpole- sitting, marathon dancing, ouija boards, crossword puzzles, miniature golf, autosuggestion, marriage ceremonies in the clouds in airplanes, capsule education through one-volume outlines of philosophy, history, art, and music.

Defiance of law, and corruption, hit places high and

low: high, in Washington, D. C., where the Teapot Dome scandals rocked even the White House; low, in the gutters of Chicago, from which sprang big-time gangsters who made fortunes from rackets, promotion of vice, and bootleg whiskey. Even Mr. Average Citizen stood in contempt of law and order. Intolerant of the Volstead Act, he did not hesitate to visit speakeasies, flaunt a hip flask, and manufacture bathtub gin at home.

It was all like some incessant carnival—gay, giddy, reckless, noisy, and brash. Everybody was hell-bent on having a good time. Tin Pan Alley stood ready to provide the theme music for this carnival with two songs that became nationwide successes because they spoke out for the entire era: Richard A. Whiting's "Ain't We Got Fun" and A. Harrington Gibbs' "Runnin' Wild."

A decade that took such delight in fads, fetishes, and fancies inevitably responded to nonsense songs. Some of the most successful ever produced by Tin Pan Alley came out during the twenties. There was Con Conrad's "Barney Google," inspired by a popular newspaper cartoon and successfully introduced by Olsen and Johnson. The lyrics were written by Billy Rose, then launched upon a profitable career as a songwriter—the profession that stood midway in his life between his past as an amateur shorthand champion and professional stenographer and his future as a millionaire showman. There was "Diga, Diga, Doo," which Jimmy McHugh wrote for Dorothy Fields' words; Adelaide Hall made her Broadway debut with it in *Blackbirds of 1928*. And there were many others, too: Harry Warren's "Where Do You Work-a, John?" and "Gidap-Garibaldi"; "I'm Wild About Horns on Automobiles That Go Ta-ta-ta-ta"; "I Faw Down an' Go Boom"; and "I Love to Dunk a Hunk of Sponge Cake."

The nonsense song that stood apart from all the others

as perhaps the most successful of its kind ever written was "Yes, We Have No Bananas." Frank Silver and Irving Cohen wrote it in 1923, after overhearing a Greek fruit peddler say these words to a customer. The authors themselves introduced their song in several New York restaurants. Then Eddie Cantor came across the manuscript in Philadelphia, where his musical *Make It Snappy* was trying out. Feeling the need for some fresh material, he interpolated it into the production one Wednesday matinee. The reaction was such that he had to repeat chorus after chorus; the show was stopped cold for more than a quarter of an hour. The audience reacted similarly at all subsequent performances. Cantor's recording for Victor was one of the several highly successful releases Victor made of the same song. By the end of 1923, everybody was singing "Yes, We Have No Bananas."

Among the places where the 1920's seemed to find a good deal of diversion was on the college campus—not in the classroom, to be sure, but in the football stadium, the varsity dance, the fraternity and sorority houses. Even young men who had never attended college started wearing the rakish hat and the huge raccoon coat over knickers and loud-striped sweaters, which the 1920's had established as collegiate uniform, and carrying a ukelele under an arm. Girls also wore an identifiable collegiate outfit: tight sweaters with college emblems, pert little caps, socks. Here, too, was serviceable material for Tin Pan Alley exploitation. One of the most popular of these songs was "Collegiate" by Moe Jaffe and Nat Box. When Fred Waring and his Pennsylvanians introduced it, they wore a collegiate outfit, a stunt that undoubtedly helped to make the song one of the big hits of the 1920's. Before the decade ended, Rudy Vallee and his Connecticut Yankees became the favorites of the collegiate factions by popularizing such new college songs as "Betty Co-Ed" (written partly by Vallee himself) and by reviving such old ones as the "Stein Song," "The Sweetheart of Sigma Chi," and "There's a Tavern in the Town." Broadway responded to the collegiate craze with one of the best musicals of the decade— *Good News*, by De Sylva, Brown, and Henderson. The ushers in the theater were dressed in college jerseys. Before the orchestra embarked on the overture, it led off with several shouts of "rah rah." Tunes in the college spirit, such as the "Varsity Drag" and "The Girls of Pi Beta Phi," maintained this rah-rah atmosphere.

# 20

## "It don't mean a thing
## if you ain't got that swing"

Possibly the most apt way of describing the 1920's is to call it the "jazz age." By "jazz" we are not here referring to the real product marketed first in New Orleans and then in Chicago and New York, by such giant jazzmen as Louis Armstrong, Bix Beiderbecke, or Duke Ellington. "Jazz," in connection with the twenties, as we are using it here, was the synthetic variety being produced in quantity in Tin Pan Alley. Ballads were still holding their own—love ballads particularly—and in the 1920's Irving Berlin was showing his mastery of the genre with such gems as "All Alone," "What'll I Do?," "All by Myself," and "Remember." But the ballad was getting plenty of competition from a more dynamic kind of song, a song more expressive of the twenties, which had captured public imagination and enthusiasm. It was exciting in its rhythmic pulse and changing meters, in its compulsive beat and dramatic accentuations, in its blues harmonies and jazz colorations. The appeal of this kind of number stemmed from its rhythmic momentum and kinesthetic force rather than from the beauty of the melody.

George Gershwin was one of the first to evolve this kind of jazz song and make it popular—with such numbers as "I'll Build a Stairway to Paradise," "Do It Again," "Fascinating Rhythm," "Fidgety Feet," and "Clap Yo' Hands." Other composers, following his direction, were also accentuating the beat and pulse of their writing and minimizing the sentiment of the lyric. There was Fred Fisher, whose "Dardanella" anticipated boogie-woogie with its recurring bass rhythm. Zez Confrey's rags are examples of this kind of jazz music—"Dizzy Fingers," "Kitten on the Keys," and "Stumbling." In the concert hall this kind of jazz found a receptive audience through the more ambitious symphonic works of George Gershwin, John Alden Carpenter, and Ferde Grofé.

The popularity of this restlessly rhythmic and nervously accented kind of song brought on a new abandon in social dance; and this new frenetic type of social dance, in turn, stimulated the writing of still other dynamically rhythmic tunes. The tango, the waltz and the fox trot—so popular before World War I—were followed in the 1920's by dances that were far more uninhibited in motions, far more in tune with the febrile spirit of the 1920's.

First there was the shimmy, the earliest dance expression of the jazz age. This was a demonstration of quivering shoulders and thighs, which was supposed to have originated on the Barbary Coast and then become popular in the dives of Chicago. The distinction of having been the first to make the shimmy famous on Broadway was hotly disputed by Gilda Gray and Bea Palmer, each of whom was celebrated for her shimmy performances. Gilda Gray had been a protégée of Sophie Tucker, who took the then-unknown dancer with her into a Sunday-night concert at the Winter Garden in 1918. There Gilda Gray did a shimmy to the music of "St. Louis Blues," with which she became the talk of the town. She kept doing the shimmy in the Broadway Theater after that—a star of the *Ziegfeld Follies of 1922* where her shimmy was performed to the strains of " 'Neath the South Sea Moon" and "It's Getting Dark on Old Broadway." Bea Palmer had also won her spurs as a shimmy artist in 1918—in the *Ziegfeld Follies*, in which she did her dance to "I Want to Learn to Jazz Dance."

There is a third claimant for the honors of first making the shimmy popular on the stage—Mae West. She had seen the shimmy (or, as it was then known, the "shimmy sha-wobble") in a Negro café in Chicago. A couple "got out on the floor," Mae West recalled in her autobiographical *Goodness Had Nothing to Do with It*, "and stood in one spot, with hardly any movement of the feet, and just shook their shoulders, torsos, breasts, and pelvises. We thought it was funny and were terribly amused by it. But there was a naked, aching sensual agony about it too." The next day, in vaudeville, Mae West improvised a dance like that for her act, and a week after that she performed the dance during her vaudeville appearances in Milwaukee. Finally she came to New York with it—in the Rudolf Friml musical *Sometime*, which opened on Broadway on October 4, 1918. "Mae West," reported Sime Silverman of *Variety*, "bowled them over with her songs and her dance known in the joints as the shimmy shawobble." There was also a fourth exponent of the shimmy, and to some she was the queen of the brood—Ann Pennington, whose shimmying was the main attraction of the *George White Scandals* of 1919 and 1920.

From the stage, the shimmy passed on into the ballroom

and even the home. Everybody was shimmying now—or, as a Dave Stamper number from the *Ziegfeld Follies of 1919* put it, "The World Is Going Shimmy Mad." The shimmy was glorified by Tin Pan Alley in such song hits as "Indianola," and "I Wish I Could Shimmy like My Sister Kate."

Then in 1923 the shimmy was rudely brushed aside by a new dance craze—the Charleston, a fast fox trot introduced in the all-Negro revue *Runnin' Wild*. The nationwide fame of the song "Charleston" accompanying this dance—the work of Cecil Mack and Jimmy Johnson—was a powerful factor in spreading the vogue of the Charleston all around the country. The vibrations of a thousand people doing the Charleston was believed to have caused the collapse of the floor at the Pickwick Club in Boston, a disaster that cost fifty lives. Nevertheless, the Charleston continued to thrive. At the Roseland ballroom on Broadway, a Charleston marathon dragged on for almost twenty-four hours. And one of the big scenes in the motion picture *Our Dancing Daughters* in 1928 showed Joan Crawford doing the Charleston.

In or about 1926, the black bottom superseded the Charleston. The phrase "black bottom" probably referred to the muddy bottom of the Swanee River, and the movements of the dance suggested the dragging of feet through the mud. In any event, Alberta Hunter is the one credited as its creator, having copyrighted it in 1926, and was the first to feature it successfully on the stage. The dance quickly made the rounds of burlesque, vaudeville, musical comedy, dance halls, and night clubs. One of the big production numbers in the *Scandals of 1926* was a black-bottom number—the song was by De Sylva, Brown, and Henderson and the dance was performed by the former shimmy queen Ann Pennington.

*

The jazz age in Tin Pan Alley emphasized the beat and the accent rather than the melody. For this reason the main distributor of Tin Pan Alley's music in the 1920's was not the singer any longer but the jazz band or orchestra. In the 1910's sheet music used to feature prominently the photographs of Nora Bayes, Al Jolson, Eddie Cantor, or Sophie Tucker; in the 1920's it concentrated on popular bandleaders. These orchestras, while hardly jazz "combos" in the New Orleans or Chicago meaning of the term, nevertheless did make effective use of jazz colors, effects, and rhythms; and many of the performers in these bands and orchestras had once been steeped in the traditions of genuine jazz.

The music of the commercial jazz band or orchestra differed from the New Orleans variety in that the emphasis lay not on improvisation but on formal arrangements. During the 1920's, the commercial jazz orchestras featured the songs of Tin Pan Alley in brilliant instrumental arrangements that made these numbers as effective for listening pleasure as for dancing. These jazz orchestras were featured prominently in night clubs, dance halls, public auditoriums, hotels, over radio and on records, in revues and musical comedies. It was now the jazz band—even more than the singing star of the stage—who would carry the songs of Tin Pan Alley throughout the United States. And it was now the band or orchestra leaders who would become the idols of a musical public.

Paul Whiteman and His Orchestra became the first of these great-name bands. For many years Whiteman had played the viola in the Denver Symphony. While performing his job there he used to enjoy gathering some of his colleagues into rag sessions. One day he dropped into a nightspot featuring New Orleans jazz. He was so taken with this music that then and there he decided to turn from symphonic to popular music. In 1917 he organized his first band. After World War I he enlarged it and called it the

Paul Whiteman Orchestra. An appearance at the Alexandria Hotel in Los Angeles was so successful that the engagement lasted more than a year. Then Whiteman hired Ferde Grofé as his orchestrator and pianist. Grofé, like Whiteman, had served a long apprenticeship in serious music before turning to jazz. The merger of Whiteman and Grofé marked the real beginnings of Whiteman's fame. With Grofé's ingenious and colorful orchestrations, and Whiteman's carefully prepared performances, the Whiteman Orchestra began gathering triumph after triumph by performing the popular songs of the day. Paul Whiteman's recording of "Whispering" in 1920 sold more than a million and a half records and was largely responsible for the immense success of that song. His rendition of "Three O'Clock in the Morning" in 1922 proved another substantial disk seller. At various times celebrated jazz artists were members of the Whiteman Orchestra, including Bix Beiderbecke, Red Nichols, Jimmy and Tommy Dorsey, and Joe Venuti; and among the vocalists affiliated with the ensemble from time to time were Mildred Bailey and the then-unknown Bing Crosby.

Besides selling millions of records, the Whiteman Orchestra appeared as a headline act in vaudeville and was starred in such revues as the *Follies* and the *Scandals*. In 1923 it made a triumphant tour of Europe. Over a period of years its performances at the Palais Royal made that night club one of the most successful on the Great White Way. Paul Whiteman was, indeed, the "king of jazz"—and that was the name used for the motion picture in which he and his orchestra appeared.

Whiteman's epoch-making achievement was a concert at Aeolian Hall in New York on February 12, 1924. For this "All-American Music Concert," jazz was featured from several different vantage points. Parts of the program consisted of Tin Pan Alley songs in Ferde Grofé's arrangements; part was made up of semiclassical pieces dressed up in jazz costume. The most significant contribution, however, came from those compositions in a symphonic-jazz idiom in which composers used the jazz style and idiom within the framework of serious musical structures. In this last category was found Gershwin's *Rhapsody in Blue*, commissioned for this very concert by Whiteman, and introduced by the Paul Whiteman Orchestra with the composer at the piano. Here the audience heard not a jazz arrangement nor an adaptation of a serious piece of music nor a popular piece in symphonic raiment, but an original work by a serious musical creator using jazz with artistic intent and with all the resources of good music at his command. "Somewhere in the middle of the score, I began crying," Whiteman later confessed. "When I came to myself I was eleven pages along, and until this day I cannot tell you how I conducted that far."

The *Rhapsody in Blue* gave meaning to Whiteman's concert, and it was the only work on the program that aroused the audience to a high pitch of excitement. For the *Rhapsody in Blue*—more than any other musical composition— caught the "roaring twenties" in tones in the same way that the Offenbach cancan reflected the French Second Empire and the waltz of Johann Strauss the Austria of the Hapsburgs. And the 1920's recognized at once that here was its testament, here its song of songs. Paul Whiteman's first recording for Victor sold a million disks in a few months' time. Before long the *Rhapsody in Blue* was heard on the stage, over the radio, in the concert hall, in the ballet theater and motion-picture palace, and then on the talking screen. It made Gershwin the most famous and most financially affluent serious composer in America. It brought a new stature to Paul Whiteman, who from then on used the slow melody of the *Rhapsody* as his theme music. Tin Pan Alley, which had thus far produced so many distinguished songs, had now witnessed one of its native sons producing a concert masterwork.

The success of Paul Whiteman—who was earning about ten thousand dollars a week for his personal appearances —made the jazz orchestra a welcome headliner in vaudeville and a star in the stage shows of leading movie houses. In the middle 1920's there were more than twenty such orchestras touring the vaudeville circuit. Many a celebrated vaudeville act that formerly had been satisfied with a piano accompanist now used full-sized jazz bands. The interest in jazz bands or jazz orchestras became so keen that one vaudeville theater—Proctor's Fifth Avenue—conducted amateur jazz-band contests.

Paul Whiteman's Orchestra encouraged some of its rivals to penetrate the concert hall with jazz performances of their own. Vincent Lopez and his orchestra offered a concert at the Metropolitan Opera House in 1925, featuring a symphonic potpourri entitled *The Evolution of the Blues*, in which Lopez played the *Maple Leaf Rag* and the number that became his signature "Nola." Though intended for the church, Lopez studied the piano from his boyhood days on. After three years of religious studies, he decided to exchange music for religion. He started playing the piano in Brooklyn saloons, beer halls and honky-tonks. In or about 1917 he was engaged as pianist and bandleader at the Pekin Restaurant in New York City, to become the youngest such maestro in the business; it was there and then that he played "Nola" for the first time. He held the job right through the era of World War I. When Prohibition threw the Pekin Restaurant out of business, Lopez and his band toured the vaudeville circuit. In 1921 they went to the Hotel Pennsylvania, there to initiate radio's first remote pickup. His salutation, "Hello, everybody, this is Lopez speaking," became as famous as the strains of his theme music. Besides his performances at the hotel, Lopez and his band were heard in vaudeville, stage shows, and at the Casa Lopez.

Neither Lopez' performance at the Metropolitan Opera, nor similar presentations by other bands in places like Carnegie Hall, achieved anything like the significance of Paul Whiteman's 1924 concert at Aeolian Hall. The main reason for this is that none of these concerts was able to produce a work in jazz idiom of the stature of the *Rhapsody in Blue*. The programs were generally filled with jazz treatments of classics and semiclassics. To provide jazz trimmings to pieces like the *Song of India*, or *Scheherazade*, or *Liebestraum*, or the *Dance of the Hours* merely demeaned and vulgarized good music without contributing an iota to the advancement of either popular music or jazz. This practice reached a low in taste with jazz versions of "The Star-Spangled Banner," the hymn "Rock of Ages," and the Spiritual "Deep River"; and it plunged to the depths of impropriety with a jazzed-up version of Chopin's "Funeral March" from the *Piano Sonata in B-flat Minor*. From across the ocean the eminent English music critic Ernest Newman bellowed, "Paws off!" while in Paris the French Society of Composers issued a formal protest.

But offering Tin Pan Alley tunes in fresh, attractive jazz orchestrations was something else again. In the 1920's the science of jazz orchestration advanced by leaps and bounds. In order to get its songs played by the leading bands, Tin Pan Alley was compelled to hire experts at instrumentation to prepare special arrangements for different orchestras, usually arrangements suiting the individual style of each ensemble. Many of these orchestrations were extraordinarily skillful. Tin Pan Alley's music was thus acquiring a new depth and dimension in orchestrations featured by ensembles led by Ben Bernie, Ted Lewis, Abe Lyman, Leo Reisman, Fred Waring, and many others, as

well as Whiteman and Lopez. There were even some authorities who liked to regard these orchestrations as a new
art form in music. Fritz Kreisler and Leopold Stokowski,
for example, found a good deal to admire in this type of
commercial jazz. Hiram K. Motherwell, a noted journalist,
had this to say about jazz orchestration: "I like to think
that it is a perfect expression of the American city, with its
restless bustle and motion, its multitude of unrelated details, and its underlying rhythmic progress towards a vague
Somewhere. Its technical resourcefulness continually sur-
prises me, and its melodies at their best delight me."

There were, to be sure, severe critics—mainly among
educators and the clergy. To John Roach Straton of the
Calvary Baptist Church in New York City, this kind of
jazz represented "music of the savage, intellectual and spiritual debauchery, utter degradation." The president of the
Christian and Missionary Alliance Conference charged that
because of jazz, "American girls of tender age are approaching jungle standards." One educator maintained that
"if we permit our boys and girls to be exposed indefinitely
to this pernicious influence, the harm that will result may
tear to pieces our whole social fabric."

Jazz, in terms of big-name bands, remained unaffected
by attack or criticism. The vogue swept right into the
1930's, when a new group of outstanding ensembles came
to the fore—headed by the Dorsey brothers, Glenn Miller,
Harry James, and Benny Goodman, the crowned "king of
swing."

Many of the big-name bands—like the big-time singers
of vaudeville and musical comedy—used identifying theme
songs from Tin Pan Alley. Just as Lopez had "Nola" and
Whiteman the slow section of the *Rhapsody in Blue*,
Tommy Dorsey had "I'm Gettin' Sentimental Over You";
Glenn Miller, "Moonlight Serenade"; Ted Lewis, "When
My Baby Smiles at Me"; Ben Bernie, "Au Revoir, Pleas-

ant Dreams"; Wayne King, "The Waltz You Saved for Me"; Kay Kyser, "Thinking of You."

Before the 1920's were over, a soothing antidote to the hyperthyroid accents and rhythms of commercial jazz had been introduced with Rudy Vallee's crooning. Sober, soft-toned, relaxed, crooning was almost like the musical warning that the inebriation of the twenties was dissipating and that the hangover of the thirties was just around the corner. To Tin Pan Alley, the greatest importance of the vogue for crooning lay in the fact that—like Jolson, Cantor, Nora Bayes, and Sophie Tucker before him—Rudy Vallee was a maker of hit songs.

Vallee started out in music by forming a band called the Yale Collegians when he was at Yale University. After leaving college, he organized the Connecticut Yankees, and in 1928 he and his band were engaged for the Heigh-Ho Club. There Vallee introduced his familiar "heigh-ho" salutation and began to use a megaphone (from then on his trademark) to amplify his small voice. After that Vallee and the Connecticut Yankees played in vaudeville, in musical comedies and revues, in motion pictures, and over the radio. For his very first broadcast on the Fleischmann Hour in 1929, he began using his identifying theme song "My Time Is Your Time." Over the radio, as well as in his public appearances, his enormous personal appeal and his infectious crooning style brought national popularity to new songs and long-forgotten songs. Among them were "I'm Just a Vagabond Lover," "Betty Co-Ed," "Stein Song," "There's a Tavern in the Town," "Good Night, Sweetheart," and Irving Berlin's "Say It Isn't So."

Before long, Rudy Vallee became involved in a "battle of crooners." A competitor, Will Osborne, came up with a claim that it was he and not Vallee who had invented the style of singing. Partly stimulated by their keen scent for a provocative news item, partly by the maneuvers of a publicity agent, journalists gave wide coverage to the feud. Now Osborne challenged Vallee to a ten-round fight to decide the issue; now he tried to instigate litigation for a half-million-dollar libel suit that never really got off the ground; now he had his lawyers issue an injunction to prevent the publication of Vallee's autobiography *Vagabond Dreams Come True*. Legal methods failing, Osborne tried to reduce Vallee's huge success with the University of Maine's "Stein Song" to the ridiculous by featuring on one of his programs a number titled "I'd Like to Break the Neck of the Man Who Wrote the Stein Song."

Vallee countered Osborne's acts, maneuvers, and attacks by pointing out that Osborne had just been a drummer when he, Vallee, had hired him, that he had taught Osborne his own approaches, techniques, and musical arrangements, and that he had started Osborne off on his career as a crooner by letting him take over the leadership of the Vallee orchestra while Vallee was out in Hollywood making a movie. "How this feud is going to end, nobody can guess," remarked the New York *Daily Mirror*. Then treating the whole affair with the facetiousness it deserved, the *Mirror* added: "Maybe the boys will hurl plums at forty paces, handfuls of confetti at a city block." What the feud ultimately accomplished was to give Osborne a good deal of publicity without in any way weakening Vallee's own position as the public's favorite crooner.

# 21

## "Looking at the world through rose-colored glasses"

During the 1920's the Broadway musical theater—the operetta, musical comedy, and the revue—began displacing vaudeville as Tin Pan Alley's prime showcase for new songs. The musical theater was now enjoying an era of unprecedented boom. The number of productions mounted were steadily increasing. Some seasons realized the opening of as many as fifty musicals, with four or five premières a night when the season was at its height. Staging and costuming had grown increasingly lavish; casts were studded with stars more plentifully than ever. Stage approaches and techniques had become slicker, dialogue and humor more sophisticated.

The opportunities offered to new creative talent by the expanding musical theater were increasing. Financial rewards were prodigious for those whose work was liked by the public. The percentage of box-office successes among produced musicals had never before—and has rarely since —been so high. With production costs low in relation to the admission prices, a musical that ran a hundred performances could expect to break even; a run of two hundred performances represented a profitable production; a three-hundred or four-hundred performance run was a smash hit. Even though the thousand-performance was as yet unknown, producing musicals in the 1920's was for the most part a profitable business.

With so many shows being put on the boards all the time, Tin Pan Alley had a ready-made market in which to display its wares. A song that went well on Broadway was sure to get recorded and heard over the radio—all of which spelled big sheet-music and record sales and large subsidiary revenues.

Except for the stars themselves, perhaps no single element of the musical theater was better calculated to bring audiences to the box office than a hit song. There was more than a single instance in the 1920's when a song—becoming a sudden hit—changed for the better the fortunes of a musical production. This happened in 1920 to *Mary* because it had Louis Hirsch's "Love Nest"; to *Little Jesse James* in 1923 because its score included Harry Archer's "I Love You"; to *The Girl Friend* of Rodgers and Hart in 1926 because the public had grown to like the title number and "Blue Room." Cole Porter's *The Gay Divorce* in 1932 became known as the "Night and Day show," and *Take a Chance*, also in 1932, as the "Eadie Was a Lady show." In each instance a song changed the tide of fortune for a production that at first looked as if it was doomed. Jerome Kern's *Roberta* in 1933 also might have had an early closing were it not for "Smoke Gets In Your Eyes."

There was much to attract and hold an audience's fascinated interest in those 1920 musicals: from the pulchritude of the chorus girls to the stupendous effects achieved by the large production numbers; from the comedy of stars like Ed Wynn, Victor Moore, or W. C. Fields to the tapping toes of Ann Pennington, Fred and Adele Astaire, and, later on, Bill Robinson. But what usually made the house electric and created a spell over the audience—what carried to the stage that touch of magic that once witnessed was never forgotten—were the times that the right song found the right singer. This was a marriage heaven-made—a marriage that made Tin Pan Alley and Broadway one.

This miracle took place in 1920 in Jerome Kern's *Sally* when Marilyn Miller brought an unforgettable glow and radiance to "Look for the Silver Lining." *Sally* was an expensive Ziegfeld production planned to glorify the one and only Marilyn Miller, whom Ziegfeld regarded as the most beautiful woman in the world and as the most glamorous personality in the musical theater of that day. Petite to the point of being precious, with a small voice which nevertheless exerted a hypnotic spell—and with a grace of body movement that was music in itself and a quality that was nothing short of ethereal—Marilyn Miller gave to her role and to the song "Look for the Silver Lining" a "curious enchantment," as P. G. Wodehouse and Guy Bolton later recalled, "that no reproduction in other lands or other mediums ever captures."

Something of Marilyn Miller's incandescence and magic flooded the stage of *Oh, Kay!* when Gertrude Lawrence sang George and Ira Gershwin's "Someone to Watch over Me." Gertrude Lawrence was a London star who was seen in the United States for the first time in *Charlot's Revue*, an importation. Broadway producers then began a scramble to get her to appear in an American-written musical comedy. Out of all the offers that came her way, she accepted that of Alex A. Aarons to appear in *Oh, Kay!*. And the reason she accepted it was that Gershwin was its composer, and she wanted to sing Gershwin's songs. For *Oh, Kay!*, produced in 1926, Gershwin wrote one of his most poignant love ballads—"Someone to Watch over Me." When Gertrude Lawrence sang it, she forthwith became one of the great ladies of the American musical theater.

"Bill"—music by Jerome Kern, words by P. G. Wodehouse—had to wait a number of years to be heard and appreciated, and it waited all that time because it could not find the right performer. "Bill" had been written in 1919 for *Oh, Lady, Lady*, but it was dropped when the proper place for it in the show—and the proper singer—could not be found. Kern then tried to fit it into *Sally*, but it was just not the right material for Marilyn Miller's small voice, and once again Kern had to admit defeat.

Then, in 1927, a dark-haired, soulful-eyed little girl with a throb in her voice was chosen for the role of the half-caste Julie in *Show Boat*. Her name was Helen Morgan. Kern knew when he auditioned her that here at last was the one to sing "Bill." The song was interpolated into the score—even though all the other musical numbers had lyrics by Oscar Hammerstein II—and "Bill" became Helen Morgan's song. Her plaintive, touching delivery has often been imitated but never really equaled.

There were many such wonderful stage moments between 1920 and 1930 when the right song and the right singer coalesced: Al Jolson singing "April Showers" in *Bombo* in 1921; Eddie Cantor with "Dinah" in *Kid Boots* in 1923 and with "Makin' Whoopee" in *Whoopee* in 1928; Grace Moore—her glamorous career in opera still ahead of her—presenting Irving Berlin's "What'll I Do?" in the *Music Box Revue of 1924*; Libby Holman's deep-throated wail of Ralph Rainger's "Moanin' Low" in the first *Little Show* in 1929 and of Johnny Green's "Body and Soul" in *Three's a Crowd* in 1930; Ruth Etting in her poignant presentation of "Love Me or Leave Me," a Donaldson song interpolated into *Whoopee;* the cataclysmic way in which Ethel Merman exploded in Gershwin's "I Got Rhythm" in *Girl Crazy* in 1930.

Tin Pan Alley's ace composers were now producing individual songs and full scores for the Broadway musical theater rather than concentrating their maximum productivity on numbers intended primarily for sheet-music distribution. Jerome Kern, for example. He came fully into his own as a Broadway composer in the 1910's. Then, in the 1920's, he went on to the heights of theatrical greatness.

One day, in 1914, Kern visited Dreyfus' office at Harms to play his songs from *The Girl from Utah* for Victor Herbert. When Kern finished playing a score that had included "They Didn't Believe Me," Herbert told Dreyfus: "This man will inherit my mantle."

Kern fulfilled this prophecy by dominating the musical theater of the 1910's and 1920's, and by revolutionizing it not once but twice. In the middle 1910's he joined with P. G. Wodehouse and Guy Bolton to evolve a new kind of musical comedy—intimate, informal, economical, sophisticated, thoroughly American. These productions came to be known as the "Princess Theater shows" because that was the theater where they were given. The most successful were *Very Good, Eddie* in 1915, *Oh, Boy* in 1917, and *Oh, Lady, Lady* in 1918. Kern's surpassing melodic charm yielded in these productions several remarkable songs, among which were "Babes in the Wood," "Nodding Roses," "Till the Clouds Roll By" (a title later used to name the Kern screen biography), and "The Magic Melody." Carl Engel, one of America's most distinguished musicologists, described "The Magic Melody" as "the opening chorus of an epoch" and went on to say of Kern: "A young man gifted with musical talent and unusual courage has dared to introduce into his tune a modulation which has nothing extraordinary in itself, but which marked a change, a new regime in American popular music. . . . It was a relief, a liberation."

Kern continued growing and developing. He wrote the music for the lavishly mounted Ziegfeld production *Sally*, in 1920. Marilyn Miller, the star of *Sally*, returned in 1925 to be the heroine in still another Jerome Kern musical, *Sunny*, where she sang "Who?" and "D'ye Love Me?" Then, two years later, Kern wrote the music for a production that once again invoked a new era for the musical theater—*Show Boat*.

With a book by Oscar Hammerstein II based on Edna Ferber's novel, *Show Boat* became the first musical to sidestep the accepted ritual of musical comedy and to use only those materials that could do justice to a play rich in atmosphere and local color, in characterizations, in dramatic interest. Here in *Show Boat* was one of the first and one of the most successful experiments to make every song basic to the development of character and story. But above and beyond that, "Ol' Man River," "Bill," "You Are Love," "Make Believe," "Why Do I Love You?" and "Can't Help Lovin' Dat Man" flooded the popular song with a glow and humanity and a deeper emotion than it had heretofore known. Songs like these—especially "Ol' Man River"— were lifted to the status of folk music. To this day, Kern's score remains a vibrant and unforgettable experience in the theater; to this day *Show Boat*, as a whole, remains a classic whose "grandeur and eloquence," as one critic said of it, "seem to increase with the passing of time."

The Princess Theater shows and *Show Boat* broke new ground for the American musical theater. This cannot be said of most of the musicals of the 1920's for which George Gershwin wrote the music and Ira Gershwin the lyrics,

Except for *Strike Up the Band!*, which came when the 1920's were just about over, Gershwin's musical comedies up to 1930 followed the accepted rule that a plot was there just to provide a means of offering songs, dances, humor, and production numbers. Indeed, the plots of these 1920 Gershwin musicals had little distinction and less originality. These musicals were contrived to offer entertainment. Any device was acceptable if it gave the stars an opportunity to shine, and provided songs that could be sung and danced to.

But there was one significant way in which Gershwin's musical comedy differed from most of those of the 1920's —and that was in the quality of the score. There was little obeisance made to formula, cliché, conventional procedures. George Gershwin could not operate that way. With his continual search for ever subtler effects, Gershwin brought to the best popular songs of these musicals a new concept of harmonic and rhythmic writing, a new pattern to the melodic line, which only Kern at his best could equal.

The first of these Gershwin musicals of the 1920's was *Lady Be Good*, in 1924, starring Fred and Adele Astaire. For this production Gershwin created "Fascinating Rhythm," infectious for its changing meters, the title song, whose repeated triplets in cut time produced a novel melodic effect, and "So Am I," with its personalized lyricism. No wonder then that the critic of the New York *Sun* described this music as "brisk, inventive, gay, nervous, delightful." But good as the score was, it would have been richer still had another song written for that show been allowed to stay in the production after the out-of-town tryouts. "The Man I Love"—its descending chromaticism providing an enchanting background for a poignant blues melody—is probably the most famous song Gershwin wrote, and it is one of his best. When *Lady Be Good* tried out, the song—intended for Adele Astaire in the opening scene—was found to slow up the action and was killed. A few years later, Gershwin thought of interpolating it into the first version of *Strike Up the Band!* Once again it was dropped. There were also plans afoot to have Marilyn Miller sing it in *Rosalie*, but these never jelled. Finally issued by Harms as an independent number, "The Man I Love" left Tin Pan Alley to become popular, first in London, then in Paris, and finally at its home base—especially in performances by Helen Morgan. By the time the second version of *Strike Up the Band!* had been crystallized and the show carried into New York City, "The Man I Love" had become too popular to be used. If any single number out of Tin Pan Alley can be said to have become a classic, its permanent survival assured, that number is "The Man I Love."

Not the least of the significance of *Lady Be Good* lay in the fact that this was the first show for which Ira Gershwin wrote all the lyrics for his brother's music. Previously he and George had collaborated only on random numbers. From *Lady Be Good* on, the songs of every important Gershwin musical comedy were a joint effort by the brothers. Just as George proved inimitable in his music, so Ira, in his masterful and subtle versification, became one of the top lyricists of his time.

There was hardly a Gershwin musical in the 1920's, even among the failures, which did not boast at least one song that stood out prominently from its context like pure gold in the company of brass. In 1925, *Tip Toes* boasted "Looking for a Boy," "That Certain Feeling," and "Sweet and Low Down." *Oh, Kay!*, in 1926, was a veritable treasure trove, with "Maybe," "Clap Yo' Hands," "Do, Do, Do," "Someone to Watch over Me," and "Fidgety Feet." *Funny Face*, in 1928, had "'S Wonderful," "He Loves and She Loves," and "The Babbitt and the Bromide," the last of which was particularly remarkable for its lyrics. In *Rosalie*, in 1928, "How Long Has This Been Going On?" was heard, while *Show Girl*, in 1929, offered "So Are You" and "Liza." "Liza" was sung not only on the stage (by Ruby Keeler) but also (for the first few nights at any rate) from the audience, where Al Jolson would jump from his seat to address a second chorus of the song to his wife.

The last of the successful traditional musical comedies by the Gershwin brothers was *Girl Crazy* in 1930. Here were born not only several extraordinary songs, but also a remarkable new musical-comedy star in the person of Ethel Merman. One-time typist in Astoria, Long Island, Ethel Merman (originally named Ethel Zimmerman) had made spasmodic appearances as a singer at small night clubs, weddings, parties, and at the Paramount Theater in Brooklyn. Without ever having appeared on Broadway, she auditioned for George Gershwin and was seized for the part of Kate Fothergill for *Girl Crazy*. Her first number there was "Sam and Delilah," which she delivered with shrill, metallic tones that electrified the audience. Later she brought down the house with "I Got Rhythm." She also sang "Boy, What Love Has Done to Me," in a resplendent score that included "Embraceable You" (sung by Ginger Rogers in her first Broadway starring role), "But Not for Me," and "Bidin' My Time."

Meanwhile, earlier in 1930, with *Strike Up the Band!* the Gershwins parted company for the first time with musical-comedy stereotypes and tried to explore new horizons for the theater. This musical was a gay takeoff on war and international politics—the book by Morrie Ryskind and George S. Kaufman tapping a vein of satire altogether fresh and novel in American musical comedy. The Gershwin music also found new resources in such songs as the title number, with its satirical overtones and with the ballad "Soon."

Finally, in 1931, came *Of Thee I Sing!*, the first musical

comedy to win the Pulitzer Prize. The book by George S. Kaufman and Morrie Ryskind here made sport of politics in Washington, D. C., and a presidential election. There were hit songs such as the title number, "Love Is Sweeping the Country" and the satirical "Wintergreen for President." But with this came all kinds of choral numbers, orchestral interludes, and large musical episodes (made up of recitatives, songs, and choruses) with which musical comedy acquired new size and dimension. "George Gershwin," wrote Brooks Atkinson, "has compounded a score that sings in many voices, simmers with ideas, and tells the story more resourcefully than the book. . . . It has very nearly succeeded in liberating the musical-comedy stage from the mawkish and feeble-minded formula that has long been considered inevitable."

Irving Berlin's first significant Broadway assignment after World War I came in 1919 with songs for the *Ziegfeld Follies* of that year. One was "A Pretty Girl Is like a Melody," sung by John Steel, and used as background music for a stunning parade of *Follies* beauties, each representing some such musical classic as "Traumerei," "Humoresque," or "Elégie." "A Pretty Girl Is like a Melody" became the theme song of the *Follies*. It is also the song heard most often at fashion shows and beauty contests all over the world. This was also the edition of the *Follies* in which Eddie Cantor presented the suggestive "You'd Be Surprised," and in which Van and Schenck sang "Mandy," which Berlin had previously written for *Yip, Yip, Yaphank*.

In 1927, Berlin once again served as composer-lyricist for the *Follies*, this time providing all the numbers (except for one or two interpolations)—the first time in the history of the *Follies* that one man was required to perform this chore. To the production Berlin contributed "It's Up to the Band" sung by the Brox Sisters and "Shaking the Blues Away" with which Ruth Etting made her *Follies* bow. (But the big song of this edition was not a Berlin number but an interpolation by Eddie Cantor—Walter Donaldson's "My Blue Heaven.")

Between 1921 and 1925, Berlin wrote the book, music, and lyrics for four editions of a splendiferous new revue that offered serious competition to the *Follies*. This was called the *Music Box Revue*, named after the Music Box Theater, a handsome new auditorium on Forty-fifth Street that opened with the première of the first *Music Box Revue*. "Such ravishingly beautiful tableaux, such gorgeous costumes, such a wealth of comedy and spectacular freshness, such a piling of Pelion on Ossa of everything that is decorative, dazzling, harmonious, intoxicatingly beautiful in the theater—all that and more was handed out in a program that seemed to have no ending." This was the way the editor of *Theater Magazine* described the show, which opened for a year's run on September 22, 1921. Berlin's top-flight score included one of his all-time favorites, "Say It with Music," and one of his last and best exercises in ragtime, "Everybody Step."

The other three editions—in 1922, 1923, and 1924— were even more lavish in costuming, scenery, production numbers, and stars. Here, as in the first production, Berlin's songs were a prime attraction—such songs as "Pack Up Your Sins," "Lady of the Evening," "Crinoline Days," "What'll I Do?" and "All Alone." The last two were made particularly memorable as sung by Grace Moore, a fledgling at the time.

During the 1920's, Berlin wrote the music for only one musical comedy. This was *The Cocoanuts*, a zany musical about the Florida real-estate boom and the phonies that helped promote it. With their improvisations and ad-libs, the Four Marx Brothers, the stars of the show, made a shambles of plot, dialogue, and situations (as George S. Kaufman had originally put them down on paper).

Season after season, Broadway was enriched by the labors of Tin Pan Alley's troubadours. Jean Schwartz wrote the scores for the *Passing Show of 1921* and *Artists and Models of 1923*. Albert von Tilzer provided the music for one of the leading musical-comedy successes of the early 1920's—*The Gingham Girl* in 1922. J. Fred Coots produced the songs for *Sally, Irene and Mary* in 1922, as well as the scores for the 1924 and 1925 editions of *Artists and Models*, for *A Night in Paris*, and the musical comedy *Sons o' Guns*. Harry Ruby was the composer of *Helen of Troy, New York*, of *The Ramblers*, and of *Animal Crackers*, the last of which was another Marx Brothers escapade. Harry Tierney created the score for *Kid Boots*, which starred Eddie Cantor in 1923, and *Rio Rita*, a spectacle that helped open the new Ziegfeld Theater on Sixth Avenue in 1927; the music of still another Eddie Cantor triumph, *Whoopee*, was the work of Walter Donaldson.

The neophytes of Tin Pan Alley, as well as its experienced hands, were now directing their main interest and attention through Broadway channels. Of these newcomers none was more productive in the 1920's than the team of De Sylva, Brown, and Henderson. Before joining forces as a trio of songwriters and coming to Broadway, each of the men had individually achieved Tin Pan Alley renown. Buddy De Sylva began writing lyrics while he was still going to college, some of which interested Al Jolson, who interpolated them in his Winter Garden shows. When De Sylva received his first Tin Pan Alley royalty check—it read sixteen thousand dollars—he decided to drop college and pursue his songwriting future more actively. He found a job at Remick's, in whose employ he wrote lyrics for George Gershwin's first musical comedy, *La, La, Lucille*, in 1919. In the next few years De Sylva provided words for the music of Kern, Victor Herbert, Gershwin, and many others. His biggest hits included Kern's "Look for the Silver Lining," Herbert's "A Kiss in the Dark," Gershwin's "Somebody Loves Me," Louis Silvers' "April Showers," and "If You Knew Susie" (the last was an Eddie Cantor specialty and was one of the rare instances in which De Sylva wrote his own music).

Lew Brown worked for the publishing house of Albert von Tilzer. There for a number of years he wrote lyrics to Albert von Tilzer's melodies. These included: "I'm the Lonesomest Gal in Town" in 1912; the World War I ballad "I May Be Gone for a Long, Long Time"; the nonsense song "Oh, By Jingo"; and "I Used to Love You." After World War I, Lew Brown's lyrics were set by composers other than Von Tilzer.

In 1922, his lyric "Georgette" (which Ted Lewis and his band introduced that year in the *Greenwich Village Follies*) had a melody by Ray Henderson.

Henderson had studied music at the Chicago Conservatory of Music, and, while there he supported himself by playing popular piano with jazz bands and at parties. Occasionally he appeared in vaudeville in an act that included an Irish tenor and a Jewish comedian. Finally arriving at the decision that his forte was composing music, Henderson came to New York City and for a while worked as Leo Feist's song plugger. After that he worked as staff pianist and arranger for Fred Fisher and later on for Shapiro-Bernstein. It was Bernstein who encouraged Henderson to concentrate on songwriting and arranged for Lew Brown to work with him. Their first collaboration, "Georgette," was a minor success. After 1922, Henderson collaborated with other lyricists. With Mort Dixon and Billy Rose he wrote "That Old Gang of Mine," which was published by Irving Berlin in 1923 and introduced that year in the

*Ziegfeld Follies* by Van and Schenck. For a number of months this song sold thirty thousand copies a day regularly. "Alabamy Bound," with words by Buddy De Sylva and Bud Green, sold more than a million copies following its publication in 1925. "Five Feet Two, Eyes of Blue" and "I'm Sitting on Top of the World"—both of which also appeared in 1925—also did extraordinarily well, the latter particularly after Al Jolson adopted it as one of his favorites.

When George Gershwin left the *Scandals* in 1924 to concentrate on musical comedies, George White engaged the team of De Sylva, Brown, and Henderson to replace him. Though Henderson had previously worked with both De Sylva and with Brown, the *Scandals of 1925* was the first time that the three men worked as a creative unit. It was truly an unusual combination. While De Sylva and Brown were lyricists and Henderson a composer, each member provided the other two with significant guidance, advice, and ideas; it could truly be said that each of their songs was a three-way collaboration, in the strictest meaning of that term.

De Sylva, Brown, and Henderson hit their full creative stride in several editions of the *Scandals*, with songs like "The Birth of the Blues," "Black Bottom," "Lucky Day," and "The Girl Is You." While employed by George White, De Sylva, Brown, and Henderson also planted their feet more solidly in Tin Pan Alley by forming their own publishing outfit that issued not only their stage music but also a series of hit songs not intended for any specific production, such as "It All Depends on You" in 1926 and "Just a Memory" in 1927.

During the year of 1927, George White produced no new edition of the *Scandals*. This was the year that De Sylva, Brown, and Henderson chose to invade musical comedy. This debut took place with *Good News,* one of the year's leading box-office attractions, a musical show reflecting the fascination of the 1920's for college life and its shenanigans. Among its principal songs were "The Varsity Drag," the title number "Good News," and "The Best Things in Life Are Free"—the last of which provided the title for the screen biography of De Sylva, Brown, and Henderson in 1956.

In *Hold Everything*, in 1928, De Sylva, Brown, and Henderson turned from college to boxing. In *Follow Through*, in 1929, they invaded the world of country clubs and golf. In *Flying High*, in 1930, they turned to air pilots and aviation. Each show had its quota of important song hits. The cream of the crop were: "You're the Cream in My Coffee"; "Button Up Your Overcoat"; "You Are My Lucky Star"; "Thank Your Father"; and "Wasn't It Beautiful While It Lasted?"

Another significant neophyte to emerge from Tin Pan Alley and achieve his full creative powers on Broadway was Vincent Youmans. Like Kern and Gershwin, he may well be regarded as a Max Dreyfus discovery. Twenty-two-year-old Youmans was the composer of a single published song when Max Dreyfus took him under his wing at Harms by employing him as staff pianist and song plugger. Youmans had been educated to be an engineer, and just before World War I he worked as a clerk in a Wall Street brokerage house. His ambition to become a popular composer was first nurtured when, as a navy man, he wrote and produced shows for naval personnel. One of the numbers he wrote during this period became popular with army and navy bands and was frequently played throughout the war. But after the war it became an even greater favorite outside the armed forces when Youmans adapted the melody for the song "Hallelujah."

How valuable Youmans regarded his apprenticeship under Max Dreyfus in Tin Pan Alley was proved by his own statement that "in less than a year I got something that money couldn't buy." He was talking about experiences as a song salesman that taught him first hand some of the secrets that made a song "tick" with the public. He then wrote his first musical-comedy score in collaboration with Paul Lannin, *Two Little Girls in Blue*. Ira Gershwin wrote all of the lyrics, and through Ira, Youmans was able to bring his music to George Gershwin's notice. George, impressed with what he heard, used his influence to get producer Alex A. Aarons to mount it on Broadway. The show opened on May 3, 1922, ran for more than a year, and yielded a modest hit song in "Oh Me, Oh My, Oh You." Youmans was on his way.

In 1923 came *Wildflower* for which Otto Harbach and Oscar Hammerstein II wrote book and lyrics; its score was a joint effort by Youmans and Herbert Stothart. *Wildflower* was an even greater box-office success than *Two Little Girls in Blue*. It ran for almost five hundred performances, and out of it came not one but two song hits, "Bambalina" and the title number.

Between 1925 and 1927, Youmans' two greatest stage triumphs, and two finest scores, made him one of the giant figures in the American musical theater. *No, No, Nanette*, in 1925, ran a year on Broadway, enjoyed over six hundred and fifty performances in London, and was seen throughout the rest of the civilized world in presentations by seventeen companies. Two of Youmans' standards were heard here: "Tea for Two" and "I Want to Be Happy." Two other Youmans standards—"Sometimes I'm Happy" and "Hallelujah"—were written for *Hit the Deck*, which opened on Broadway in 1927.

*Hit the Deck* was Youmans' last successful Broadway musical for which he wrote the entire score; but it was not the last of his Broadway productions for which he created song classics. In fact, one of his greatest fiascos—*Great Day*, which lasted only thirty-six performances—had no less than three Youmans gems: the title song, "More than You Know," and "Without a Song." *Smiles* in 1930 (sixty-three performances) introduced "Time on My Hands." *Through the Years* in 1932 (twenty performances) was the source of the title number—the composer's own favorite among his creations—and "Drums in My Heart." With *Take a Chance* the same year—for which Youmans wrote "Rise 'n Shine"—Youmans finally was able to break his losing streak on Broadway. *Take a Chance* was a moderate success, but that success was not exclusively Youmans' since part of the score was the work of Richard A. Whiting.

# 22

## "Some enchanted evening"

The highway that stretched from Tin Pan Alley to the Broadway theater went in two directions. Just as many a Tin Pan Alley tunesmith made the trip from his home base to the Great White Way, many a composer and songwriter from Broadway made his way to Tin Pan Alley. These composers had received their experiences and first successes within the theater and wrote their finest numbers for Broadway before these songs passed on to Tin Pan Alley for publication and further exploitation.

Rudolf Friml—his world being operetta—was such a composer; he had come from obscurity to fame inside a theater. In the 1920's the operetta was arriving at the sunset of its long rich day. With Friml—and with Sigmund

Romberg—it was still able to cast a wondrous light before twilight set in.

During the last years of his life, Victor Herbert, the prince of American operetta, was on the downgrade, both as to the quality of his music and the stature of his successes. His last profitable operetta was *Sweethearts* in 1913; for this production Herbert wrote two fine songs, the title number and "The Angelus." *Eileen*, in 1917, was a failure, despite the fact that out of it came one of Herbert's most remarkable and most successful ballads "Thine Alone."

Though Herbert remained productive until the end of his days, all he managed to produce of value after 1917 were one or two good songs such as "A Kiss in the Dark." As far as operettas went, he had lost the golden touch. "My day is over," he remarked sadly to one of his friends. "They are forgetting poor old Herbert." When he died in New York City on May 26, 1924—while working on some material for the *Ziegfeld Follies*—he had long since lost his place as America's foremost operetta composer.

But there were others to take his place, especially Rudolf Friml. Friml, indeed, came upon the Broadway scene while Herbert was still in his prime; and it was because of Herbert that Friml got his first chance to write for the theater. In 1911, Herbert was writing an operetta for Emma Trentini, the star of Herbert's *Naughty Marietta* in 1910. Before Herbert could get to work on his score, he and his star had a serious falling-out. Heatedly, Herbert announced that under no circumstances would he ever have any further traffic with Madame Trentini; and the prima donna was just as resolute in her decision never to appear again in a Herbert operetta.

With a new operetta scheduled for Emma Trentini in 1912, another composer had to be found to replace Herbert. When the choice was finally made—and it was made by the publishers Max Dreyfus and Gus Schirmer—the prize went to a completely obscure composer, one who thus far had written no popular music whatsoever and who had had no experience on Broadway. He was Rudolf Friml, a Bohemian concert pianist who had settled in the United States in 1906. Since then he had pursued a career as pianist, teacher, and composer of concert songs and serious piano pieces published by G. Schirmer. Both Schirmer and Dreyfus were convinced that Friml had the potential for a successful operetta composer. They convinced Arthur Hammerstein, producer of the Emma Trentini production, to take a chance on him. The gamble paid off handsomely. The operetta was *The Firefly*, which opened for an extended run on December 2, 1912. And Friml's score—his first attempt at writing popular music—yielded such gems as "Giannina Mia," "The Dawn of Love," "Love Is like a Firefly" and "When a Maid Comes Knocking at Your Heart."

Actually not even in publication did these remarkable songs become part and parcel of Tin Pan Alley, since they were issued by G. Schirmer, whose main activity lay in the publication of serious music and musical exercises. But as Friml's career unfolded on Broadway with all its richness and variety, he too became a legitimate son of Tin Pan Alley. By the time he had written and had produced his greatest operettas—*Rose Marie* in 1924, *The Vagabond King* in 1925, *The Three Musketeers* in 1928—Max Dreyfus had contracted him for Harms. And it was under the Harms imprint that Friml's song classics of the 1920's flowed throughout the country in their sheet-music publications: "Rose Marie," "Indian Love Call," "Only a Rose," "Song of the Vagabonds," "Huguette Waltz," "Heart of Mine," and "All for One."

Sigmund Romberg was the last of America's great operetta composers. Before 1913 he was busily occupied: as the director of a restaurant orchestra he had become a pioneer in initiating social dancing in an eating establishment; and he had written two two-steps and a waltz that were published. Then, in 1913 he was engaged as staff composer for the Broadway producing firm of J. J. Shubert. In this job, over a three-year period, he completed seventeen scores for revues, extravaganzas, and other musicals produced by Shubert, including several starring Al Jolson at the Winter Garden.

In 1915, Romberg directed his rare gift at melody into operetta. *The Blue Paradise,* produced that year, was set in Vienna, a city Romberg had known intimately; it had the kind of European background and atmosphere to which Romberg could respond instinctively. For this reason, perhaps, his music for *The Blue Paradise* was the best he had thus far created; and it was the source of "Auf Wiedersehen," the first of his remarkable waltzes and the first of his formidable song hits. In 1917, Romberg scored an even greater success with *Maytime.* Here several Romberg hits were born, most notably the waltz "Will You Remember?" which served as a recurring leitmotiv throughout the production.

Up to this point, Romberg's music had been published by Schirmer, a fact that put him outside the periphery of Tin Pan Alley. But in 1919, Romberg signed a lucrative contract with M. Witmark and Sons. Now as a Witmark and a Tin Pan Alley composer, Romberg headed for the greatest song triumphs of his career. In 1921 came *Blossom Time,* an operetta supposedly based on incidents in the life of the great Viennese composer Franz Schubert, whose music Romberg adapted and commercialized. *Blossom Time* ran on Broadway almost two years and was produced by four road companies. *The Student Prince* followed in 1924, amassing six hundred and eight performances and boasting nine road companies. After that followed *The Desert Song* in 1926 and *New Moon* in 1928—each a box-office attraction of the first order. Hit song after hit song emerged from each of these many Romberg productions: "Song of Love," "Deep in My Heart," "Serenade," "Golden Days," "One Alone," "Blue Heaven," "Softly As in a Morning Sunrise," "One Kiss," "Wanting You." They made Romberg the main cog in the Witmark hit machinery. In fact, these songs—particularly those from *The Student Prince*—were directly responsible for saving the Witmark company from bankruptcy. As Isidore Witmark revealed in his autobiography, *From Ragtime to Swingtime*, the Witmark firm had been in serious trouble after 1923. It had made an expensive move uptown to a new building and had instituted a major expansion program. Despite its catalogue of standards, and two recent hits in "I'm Goin' South" and "California, Here I Come," the house had fallen upon bad days. In the face of seemingly inevitable doom, the lawyers urged the Witmarks to start bankruptcy proceedings.

At that time one of Witmark's competitors tried to induce Romberg to leave Witmark and come to its company. The publisher even promised to pay all lawsuits and damages if Witmark were to bring a breach-of-contract action against Romberg; and, as additional bait, he dangled before Romberg a bonus of fifty thousand dollars. But Romberg refused to listen to such siren calls. He insisted he would stick by his agreement with Witmark to the end; thus the songs from *The Student Prince* remained a Witmark property. With nine road companies and a box-office return in excess of eight million dollars, *The Student Prince* inevitably inspired a sustained interest in its rich storehouse of wonderful melodies. The Witmarks made a fortune from these songs and through them were able to catch their second wind. The songs from *The Desert Song* and *The New Moon*, which Witmark later published, were the insurance that this publishing house needed to keep its prosperity permanent.

Musical comedy also yielded its quota of composers who first grew successful in the theater before their work was profitably used by Tin Pan Alley. And the greatest of them all was Richard Rodgers.

Born in Hammels Station, near Arverne, Long Island, in 1902, Dick Rodgers began writing songs when he was fourteen, and was soon contributing numbers for various amateur shows. While attending Columbia College he became the first freshman to create the music for its annual varsity show. In this production Rodgers found a valuable helpmate in Lorenz Hart, the author of the song lyrics. Hart remained Rodgers' lyricist for the next quarter of a century and was his partner as Rodgers first scaled the heights in the musical theater.

As a high-school student, Rodgers had tried to penetrate the stronghold of Tin Pan Alley. He came to Harms with a letter of introduction to Max Dreyfus, for whom he played some of his tunes. Dreyfus listened, his face inscrutable. When Dick finished, Dreyfus asked: "What do you do with your time when you're not writing songs?" Rodgers told him he was going to high school. "Then," remarked Dreyfus icily, "pay attention to your schoolwork and leave songs to professionals."

After he had completed his first Columbia varsity show in 1920, Rodgers tried again to interest Dreyfus, this time playing for him the varsity show music. "There's nothing there worth anything," Dreyfus told him. But by 1920, Rodgers had managed to get one of his songs published in Tin Pan Alley and sung in the Broadway theater. Named "Any Old Place with You," it was interpolated into *A*

*Lonely Romeo,* at the Casino Theater, on August 26, 1919, after which it was published by Remick.

But like Friml and Romberg before him, Rodgers did not become a significant creator of songs for Tin Pan Alley until he had made his mark on Broadway indelibly. But this was a development still a number of years away.

In 1920, Rodgers and Hart contributed half the score for the Broadway musical comedy *Poor Little Ritz Girl,* the other half of which was the work of Sigmund Romberg. *Poor Little Ritz Girl* got some good notices, but it did practically nothing to further Rodgers' career. For several years, the only place he could find for his songs was in amateur productions. Meanwhile, in an effort to learn something more about his craft, Rodgers went for a two-year period of intensive music study at the Institute of Musical Art.

The first sweet taste of success came in 1925 with *The Garrick Gaieties.* This was an intimate, sophisticated revue put on by the young members of the Theater Guild to raise money for draperies for the new Broadway theater that would house Guild productions. Rodgers and Hart contributed a few songs, out of which leaped their first two hits—"Manhattan" and "Sentimental Me." On the strength of this success—and on the strength of the popular appeal of the two main songs, which were put into sheet music by Edward B. Marks—Max Dreyfus summoned Rodgers and Hart into his office to sign an exclusive Harms contract. Diplomatically, Rodgers did not recall to Dreyfus his earlier frustrated attempts to interest the publisher. He did his best to suppress a smile of victory when Dreyfus growled to him that he should have brought Harms "Manhattan" before allowing Marks to publish it. "Manhattan" had been one of the numbers Rodgers had played for Dreyfus when the young composer had come to him with his Columbia varsity show, only to be soundly and decisively rejected!

After 1925, Rodgers and Hart wrote, and had produced, a number of musical comedies that not only carried them to a high elevation of Broadway success but that also introduced new sophistication, freshness of viewpoint, and progressive techniques into the musical theater. In all this they were aided and abetted by Herbert Fields, who provided them with their librettos. By seeking out unusual subjects, by insisting on trying out all kinds of new approaches, the trio of Rodgers, Hart, and Fields helped to rid musical comedy of some of its stultifying platitudes. As I have written elsewhere: "In an age when musical comedy still was a machine-made product, Rodgers, Hart, and Fields introduced the handmade creations of craftsmen who touched their work with an artistic and personal stamp."

*Dearest Enemy* in 1925 tore a page from the American history book. It amplified on a Revolutionary War episode in which Mrs. Robert Murray, on instructions from General Washington, delayed some British soldiers at her New York home long enough to permit the Continental Army to manage a strategic withdrawal. *Peggy-Ann* in 1926 was a fantasy that exploited dream psychology—a subject still virgin soil for Broadway. *A Connecticut Yankee* in 1927 was an adaptation of a literary classic by Mark Twain.

These and other musical comedies by Rodgers and Hart —some seasons found as many as four of their productions on the boards—were filled with methods and materials that changed musical comedy. *Peggy-Ann,* for example, had no dancing or singing for the first fifteen minutes. Thus the age-old tradition that the opening curtain must rise on a big musical scene was defied. Musical comedy was also supposed to end in a similar way, with the full cast crowding the stage and singing at the top of their lungs. But *Peggy-*

*Ann* closed with a slow comedy dance performed on a darkened stage.

No less original, no less striking, and no less imaginative were the lyrics of Lorenz Hart and the melodies of Dick Rodgers. All these musical comedies contained hit songs galore, to the delight of Max Dreyfus: "Here in My Arms"; "The Girl Friend"; "The Blue Room"; "My Heart Stood Still"; "You Took Advantage of Me"; "With a Song in My Heart." Hart's rhyming and rhythms marked a new age for the song lyric—with his exterior and interior rhymes; male and female rhymes; inventive turns of phrases and figures of speech; insouciant attitudes; and his capacity to create shock through the sudden introduction of an unexpected thought or mood. He was, indeed, as was so often said of him, the first lyricist "to make any real assault on the intelligence of the song-listening public."

As different, as brilliant, as varied as Hart's words, were the melodies Rodgers wrote for them. Now his melodic line veered refreshingly in an unexpected direction; now a phrase was marked by an unusual melodic structure; now a new concept for popular music of rhythm, harmony, modulation was realized; now the song structure underwent expansion; and now the lyricism gained in expressiveness and poignancy, or in wit and sophistication, through its unusual design. Like the best songs of Gershwin and Kern, those of the young Rodgers represented a shining new era both for Broadway and for Tin Pan Alley.

Before the 1920's ended, Max Dreyfus added to the already well-stocked Harms lists another formidable creator of theater music—Cole Porter, who, in 1928, was represented on Broadway with *Paris*, starring Irene Bordoni. *Paris* was Cole Porter's first successful musical comedy, and from its score Harms lifted for exploitation Porter's most successful song up to that time, "Let's Do It."

Porter was born to wealth, in Peru, Indiana, in 1893. Though he early showed an unusual musical gift, he was directed to law. At Yale he distinguished himself by writing two still-popular football songs—"Bulldog" and "Bingo Eli Yale." He also made a brief entry into Tin Pan Alley in 1910 with "Bridget," a song published by Remick. By 1913 he had entered Harvard Law School. There, its perceptive dean convinced him to transfer to the school of music. It was while he was deep in music study that Porter wrote his first musical score for Broadway—*America First*, which lasted only two weeks in 1916.

Porter made a second appearance on Broadway as composer three years after that. Meanwhile he had served in the French Foreign Legion; then, during World War I, he taught French gunnery to American soldiers at Fontainebleau. His return to Broadway came through the music and lyrics for *Hitchy Koo of 1919*, which offered his first song hit, "An Old-Fashioned Garden."

Before Porter challenged Broadway for a third time, several important things had happened to his personal life. He had married an American socialite, Linda Lee Thomas; he had inherited a million dollars from his grandfather; and he had set up a swank home in Paris to embark upon the life of a playboy. He gave grandiose parties attended by the bright lights of Europe's social, political, and cultural life. A child of the 1920's, Porter lived life to a full measure—in Paris, on the Riviera, at the Lido in Venice. But all the time he kept on writing songs, already significant for their scintillating and sophisticated lyrics, with all kinds of esoteric, exotic, and erotic allusions that set them apart from the work of the other lyricists of that day, just as his sensual melodies, with the broad sweep of the lyric line towards an exciting climax, separated his work from that of composers of the day. "You are much too good," Elsa Maxwell once told him. "Your standards are too high.

But one day you will haul the public up to your own level, and then the world will be yours."

In 1924, Porter contributed five songs to the *Greenwich Village Follies;* nobody paid much attention to them. It was with *Paris* in 1928—with Irene Bordoni's infectious and provocative rendition of "Let's Do It" in her saucy French accent—that Cole Porter first emerged, both as lyricist and composer, as the voice of the roaring twenties (even though the twenties were now drawing to their close). That voice sounded louder and stronger in 1929 in the score of *Fifty Million Frenchmen,* for which Porter wrote "You Do Something to Me" and "Find Me a Primitive Man." The following year, 1930, brought "What Is This Thing Called Love?" in *Wake Up and Dream* and "Love for Sale" in *The New Yorkers.* The Cole Porter way with a song was now fully realized.

## 23

## "The music goes 'round and 'round"

In 1919, Irving Berlin formed his own publishing company. Max Winslow, the man who had discovered Berlin a decade earlier, was made its vice president. The new firm opened its offices not on Twenty-eighth Street but within the Broadway sector. Irving Berlin was not the first publisher to operate away from Twenty-eighth Street. In fact, the organization from which he had broken away—the firm of Waterson, Berlin and Snyder—had for some time been located in the Strand Theater Building in the heart of the theatrical district.

Tin Pan Alley had always followed the theater. It had moved from Union Square to Twenty-eighth Street to follow the theater. After World War I, it happened again.

The minstrel show was dying: there were hardly more

than six or seven companies left in the entire country. Vaudeville was beginning to peter out. In 1926 only twelve theaters catered exclusively to vaudeville; two-a-days had given way to continuous performances; the Palace Theater, the last stronghold of great vaudeville entertainment, was now offering movies with its live acts. This was the beginning of the end for vaudeville—and the end was not far off now.

The main stage outlet for the songs of Tin Pan Alley, therefore, was now operetta, musical comedy, and revue. With the hub of the theater world concentrated on or near Broadway—roughly between Fortieth and Fiftieth Streets —the locale of Twenty-eighth Street for publishing was no longer practicable. By the middle 1920's, Feist and Remick were located on West Fortieth Street. F. B. Haviland had come to West Forty-fourth Street; Harms to West Forty-fifth Street; and Charles K. Harris to West Forty-seventh Street. Von Tilzer, Irving Berlin, and Witmark planted themselves on Broadway proper. No longer concentrated on a single street as it had been since 1900, Tin Pan Alley was becoming decentralized for the first time in more than a half-century. But, though scattered over a larger area than heretofore, the various firms still operated with a common program and toward a common goal. Twenty-eighth Street might no longer be the street of song, but Tin Pan Alley was still alive.

A number of new firms came into being after 1920: Jack Mills, Inc., which published Zez Confrey's piano rags, of which the most famous was "Kitten on the Keys"; Fred Fisher, Inc., controlled by that song composer; Edward B. Marks Music Company (successor to the historic Joseph W. Stern & Company); Yellen and Borenstein, which before long also included Milton Ager, the composer, and was renamed Ager, Yellen and Borenstein; Richmond-Robbins, which started out as the Maurice Richmond Company. Most of these were found in or close to the theaters of Broadway; and some introduced new viewpoints and new methods to song publishing. Jack Robbins, for example, was one of the first in Tin Pan Alley to recognize the significance of name bands to the song business. He is credited with having encouraged Vincent Lopez to start a band; to have brought Paul Whiteman and His Orchestra to the attention of the recording industry; to have helped make famous the George Olsen Orchestra.

The offices of the more affluent of these publishers along Broadway were growing increasingly spacious and more opulent. The one-time plugger's cubicles were now frequently handsomely appointed professional parlors where performers could drop in for their copies of current hits. Rehearsal rooms were available where these numbers could be tried out. Elegant parlors, with grand pianos, provided the leading composers of the different firms—together with their friends and colleagues—with a comfortable place to transact business or to use for social engagements.

One of the most celebrated of these professional parlors in the 1920's was the one at Harms at 62 West 45th Street. There held sway such kings of Tin Pan Alley as Kern, Gershwin, Rodgers, Youmans—and, later on, Cole Porter. Important composers and lyricists of that day made it a habit to drop in at Harms during the noonday hour for some music, shoptalk, social palaver. George Gershwin could be found there several times a week. Harry Ruby, Bert Kalmar, Joe Meyer, Buddy De Sylva, Vincent Youmans, Irving Caesar, Paul Charig—later on, Arthur Schwartz, Vernon Duke, and Harold Arlen—hovered around Gershwin like satellites. In *A Journey to Greatness*, my biography of George Gershwin, I wrote: "George often played for his friends his latest creations or works in progress. Irving Caesar was something of the court jester, delighting the group with impromptu parodies and improvised opera arias. Once, while waiting for the others, Bill Daly (the orchestra leader and one of Gershwin's closest friends) accompanied Caesar on the piano as the latter hummed the "Depuis le jour" aria from the opera *Louise*. When Youmans and Gershwin appeared, they listened to the air with rapt attention, Gershwin exclaiming, 'Why, it's wonderful, really wonderful, when did you write it?' He thought it was a new song by Bill Daly, which Daly and Caesar were trying out for the first time. The younger composers and lyricists would sometimes use this social period at Harms to discuss new projects with the Harms editor, Dr. Albert Sirmay, and their patron saint, Max Dreyfus. Dreyfus would then take a few of them out to lunch at the Hunting Room in the Hotel Astor where the special Dreyfus table was reserved for them."

Young composers, still wet behind the ears, would come up to Harms at this noon-hour session to play their unpublished pieces for Gershwin. He saw all visitors, welcomed them as warmly as if they were friends. One visitor was the lawyer Arthur Schwartz, for whom the writing of songs, in 1925, was still a diversion. Schwartz had been so overwhelmed by the *Rhapsody in Blue* that he wrote a song whose main melody quoted some of its thematic material. The lyric, an unashamed paean to Gershwin, began with the lines: "O wonderful, wonderful, Georgie. What you've done to me!" As he began playing for Gershwin, Schwartz was suddenly seized by the awareness that this was something less than a masterpiece. He stopped short with obvious embarrassment. Gershwin gently invited him to play some of his other songs, which he did. "I found his reaction the warmest, most encouraging I had yet received," says Schwartz. Schwartz gave up law practice in 1928 to devote himself completely to songwriting. Success came about a year after that when, with Howard Dietz as his lyricist, he wrote a majority of the songs for the successful, intimate, and sophisticated revue *Little Show*, the best of which were "I Guess I'll Have to Change My Plan," "I've Made a Habit of You," and "Little Old New York." Writing hit songs now became a habit with Schwartz. For *Three's a Crowd* in 1930 he did "Something to Remember You By," a highlight of that show as sung by Libby Holman. From the musical comedy *The Bandwagon*, in 1931, came what is probably the most famous song he ever wrote, "Dancing in the Dark," as well as "I Love Louisa" and "New Sun in the Sky."

Another newcomer to drift into the Gershwin orbit at Harms was Vernon Duke. Duke had come from his native Russia to the United States in 1921. En route to the new world, he stopped off at Constantinople. There, at a Y.M.C.A. run for refugees, he came upon a copy of Gershwin's "Swanee." His enthusiasm for Gershwin, and for American popular music, was born that day. Arriving in New York, he sought out Gershwin and found him both accessible and encouraging. It was Gershwin who urged Duke (up to then exclusively a writer of serious concert and ballet music) to try his hand at popular music. And since the Russian was still using the name with which he had been born, that of Vladimir Dukelsky, Gershwin also coined the pseudonym of "Vernon Duke" for the young man's popular efforts. Duke profited immeasurably from Gershwin's advice and criticism, as Gershwin dissected and analyzed for him the elements that made a popular song popular. Gershwin also introduced Duke to Max Dreyfus, who soon thereafter became Duke's publisher.

It was several years, however, before Vernon Duke proved as successful in the popular field as he was in the serious one. As Dukelsky he had written a ballet produced by the renowned Ballet Russe de Monte Carlo in 1925 and symphonies and concertos that Serge Koussevitzky directed in Paris and Boston. But while thus making an impressive place for himself in the concert world, Duke was writing popular tunes which he hoped would enable him to invade both Tin Pan Alley and Broadway.

Finally, in 1930, Duke had a modest hit—"I'm Only Human After All," with lyrics by E. Y. Harburg and Ira Gershwin; it was introduced in the *Garrick Gaieties* of that year. In 1932, Duke was the father of a popular-song classic: "April in Paris"; with lyrics by E. Y. Harburg, it was born in the Broadway revue *Walk a Little Faster*. After that, Duke (like Gershwin) became a split personality, musically speaking. As Vladimir Dukelsky he continued writing ambitious compositions for the concert stage; as Vernon Duke he wrote hit songs and some excellent scores for the Broadway theater. His best songs included "Let Me Match My Private Life with Yours," "Autumn in New York," and "I Can't Get Started with You"; his most eminent musical-comedy scores were for *Banjo Eyes*, starring Eddie Cantor, and for the Negro musical play *Cabin in the Sky*, for which he did "Taking a Chance on Love," "Honey in the Honeycomb," "Love Me Tomorrow," and the title song.

"April in Paris," which has remained Duke's most famous song, started out as a most dismal failure. Evelyn Hoey introduced it in *Walk a Little Faster*, in a scene set in Paris' Left Bank district. Nobody among the audience or critics found "April in Paris" appealing or worthy of note —possibly because Evelyn Hoey, suffering from laryngitis, could hardly do vocal justice to it.

What spelled the difference between failure and success for "April in Paris" was—a phonograph record. The recording was made by Marian Chase, a popular society chanteuse, for Liberty Records. Marian Chase was by no means a big name in the record business, nor was Liberty an important company. Nevertheless, this recording became a huge seller, and "April in Paris" was carried by it to a peak of popularity from which it never again descended.

The influence of a phonograph record on a popular song, as illustrated by the fate of "April in Paris," underscores the importance that recordings had begun to assume in Tin Pan Alley.

Sheet-music sales were on a sharp decline. A hit song was now measured in terms of a hundred-thousand-copy sale, with million-copy sales considered a phenomenon. Nobody was playing the piano any longer in the country's living rooms. The one-time practice of standing around a piano and singing current hits had become as obsolete as the horsedrawn carriage. In the 1920's people no longer seemed to want to make music for themselves. They wanted music to be played *at* them: in theaters, hotels, dance halls, and now at home. Thus the phonograph industry, which started to gain momentum in the 1910's, was beginning to enter the first of its boom periods. Record sales mounted—some recordings selling a million, two million disks, even more. Where once the popularity of a song was measured in terms of sheet-music sales, the yardstick now used most often was the number of records sold.

For a while, after World War I, Tin Pan Alley was thrown into a panic at the collapse of the sheet-music market; several publishing firms even had to go out of business for good. Suddenly, in the early 1920's, Tin Pan Alley found itself entering a new era of prosperity—this time thanks to the revolving disk. The revenues that record sales brought in by way of royalties—once dismissed by Tin Pan Alley as altogether negligible—were beginning to assume impressive figures. But what was even more important for Tin Pan Alley than this new-found revenue was the fact that records were becoming a new method and means of promoting songs, of taking an unknown and newly born number and building it up to national acceptance. This is something the piano roll had never been able to do. What Abel Green was to write in *Variety* in the 1950's was proving true thirty years earlier. "More than ever an inanimate object—a platter . . . running three minutes . . . is king of Tin Pan Alley. The popular-music business seems to revolve almost entirely around the revolving biscuit."

The first popular song believed to have been made a hit through records alone was George Stoddard's song "Mary" (not to be confused with the more familiar items of the same name by George M. Cohan and by Louis Hirsch). In 1919, Stoddard induced Victor to record it, even though the song had not yet been publicly performed or published. In three months three hundred thousand disks of that recording were sold, earning for its composer a royalty of fifteen thousand dollars. Tin Pan Alley could hardly have realized it at the time, but "Mary" was opening up for it a new world of income, exploitation, and distribution.

Al Jolson and Eddie Cantor had been recording songs from the middle 1910's on—often with the most rewarding results. We have already had an opportunity to point out how Jolson's recording of Gershwin's "Swanee" became one of the biggest-selling records of 1920. By 1920, Eddie Cantor—as well as Jolson—had become a best-selling recording artist. Cantor's first big hit record was "That's the Kind of Baby for Me" in 1917; this was followed by "You'd Be Surprised" in 1919, which sold a million disks. In 1920, Cantor became one of the first of Broadway's singing stars to sign a long-term exclusive contract with a recording firm. His agreement with Brunswick extended for five years and brought him a guarantee of about a quarter of a million dollars.

In the 1920's a powerful impetus was given to the success of songs previously introduced on the stage or over the radio through recordings by such popular performing artists as Rudy Vallee, Ruth Etting, Sophie Tucker, and the big-name bands of the time, including the Paul Whiteman Orchestra. Whiteman's rendition of "Whispering" and "Three O'Clock in the Morning" for Victor each had a sale of almost two million records. An equally formidable sales figure was achieved by Frank Crumit's recording of "The Gay Caballero." Frank Munn, a star on the Brunswick label (and later the star of the Brunswick Radio Hour) sold his recording of "Little Mother o' Mine" by the hundreds of thousands. Gene Austin's recordings of "That Silver Haired Daddy of Mine" and "My Blue Heaven," in 1927, not only helped to establish both songs as solid hits but were also responsible for making him one of the decade's most highly paid recording artists. Clyde McCoy's Brunswick recording of "Sugar Blues" in 1923 and the Victor recordings of "The Prisoner's Song" by Vernon Dalhart in 1924 and of "Ramona" by Gene Austin each sold over a million disks. Bing Crosby's record of "I Surrender" in 1930 helped make this song successful while bringing Bing his first big break in show business. This record led to a C.B.S. radio contract, on the one hand, and a Hollywood contract on the other.

Many a song such as "April in Paris" was snatched by a single phonograph record from undeserved neglect. Hoagy Carmichael's classic, "Star Dust" was such a song. Hoagy Carmichael first wrote this piece of music as a piano rag in 1927. An arranger suggested to him that the music would sound better in a slower tempo and in a more sentimental style of performance. Carmichael complied by making the necessary changes and Isham Jones made a "schmalzy" recording—but without any appreciable results as far as public acceptance went. Then in 1929 the publishing house of Mills commissioned Mitchell Parish to write words to the sentimental melody. This version recorded by Artie Shaw and his orchestra for Victor sold over two and a half million disks. Now a hit, "Star Dust" went on to become a standard. It has since been recorded almost five hundred times in forty-six different arrangements. It was the only song up to then recorded on both sides of a single disk: one side featured a Tommy Dorsey arrangement and performance, and the other side, Benny Goodman's version. "Star Dust" has also been transcribed for every conceivable instrument or combination of instruments: piano, two pianos, organ, brass band, accordion, violin, Hawaiian guitar, chorus, xylophone, string septet, woodwind octet, and so forth.

An Artie Shaw recording lifted still another remarkable song out of the depths of neglect to the heights of fame. That song is "Begin the Beguine," now recognized as one of Cole Porter's greatest, and the one Porter himself likes best. The song was part of a score Porter produced for the unsuccessful Broadway musical comedy *Jubilee* in 1935. Nobody seemed impressed, and for a while the song was completely forgotten. Then Artie Shaw and his orchestra issued it on a Victor record—almost as an afterthought. Victor wanted Artie Shaw to record a swing version of Rudolf Friml's "Indian Love Call." Artie Shaw was ready to comply if the company allowed him to put the forgotten Cole Porter song "Begin the Beguine" on the reverse side. "Begin the Beguine"—and not Friml's "Indian Love Call"—sold two million records of that Artie Shaw release. Artie Shaw has since conceded that this recording was "the real turning point" in his own career; but it was also the turning point in one of the most remarkable American popular songs ever conceived.

# 24

*"The best things in life are free"*

Two big booms in the record business (the first in the 1920's, the second a decade later) were separated by a searing depression. Once again Tin Pan Alley began to sniff the acrid odor of disaster. Just as the phonograph had helped deplete the sales of sheet music, so during the course of the 1920's the vitality of the rapidly expanding record business was slowly being sapped by a competing electronic miracle—the radio. To Tin Pan Alley the growth of radio broadcasting represented a cancer that, it felt, must eventually destroy both the sheet-music and the record industries. The radio was providing the home free of charge with music and other forms of entertainment from morning till late at night. It was unthinkable that in the face of such competition the public should be willing to spend its hard-earned cash on printed music or records.

The radio caught and held the enthusiasm and imagination of the American people beginning with 1920 when the Detroit *News* and the Westinghouse Broadcasting Company usurped radio broadcasting from amateurs and opened the first two commercial stations—WWJ in Detroit and KDKA in Pittsburgh. By 1921 commercial radio stations were mushrooming all over the country, their programs reaching into millions of homes. In 1926 the National Broadcasting Company inaugurated the first network of stations, whereby a single program could now be transmitted from a central point across the country. With so much good popular music available with a flip of the dial, the worst fears of Tin Pan Alley and the record business were quickly being realized. Sales of sheet music and disks plunged to an all-time low. Most of the small radio stations of the country were now using phonograph records as a basic part of their daily program, creating the crowning irony of having records themselves destroy the record business.

But once radio outgrew the status of a gadget or a toy to become a basic fixture in the American household, it no longer threatened either Tin Pan Alley or Record Row. On the contrary—radio endowed both with a new strength and vitality. A single radio program, a single singing star over the air, could create a hit song overnight. Once the song became a hit, the public went back in droves to their record shops. "The music you want when you want it"—a slogan devised by the record industry to combat radio competition—carried a basic truth. The American public liked to hear hit songs by favorite performers again and again. The only way such a need could be satisfied was through recordings. This is the reason a new and greater wave of prosperity inundated recorded music in the 1930's. About forty million records were now being sold annually, where the figure a decade earlier had been only a little more than half that amount.

There was even a boom in the sale of printed music—thanks to radio—though this time the selling item was song collections. Folios combining the favorite songs of some radio singing star—his or her picture prominently on the cover—provided a new and unexpected way of distributing published music in large quantities, and became a big business operation.

For radio was creating its own stars, and these stars were creating their own song hits. Among the first to become household names were the Happiness Boys, Frank Munn, Arthur Tracey ("The Street Singer"), Whispering Jack Smith. A new breed of radio singing stars followed in their footsteps with the Mills Brothers, Rudy Vallee, Morton Downey, Bing Crosby, Kate Smith, Jane Froman. Beginning with 1931, Sunday evenings belonged to Eddie Cantor and the Chase and Sanborn Hour, whose weekly program was then playing to the largest audience in radio history up to that time.

These and other stars of the air waves became the new salesmen of songs. They could take a number fresh from the presses and have the entire country singing it the very next morning. Eddie Cantor did this for "Now's the Time to Fall in Love" ("Potatoes Are Cheaper, Tomatoes Are Cheaper") and "Santa Claus Is Coming to Town"; Rudy Vallee, for "Vagabond Lover" and "Good Night, Sweetheart." These stars were also able to resurrect and revive long-forgotten songs and create for them a new popularity with a new audience—just as phonograph records were doing at the same time. Donaldson's "My Blue Heaven" had lain dormant for three years before Abe Lyman used it as a radio theme song and started it off on the road that led to the *Ziegfeld Follies* and the fabulous recording by Gene Austin. Rudy Vallee accomplished a similar miracle for the University of Maine "Stein Song." That number was written in 1901 by E. A. Fenstad, and nine years after that it became the song of the University of Maine in a new version made by A. W. Sprague. For twenty years nobody outside the Maine campus knew the song until Rudy Vallee began to sing it on his radio show. In no time at all, three hundred and fifty thousand copies of sheet music and a half-million disks of Vallee's recordings passed over the counters. The same thing happened to a students' song of 1883, "There's a Tavern in the Town," and to a neglected and forgotten ballad by Irving Berlin, "Say It Isn't So." In each case, Rudy Vallee revived it over the radio and made it successful.

Perhaps the songs made most popular over the radio were those that the stars used as their theme music. Some of these were old numbers being revived; others were newly written. All became hits of the first importance because of the repeated plugging they got at the beginning and end of each broadcast. "Marta" served Arthur Tracey; "My Time Is Your Time," Rudy Vallee; "When the Blue of the Night Meets the Gold of the Day," Bing Crosby; "One Hour with You," Eddie Cantor; "When the Moon Comes over the Mountain," Kate Smith; "Carolina Moon," Morton Downey.

The American way of life, of which radio had just become an integral part, was in a bad way. The twenties were roaring straight toward disaster. The fortunes of the rich, and the modest savings of the middle and lower classes, had been swallowed up by the stock-market crash in October of 1929. An economic depression was gaining hurricane strength. Wall Street tycoons were jumping out of windows. Six million people were unemployed. An economic disease was ravaging the whole country whose symptoms included crowded soup kitchens, shantytowns and Hoovervilles, apple vendors (five thousand of them in New York alone), a bonus march on Washington. Hotels and theaters were three-quarters empty. One actor remarked at one matinee that the balcony was so empty you could shoot an elk there. Uncertainty poisoned the air. Labor and management were at each other's throats.

In Washington, D. C., a new President—Franklin D. Roosevelt—closed down the banks, promised to chase the moneychangers from the marketplace, and emphasized that the only thing to fear was fear itself. To banish that fear, he embarked on a "new deal" for the underprivileged. Food, work, even culture were now to be meted out on a national scale. The day of the flapper and the collegiate was over. Young men and women now looked upon life with greater sobriety, with a healthier and more realistic set of values. They began to interest themselves in political and social problems, in crusades, in the common man. Feverishly the search began for economic cure-alls, such as Upton Sinclair's EPIC ("End of Poverty in California"), Huey Long's Share the Wealth, and the Townsend Plan.

Nobody remained untouched by the Depression, and no facet of art or culture was not affected by it. Out of the Depression came such novels as John Steinbeck's *The Grapes of Wrath*, such plays as Clifford Odets' *Waiting for Lefty* and the stage adaptation of Erskine Caldwell's *Tobacco Road*, such musical comedies as *Face the Music*, with text by Moss Hart and music by Irving Berlin. The temper of the times filtered as well into the songs of Broadway and Tin Pan Alley. One of the hits from *Face the Music* was "Let's Have Another Cup of Coffee," its message being that in these dark times pleasures can be found in life's simpler pursuits. Other composers and lyricists wrote songs that eulogized love found in humble places instead of palaces and penthouses: "In a Shanty in Old Shanty Town" and "I Found a Million Dollar Baby in a Five and Ten Cent Store." Rodgers and Hart had a Depression song in their musical comedy *America's Sweetheart*, in 1931, in "I've Got Five Dollars"; here Hart's lyrics spoke about debts "beyond endurance on my life insurance," but added that all was well so long as there were five dollars in the pocket. This effort to find the silver lining behind the pitch-black financial clouds gave Eddie Cantor his big radio song hit of 1932 in "Now's the Time to Fall in Love," since potatoes and tomatoes were then becoming cheaper. Another song suggested that since there was no more money in the bank, "let's turn out the light and go to bed." In a somewhat more serious vein, Vincent Youmans' hymn "Rise 'n Shine" pointed up a moral: black days notwithstanding, life was precisely what one chose to make it. One song more than all the others sounded the keynote of the Depression. It was "Brother, Can You Spare a Dime," which Jay Gorney wrote for the revue *Americana*.

But even in the thick of their misery and financial distress, Americans were beginning to face their troubles with courage and a touch of defiance. It is certainly no coincidence that one of the biggest song hits of 1933 was a number called "Who's Afraid of the Big Bad Wolf?" Frank E. Churchill and Ann Ronell wrote it for the Walt Disney animated cartoon about the three pigs and the houses they built. When Americans whistled the tune, they were correlating the big bad wolf with the Depression. Defiance soon led to a cautious optimism. Many people sang Milton Ager's "Happy Days Are Here Again" as a portent of the future rather than as a present reality. As such a portent it became the theme song for President Roosevelt's campaigns in 1932 and 1936. In the *Scandals of 1936*, Ethel Merman also sounded a shrill note of optimism with "Life Is Just a Bowl of Cherries."

If there was any one segment of American society that

remained least touched by the devastation of the Depression, that group was made up of the writers and composers of Tin Pan Alley. There was a good reason for this. Just before the economic bubble burst, talkies had come to Hollywood. A huge, new, insatiable market for songs had suddenly opened up, willing to pay fortunes for the badly needed services of Tin Pan Alley's and Broadway's leading songwriters. "California, Here I Come" was a slogan as well as a song, now on every songwriter's lips. A new gold rush was on. The forty-niners of the nineteenth century were succeeded by the "twenty-niners" of the twentieth.

## 25

## *"If I had a talking picture"*

When the screen burst into song and speech toward the end of the 1920's, Tin Pan Alley entered upon another rich era —and its last.

There had always been a tie-up between Tin Pan Alley and the movies, even in the silent days. The movie house had from the beginning been a happy hunting ground for song pluggers—through the use of song slides; through songfests; through contests; through amateur nights; and most of all through the use of accompanying music for the screen played by the pianist in the pit.

Tentative efforts were then already being made to derive song material from popular movies. "Poor Pauline" was inspired by the Pearl White serial *The Perils of Pauline;* "Oh, Those Charley Chaplin Feet," by the two-reel comedies starring that sad little man with a derby, cane, the caricature of an evening suit, and that rocking walk; "Sweet Little Mary Pickford," by the screen's first sweetheart; "Those Keystone Comedy Cops," by the Mack Sennett two-reelers; and "Civilization," by the first million-dollar motion-picture spectacular, produced by Ince. The first attempt made to write a theme song for a movie came in 1918 with "Mickey," a song by Neil Williams, for the motion picture of the same name starring Mabel Normand.

Even during the days of the silent screen, the theme song was beginning to gain considerable popularity. In the middle 1920's, Tin Pan Alley was making an earnest effort to issue songs inspired by, and written for, major screen productions. The song then became the heart of the accompanying score, repeated (*ad nauseam*) throughout the course of the picture. The first such theme song to become a major hit in Tin Pan Alley was "Charmaine" in 1926, with melody by Erno Rapee, for the picture of the same name. Rapee also produced one of the most widely heard movie theme songs of 1927 in "Diane," which had been written for *Seventh Heaven*, the picture starring Janet Gaynor that won the Academy Award that year. "Ramona," also in 1927, was written by Mabel Wayne (to L. Wolfe Gilbert's lyrics) for the motion picture of the same name—the song's popularity was given an enormous boost by Gene Austin's recording that sold about two million disks. In 1928, with the silent movie breathing its last gasps, two theme songs became popular: Nathaniel Shilkret's "Jeannine, I Dream of Lilac Time" for *Lilac Time*, and Erno Rapee's "Angela Mia" for *Street Angel*.

Then the screen burst into sound, creating a revolution in Hollywood and carrying motion pictures to the dawn of a new age. On August 6, 1926, the Warner Brothers presented in New York the first feature motion picture with a synchronized accompaniment written expressly for that film by Major Edward Bowes, David Mendoza, and Dr. William Axt. The feature film was *Don Juan* with John Barrymore. It was preceded by a screen concert, in which leading virtuosos and the New York Philharmonic Orchestra under Henry Hadley participated.

The full possibilities of talking pictures as a new medium of screen entertainment, however, did not become apparent until October 6, 1927. That was the evening when Warner Brothers offered in New York *The Jazz Singer*, starring Al Jolson. This, for the most part, was still a silent picture. But at a few points in the story—it told the tale of a synagogue cantor's son who was trying to become a jazz singer —the screen found a voice that allowed Jolson to sing a few of his particular specialties: "Dirty Hands, Dirty Face," "Toot, Toot, Tootsie," "Blue Skies," and the number that brought the picture to its poignant conclusion, "Mammy."

In one of these scenes Jolson was performing his jazz tunes for his mother, accompanying himself on the piano. In his characteristic way, he suddenly began to ad-lib in front of the camera: "Wait till ya hear this, Mama. . . . When I'm a hit I'm gonna take ya to Coney Island and I'm gonna buy ya the prettiest black silk dress that'll make a noise when ya walk. Will you like that, Mama?" Then he went into his song. When the Warner brothers saw the rushes of this scene, with the talk as well as the singing, they decided to keep Jolson's monologue in the movie. This was the first time that speech was heard in a full-length motion picture; and it was this scene that provided the ultimate proof that sound in the movies was here to stay.

*The Jazz Singer* proved a sensation. It grossed the then-unprecedented sum of more than three million dollars. Al Jolson was Hollywood's new king, and the Warner Brothers its major power. The songs Jolson sang in *The Jazz*

*Singer* became nationwide hits once again, just as they had been years earlier when he first introduced them at the Winter Garden.

The age of the talking picture had arrived. Warner Brothers and their competitors now went into a mad scramble to produce all-talking, all-singing motion pictures. The first cinema revue was *The Broadway Melody* in 1929, with songs written directly for the production by Nacio Herb Brown to Arthur Freed's lyrics; this became the first motion-picture musical to win the Academy Award. It also brought to Tin Pan Alley (by way of the progressive publishing house of Robbins) two substantial hit numbers in the title song and in "The Wedding of the Painted Doll."

"The Broadway Melody" was, of course, the theme song of that movie, and drew to the attention of Hollywood moguls more forcefully than ever the importance of using theme songs. Repeated performances of such songs on stage, records, and over the radio was a rich source of free publicity for the movie in question. Hollywood, consequently, now issued an order that wherever possible—and even for nonmusical motion pictures—a theme song was to be used, and that, wherever possible, the theme song was to bear in its title the name of the movie for which it was intended. Thus for Maurice Chevalier's film *The Love Parade*, the song "My Love Parade" was written. In what now became a frantic effort to tie in the name of a movie with the theme song, Tin Pan Alley joined hands with Hollywood. "Varsity Girl, I'll Cling to You" was written for *Varsity Girl*; "Woman Disputed, I Love You," for *Woman Disputed*; "My Wild Party Girl," for *Wild Party*; "The Pagan Love Song," for *The Pagan*; "Speedy Boy," for Harold Lloyd's comedy *Speedy*; "Weary River," for *Weary River*; "The Mating Call," for *The Mating Call*; "Coquette" for *Coquette*; and "The Sacred Flame," for

*The Sacred Flame.* It took Dorothy Parker to reduce to absurdity what was rapidly becoming a silly practice. Called upon for lyrics for *Dynamite Man* she proceeded to submit a little classic entitled "Dynamite Man, I Love You." This theme-song craze was also ridiculed on Broadway in the sophisticated revue *The Little Show,* which contained a number purporting to be the theme song for the famous New York store (at that time a hardware store), "Hammacher, Schlemmer, I Love You."

With *The Broadway Melody* smashing all known box-office records, competing star-studded musicals were hurriedly being rushed into production. During 1929 to 1931 the following were released: the *Fox Movietone Follies; The King of Jazz,* starring the Paul Whiteman Orchestra; *The Gold Diggers of Broadway,* with Nancy Welford, Conway Tearle, Winnie Lightner, Ann Pennington, and Lilyan Tashman; and *Hollywood Revue, The Show of Shows,* and *Paramount on Parade,* into which the three respective studios (M.G.M., Warner Brothers, and Paramount) each threw their stars into a single giant grab bag. From these and similar productions emerged an avalanche of new song hits to flood Tin Pan Alley, and through Tin Pan Alley, the song market; among those were "Am I Blue?," "Painting the Clouds with Sunshine," "Tip-toe Through the Tulips," "Singin' in the Rain," "Happy Feet," "It Happened in Monterey."

Musical comedies as well as revues enjoyed a veritable heyday during the first years of the talking pictures. Some were transplantations from the Broadway stage, while others were written directly for screen production. Maurice Chevalier made his American screen bow in 1929 with *Innocents of Paris,* in which he sang "Louise." During the next two years, Chevalier assumed the role of America's leading romantic hero—in *The Love Parade, The Smiling Lieutenant,* and *The Big Pond,* in the last of which he introduced "You Brought a New Kind of Love to Me." Fanny Brice was starred in *My Man*, in which she sang the title song and several others that she had formerly made so famous in the *Ziegfeld Follies*. Radio's blackface comedy team, Amos 'n Andy, were starred in 1930 in *Check and Doublecheck*, with songs by Harry Ruby including one of his biggest, "Three Little Words." Jeanette MacDonald appeared in 1930 in *Monte Carlo*, there to introduce "Beyond the Blue Horizon." De Sylva, Brown, and Henderson wrote "Sonny Boy" and other songs for the Al Jolson triumph *The Singing Fool*, as well as the score for *Sunny Side Up* starring Janet Gaynor and Charles Farrell, which gave the public "Keep Your Sunny Side Up," "Aren't We All," and "If I Had a Talking Picture of You."

The great of Broadway and Tin Pan Alley were beating a straight path to Hollywood. Irving Berlin's first stint for the screen was the ballad "When My Dreams Come True," for *The Cocoanuts*, the first of the screen-comedy extravaganzas with the Four Marx Brothers, in 1929. Between 1929 and 1930, Jerome Kern went to the coast to write the music for *The Three Sisters*, Walter Donaldson for *Hot for Paris*, and Sigmund Romberg for *Viennese Nights*. In 1931, George and Ira Gershwin made their appearance in Hollywood to do the songs for *Delicious*, and Rodgers and Hart to create songs for *The Hot Heiress*. Vincent Youmans was brought West in 1933 for *Flying Down to Rio*, the first of the Fred Astaire-Ginger Rogers singing-and-dancing triumphs; here Youmans maintained his previously high Broadway standards by producing "Carioca" and "Orchids in the Moonlight."

The huge net that Hollywood spread all over Broadway and Tin Pan Alley scooped up not only composers and lyricists but also most of Broadway's successful musical comedies, operettas, and revues. These included (during the first few years of talking pictures), *Show Boat, Sally*, and *Sunny*, all of them with music by Kern; *Whoopee*, in which Eddie Cantor made his bow on the screen; Rudolf Friml's *The Vagabond King*, which became the first major production in Technicolor; Romberg's *The Desert Song* and *The New Moon* (in the latter Grace Moore made her screen debut); and such outstanding musical comedies of the 1920's as *Good News* and *Follow Through*, by De Sylva, Brown, and Henderson, and *No, No, Nanette* by Vincent Youmans.

Surely it is only poetic justice that the first screen musical to win the Academy Award—*The Broadway Melody* —had its musical score written by a composer whose career is almost entirely identified with the screen. For like the Broadway musical theater, the Hollywood talking picture was responsible for the emergence of a new school of popular-song composers. These men may or may not have gained their initial experiences in Tin Pan Alley or Broadway, but all of them came fully into their own as popular composers of outstanding significance and popularity by writing for the screen.

Nacio Herb Brown was one of the first of this new group, one of the most successful—and one of the best. He had come to California in 1904 when he was just eight. For a while he worked in vaudeville as piano accompanist for Alice Doll, after which he opened a tailor shop in Hollywood. Investments in Hollywood real estate in the early 1920's made him a wealthy man.

Though he had published a popular song in 1920, and had one of his numbers interpolated in a Hollywood revue in 1926, he had no intention of devoting himself to songwriting. Then, one day in 1928, Irving Thalberg, the distinguished producer at M.G.M., persuaded him to write the music to Arthur Freed's lyrics for *The Broadway Melody*. The fantastic success of that movie musical started

Brown off on a new life. In 1929, with Freed, he wrote the songs for the *Hollywood Revue*, in which two more of his hits were born—"You Were Meant for Me" and "Singin' in the Rain." His many and varied screen productions after that brought to popularity other songs of his, such as "The Pagan Love Song," "The Chant of the Jungle," "All I Do Is Dream of You," and "You Are My Lucky Star."

Early in 1930, Harry Revel, a composer, teamed up with Mack Gordon, a lyricist, to form one of the most successful songwriting combinations in the early history of talking pictures. Revel was born in London and had received his early musical training and experiences in Europe by playing in Parisian jazz bands and in a Hawaiian orchestra. Even before coming to America he was the proud father of a hit song that, curiously enough, was inspired by an American setting—"I'm Going Back to Old Nebraska."

Revel came to the United States in 1929 and for a while toured in vaudeville. Then, teaming up with Mack Gordon, he concentrated his hopes for success on songwriting. In 1933, Gordon and Revel went to work in Hollywood, and it was not long before they were flooding the movie industry with hit songs. One of their earliest efforts was "Did You Ever See a Dream Walking?" which, after being sung in *Sitting Pretty*, swept the country. Within the next few years they wrote "Love Thy Neighbor," "Good Night, My Love," and "With My Eyes Wide Open I'm Dreaming." In 1935 they received special awards from ASCAP for no less than nine songs!

Harry Warren may have had his songwriting beginnings in Tin Pan Alley and Broadway in the 1920's, but his greatest triumphs were realized in Hollywood. Actually he was a graduate of both schools—Tin Pan Alley *and* Broadway. In Tin Pan Alley he worked as a song plugger. On Broadway, he wrote "You're My Everything," "I Found a Million Dollar Baby in a Five and Ten Cent Store," and

"Cheerful Little Earful." Finally, in 1930, he went to Hollywood. His first assignment was *Spring Is Here*, the screen adaptation of a Rodgers and Hart Broadway musical. After that, working with Al Dubin as his lyricist, Warren wrote the songs for *The Gold Diggers of 1933* and *Forty-second Street*, each a major screen success. His leading numbers included "You're Getting to Be a Habit with Me," "Forty-second Street," "Shuffle Off to Buffalo," and "We're in the Money."

Jimmy McHugh had also done well for himself on Broadway before emigrating to the screen capital. His greatest success on Broadway had come with the all-Negro revue, *Blackbirds of 1928*, for which (with Dorothy Fields as lyricist) he wrote "Diga, Diga, Doo" and "I Can't Give You Anything but Love, Baby."

As an office boy at the Boston Opera House, young McHugh used to entertain famous opera singers and conductors with his improvisations on opera arias. Then he stepped out of grand opera into Tin Pan Alley by taking on a job as song plugger for the Boston branch of Waterson, Berlin and Snyder. Later on, as an employee at F. A. Mills, McHugh realized his first publication, "Emaline." For almost a decade after that he wrote songs for the revues mounted at the Cotton Club in Harlem. Two were particularly successful: "I Can't Believe That You're in Love with Me" and "When My Sugar Walks Down the Street." Then in 1927 he and Dorothy Fields became working partners and celebrated their newly formed collaboration with a resounding stage success—the *Blackbirds of 1928*.

In 1930, McHugh and Fields invaded Hollywood, their maiden effort there being "Go Home and Tell Your Mother" for *Love in the Rough*. The pair then scaled the highest mountains of success in the movies with a long and formidable list of song hits. A few of these were the "Cuban Love Song," "Singing the Blues," "Don't Blame Me,"

"Thank You for a Lovely Evening," "I'm in the Mood for Love," "I Feel a Song Coming On," and "You're an Angel."

The significance of the popular song in the motion-picture industry was officially recognized in 1934 when the Academy of Motion Picture Arts and Sciences added the song to the list of its annual awards. The first Oscar went to Con Conrad for "The Continental," from the Fred Astaire-Ginger Rogers musical *The Gay Divorcee*. (The movie *The Gay Divorcee* was an adaptation of the Cole Porter musical *The Gay Divorce*, and Con Conrad's "The Continental" was an interpolation into the Cole Porter score for the movie version.) But this and subsequent Academy Awards are outside the periphery of a history on Tin Pan Alley, for, to all intents and purposes, by 1934 Tin Pan Alley was no longer in existence.

# 26

## *"The song is ended but the melody lingers on"*

The death of Tin Pan Alley as such coincided with the birth of talking pictures. The two events were not disconnected. By the time *The Jazz Singer* had established the validity of talking and singing pictures—and was sending the silent film to permanent oblivion—sheet-music sales had sunk to the lowest levels in Tin Pan Alley history, about seventy-five percent below what was considered normal a few decades earlier. Most hit songs now sold fewer than a hundred thousand copies. A publisher, therefore, had to realize that he could no longer keep the machinery of his business oiled through the profits of sheet-music publication. Other income had to be found if he was to survive. Royalties from recorded music provided some relief, but it was not enough to fill the gap made by the vanishing sheet-music business. The situation in Tin Pan Alley had grown so serious toward the end of the 1920's that nine publishers talked of a giant merger (with backing from banks) with the hope that disaster could be averted by a centralization of their activities and market. Then the talking pictures arrived, and the plan was forgotten. The enormous demand for music by talking pictures represented welcome manna from heaven to a starved industry; Tin Pan Alley expected it would once again grow fat and prosperous.

The insatiable appetite of the screen for songs soon led a number of Hollywood's most important motion-picture studios to buy firms in Tin Pan Alley. By doing so, they got a rich backlog of songs from which to draw; at the same time they acquired the services of experienced and successful composers and lyricists who might be contractually affiliated with those publishers. Warner Brothers paid ten million dollars for three houses, Harms, Witmark, and Remick, which were assembled into one giant organization and renamed the Music Publishers Holding Corporation. Other movie studios followed suit. Metro-Goldwyn-Mayer, for example, acquired Leo Feist, Robbins, and one or two lesser firms.

In this way, some of Tin Pan Alley's historic and powerful publishing houses became offshoots of the movie industry, subservient to the needs and demands of the screen. It was now the studio executive who called the tune—figuratively as well as literally. He told composers and lyricists the type of material needed for specific productions. Once these songs were written, their publication became an automatic procedure in which the publisher himself had little say.

This was the first significant change in publishing, and one that doomed Tin Pan Alley. In the Alley, the publisher had been the central force around which everything connected with songs gravitated—the writers, performers, salesmen, pluggers. It was the publisher who selected what songs were to be printed, and he picked them because he liked them and felt that the public would like them. Then he set about the necessary business of getting the songs performed and popularized. Of all the people in the trade, it was the publisher above all others who sought out latent talent and nursed it to fulfillment; the publisher who told a performer about a song suited to his particular gift; the publisher who worked out methods of promotion.

But now, in the new scheme of things created by the movie industry, the publisher was dictated *to*. He resigned not only his basic function of selecting songs for publication but also of determining the best ways of making them popular. One publisher put it this way, wistfully and sadly: "All we do now is clip coupons like bankers, where once we were the makers of song hits and great composers. The thrill and glamour of old Tin Pan Alley are gone forever."

Hollywood was not the only force to destroy Tin Pan Alley. The record industry was responsible for contributing the finishing death strokes.

Decade by decade the record business was growing into Gargantuan size. Where in the 1930's forty million records were sold each year, the number swelled to a hundred million by 1949, a hundred and fifty million by 1959, and almost two hundred million by 1963. This was a giant market from which publishers could profit no end—but only if the publisher happened to have a direct line into the recording organization. Consequently, it was not long before the one-time Tin Pan Alley song plugger had to be jettisoned and replaced by the "office manager" who had an "in" with the "mechanical man"—the latter being the one in the recording business who served as a liaison with publishers. The brains of the record firm was the "A and R director"—the director of popular artists and repertory. It was he who decided what songs should be recorded and by whom—and, by selecting a big-name artist for a song, he could create the hit record that in turn could bring about the hit song. The "A and R director" often dictated what a publisher's output should be in very much the same way that Hollywood was doing to its own publishing affiliates. In the 1940's the main thoroughfare of the song industry was no longer Tin Pan Alley but Record Row. When a song had to depend exclusively for its popularity and commercial success on a recording—instead of on a published sheet of music—that was the time that Tin Pan Alley was through.

A publisher hoping to succeed in his business now simply had to have a tie-up—if not with a record company or a movie studio, then with Broadway show business in the way that Chappell and Company was inextricably bound up with Broadway musical comedies and plays (Chappell was directed by Max Dreyfus after Harms had gone to Hollywood). Just as Harms had done before 1930, Chappell drew most of its publications from Broadway's foremost musical productions. Chappell also had important subsidiaries with Broadway affiliations: the New World Publishing Company and the George Gershwin Publishing Company (both formed to issue music by Gershwin other than that owned by the Music Publishers Holding Corporation); and the Williamson Music Corporation, founded to issue the music of Rodgers and Hammerstein.

The need for tie-ups brought about complex and at times subtle business interrelationships between the publishers on the one hand and various media of song distribution on the other. This by no means redounded to the best interests of popular music. Leading singing stars and bandleaders acquired interests in publishing houses to profit more directly from songs they helped make popular. Nat King Cole has two publishing firms, Sweco and Comet, the one affiliated with ASCAP, the other with BMI. Frank Sinatra owns a handful, including Barton, Ding Dong, Midwood. So do Connie Francis (Efsee, Francon, Merna, and three others) and Paul Anka (Spanka and Flanka). It stands to reason that performers, being human after all—and generally having highly efficient business managers to take care of their affairs—should be more partial to their own firm's publications than to the songs of rival organizations. It is surely no coincidence, for example, that Connie Francis—who today is one of the most successful female singers on records, having sold over forty million disks—used eleven of her own publications among the first twenty she recorded early in 1963. Surely it is also no coincidence that Nat King Cole's biggest record of 1962, "Ramblin' Rose," is a song issued by Sweco, his own company.

A publisher trying to interest a famous singer in one of his new numbers often finds that he is competing with a fellow publisher. This fact was strongly accented by William H. A. Carr and Gene Grove in the New York *Post* when they described how one publisher tried to interest Frank Sinatra's business associates to get the singer to use one of his songs. The associate replied: "Do you want me to get my head knocked off? The first thing Frank will ask me is if we own the song. If I tell him no, I'll be out of work."

Some publishing houses even have artist bureaus under their wing. This may simplify the way of getting songs performed, but by the same token it is also likely to compel an artist in his programming to be partial to the publisher's lists. Radio stations and motion pictures own their own record companies: C.B.S., Columbia; R.C.A., Victor; Paramount and M.G.M., companies bearing those names. Thus the radio station and the movie company can hardly be expected to be indifferent to the affairs of its affiliated record company, and vice-versa. The involvement of motion pictures in recording has been accentuated in recent years with the acquisition of Dot Records by Paramount, Verve Records by M.G.M., Aldon and Dimension Records by Columbia Pictures, and most of all by a giant deal in August of 1963 whereby Warner's acquired Reprise Records (a Frank Sinatra operation) in return for a sizable block of Warner Brothers stock and a one-third stake in the new record company merging Reprise with Warner Brothers Records.

Beginning with the 1940's, one of the most important and fruitful tie-ups sought by record companies was with disk jockeys. The disk jockey was a phenomenon born through the marriage of radio and records. The term itself was coined by *Variety* in 1957 to identify a species emerging to public notice with the Make Believe Ballroom, a radio program at which Al Jarvis presided in Hollywood and Martin Block in New York. By spinning the latest records, and interspersing the musical selections with light banter about the performer or the composition, the disk jockey soon acquired a vast, faithful audience. It was estimated that only four months after Martin Block introduced his program in New York he had four million regular listeners tuning in day after day. In time, the disk jockey dominated radio entertainment. By 1960 there were some three thousand disk jockeys operating on thirty-five hundred stations all over the country. By their choice of records, and the frequency with which they played any single number, jockeys such as Jarvis, Block, Bob Clayton, Albert Jazzbo Collins, and Dick Clark became the most potent single force in directing and influencing public taste in popular songs.

One of the first up-and-coming publishers to realize the

value of the disk jockey to popular music was a young man named Harry Richmond. He conceived the idea of making records of the songs he wanted to publish, or had just published, and distributing them to a select group of disk jockeys. He would then rely on their advice as to whether the song was worth promoting and the best way to do it. He also counted on some of these disk jockeys to start the ball rolling by plugging one of the songs they had singled out for special praise. How right he was in sensing the importance of the disk jockey to his publishing business was proved eloquently when he issued a number called "The Thing," recorded by Phil Harris on the Victor label. Richmond sent out advance copies of this recording to twenty-five disk jockeys, one of whom was Bob Clayton in Boston. It happened that at that very time a railroad strike had paralyzed shipments in and out of Boston, making it impossible for Victor to fill any orders in Boston for "The Thing." The recording that Richmond had placed in Clayton's hands was, therefore, an "exclusive" for Clayton, who took full advantage of his solitary position by playing the recording once each hour for several days. Soon there was such an enormous demand in the shops for the recording that the Victor distributor in Boston had to send his truck into New York to pick up twenty thousand disks.

Elvis Presley's first recording (for Sun) was "That's All Right, Mama" and "Blue Moon Kentucky" in 1954. Dewey Phillips, a Memphis disk jockey, was so taken with the performance that he played each side seven times consecutively. A week later six thousand disks of that recording were sold in Memphis, starting the Presley boom soon to grow to fabled proportions. Also early in the 1950's Bill Randle, then a disk jockey in Cleveland, frequently played a recording of the old-time hit "Charmaine," in a performance of Mantovani and his strings. That record at once became a best seller and went a long way toward establishing not only Mantovani's popularity in America but also the vogue for string recordings. A few years before, a disk jockey in Charlotte, North Carolina, had come upon an old Ted Weems record of "Heartaches." By playing it again and again he started a demand that resulted in a three-million-disk sale before the year was over; on the strength of this revival, Ted Weems returned to big-time booking after a hiatus of several years.

It was the power of a local disk jockey in Louisville, Kentucky, that was responsible in 1951 for two major hit songs and the emergence of a new composer. Mrs. Chilton Price, a Louisville housewife, wrote two songs (her first attempts)—"Slow Poke" and "You Belong to Me." A local disk jockey liked them and played their recordings, after which the Pee Wee King record of "Slow Poke" sold well over a million disks.

Scattered as he was over the whole country, the disk jockey was able to effect the complete disintegration of Tin Pan Alley through the decentralization of the song industry. No longer were the country's leading songs published in New York as they had been between 1880 and 1930. Now a large percentage of music publications flowed from a new capital, Hollywood, and from numerous other cities.

Early in the 1950's, for example, the joint efforts of a number of high-pressure disk jockeys and a few young, far-sighted publishers made Nashville, Tennessee, a center of hit-song production. Out of Nashville came Patti Page's successful number "The Tennessee Waltz," Jimmy Dean's sensational-selling song "Big Bad John," and other songs, many of which sold a million or more disks, such as "Your Cheatin' Heart," "Bye, Bye, Love," "Little Darlin'," "Half as Much," "Cold, Cold Heart," "Bird Dog," "Too Much," and "Ebony Eyes."

Hit songs also emerged from other points of the compass. "Witch Doctor" and "Raindrops" came from Chicago; "Young Love" from Atlanta; "I Went to Your Wedding" from St. Louis; "Whole Lot-a-Shakin' Goin' On" and "Rock Around the Clock" from Philadelphia; "A Rose and a Baby Ruth" from Chapel Hill, North Carolina; "This Ole House" from Arcadia, California. In short, the song industry had come full circle. With the disintegration of Tin Pan Alley, publishing houses were once again scattered all over the country, just as they had been before 1880.

As soon as publishers became aware of the power of the disk jockey, bribery (or, as *Variety* baptized the practice, "payola") followed as an inevitable reaction and development. Expensive gifts, a percentage of song royalties, an interest in the publishing house, hard cash in sizable amounts—this was the oil for the machinery that kept a record spinning on radio day after day. Payola was, to be sure, a dishonest practice, since a disk jockey was presumably being paid to be objective in his choice of records and in the frequency with which he played a tune. But payola represented not only a degeneration of moral and ethical values but of musical standards as well. Many a song that should have been relegated to the refuse heap as soon as it was issued—either because of gibberish lyrics or an infantile tune—was instead orbited to the outer-space regions of public acclaim because a number of highly influential disk jockeys were themselves reaping a harvest from this success, a success that they had set into motion in the first place.

The disk jockey not only helped to popularize bad songs—he also helped to kill good ones. The frequency with which a popular tune was now being plugged over the radio brought about a point of saturation, quickly and permanently. Here's the way J. Fred Coots, the famous composer, once put it: "Years ago it took months to establish a song, and a hit could last for several years until it grew into a standard. Today a song is over and forgotten in a few weeks. The song turnover is enormous, and it has resulted in a writing pattern that is more high pressure and fight than it is fun." Before 1925 a hit song was expected to survive in public interest for about sixteen months. But in the heyday of the disk jockey, few songs could last more than a couple of weeks. The old way—the Tin Pan Alley way—often transformed a popular tune into a permanent classic. That way had now become obsolete. The new method—that of the disk jockey and Record Row—is to capitalize on a song in a big way as quickly as possible and to send it off to permanent oblivion. The slower processes of Tin Pan Alley had helped to create a rich body of songs that has survived. The newer procedures of the disk jockey and the recording industry—and the subtle and complex interrelationships that now exist among publisher, recording company, performer, and disk jockey—have contributed few songs, indeed, that can hope to be remembered tomorrow.

Few and far between are the standards produced since 1940. Some of the best songs still heard today are those for which Tin Pan Alley had been responsible. For example, in 1953 the *Encyclopedia of American History*, edited by Richard B. Morris, listed what it considered the fourteen greatest popular song hits since 1890. Only three of these were written after 1930, and those three were the work of a creator who had learned his craft in Tin Pan Alley—Irving Berlin. This historian then could not find a single number worthy of being including in its list from the post-Tin Pan Alley era!

A decade later, in 1962, *Variety* presented what it considered the "golden hundred" in American popular music—those songs that have become standards, that are most often performed today, whose sale of sheet music and records has been most substantial. Excluding the work of composers who were raised in Tin Pan Alley, or who were products of Tin Pan Alley influence—and in this category I put such composers as Irving Berlin, Jerome Kern, Richard Rodgers, and Cole Porter—only 18% of the songs on the *Variety* list were produced in the thirty-year period between 1932 and 1962, and 82% in the thirty-year period between 1902 and 1932. Such a lopsided score in favor of Tin Pan Alley over the efforts of the post-Tin Pan Alley music industry speaks for itself.

And so, it is not too much to maintain that something more than just a tradition passed away when Tin Pan Alley died in or about 1930. The end of Tin Pan Alley is also the ending of a rich, incomparable epoch in American popular music. The open-door policy that had prevailed in Tin Pan Alley, a policy that made publishers receptive to manuscripts by unknowns and to composers and lyricists who had still to make their reputations—this door was shut tightly after 1930. The two hundred thousand or so manuscripts that now pour regularly into publishing houses from aspiring writers are never looked at. Publishers are now interested only in the song that has already found an outlet on Broadway or in Hollywood, over TV, with a major recording company, or with important disk jockeys. Besides, publishers are in dread of plagiarism suits from composers who continually find in a hit song the recollection of something they themselves had written and submitted to the publisher. Mail, therefore, is returned unopened; newcomers with songs under their arms are not interviewed.

Tin Pan Alley had been a university at which great popular composers could grow to full maturity while learning their craft from the ground up, in all its varied facets.

The present-day music industry no longer provides such training. Today a song has to be big time before a publisher is interested; a composer has to be big time before he is taken under a publisher's wing. In Tin Pan Alley an obscure song, by an equally obscure composer, which grew into a million-copy hit, was so frequent as to be almost normal; today it is a fluke that comes at long-spaced intervals.

In my Introduction to this book, I remarked that the term "Tin Pan Alley" is still being used to identify the music business, that it has become a synonym for American popular music. But American popular music is Tin Pan Alley no more. At times that concentration of small publishing houses in the Brill Building at 1619 Broadway is identified as Tin Pan Alley. But this is a misnomer. This concentration of music publishers, most of which are small-time, bears about the same relation to old Tin Pan Alley that rhinestone does to pure diamond. In a New York *Post* story, William H. A. Carr and Gene Grove made this plain when they described the Brill as "this old, gray building in which the offices run the gamut from plain to dingy, from ordinary to tiny. The doors of many are emblazoned from lintel to sill with the names of music companies, many of whose entire existence is contained in the gold leaf on the door and the black ink on the letterheads. The lobby is a clutter of youngsters mostly over-eager and under-talented, and their jaded elders, entering and leaving the elevators in a line that would seem more in place before a Coney Island fun house."

In 1950, *Downbeat* magazine realized that the term "Tin Pan Alley" meant something quite different from the big plush offices of music-publishing houses in Radio City and Hollywood which were completely dominated by the movies, Broadway, records, radio, TV, and other interests. It initiated a national contest to find a new name for America's song business. No appropriate name was hit upon—no new term seemed to fit the new age of popular music in the way that Tin Pan Alley had identified the old.

Perhaps what is needed most today is not just another name for Tin Pan Alley. Perhaps the vital need is for *another* Tin Pan Alley—with Tin Pan Alley's overall *Weltanschauung*, methods, traditions; with Tin Pan Alley's high regard for the song and the writer of the song. Today the cart is pulling the horse. It is the means of distribution and the performance that is of prime significance, not the composer or lyricist. (In fact, when a popular song is played by a disk jockey he remembers to identify everybody and everything connected with the recording—except the composer and the lyricist!) In Tin Pan Alley, for all its emphasis on song-plugging, it was the other way around. And that is why, for all its seemingly haphazard, unschooled ways and its crass commercialism, Tin Pan Alley made musical history, why the fifty years of its existence is the golden age of American popular music.

*The Golden Hundred:*
*Tin Pan Alley Standards, 1880–1930*

*(compiled by David Ewen)*

*A Bird in a Gilded Cage*  1900
Arthur J. Lamb / Harry von Tilzer

*A Hot Time in the Old Town*  1886
Joe Hayden / Theodore M. Metz

*A Pretty Girl Is like a Melody*  1919
Irving Berlin

*After the Ball*  1892
Charles K. Harris

*Ah, Sweet Mystery of Life*  1910
Rida Johnson Young / Victor Herbert

*Ain't Misbehavin'*  1929
Andy Razaf / Thomas Waller, Harry Brooks

*Alexander's Ragtime Band*  1911
Irving Berlin

*All Alone*  1924
Irving Berlin

*All Coons Look Alike to Me*  1896
Ernest Hogan

*April Showers*  1921
Buddy De Sylva / Louis Silvers

*Auf Wiedersehen*  1915
Herbert Reynolds / Sigmund Romberg

*Beautiful Ohio*  1918
Ballard MacDonald / Robert A. King

*Bedelia*    1903
William Jerome / Jean Schwartz

*Bill*    1927
P. G. Wodehouse / Jerome Kern

*Bill Bailey, Won't You Please Come Home?*    1902
Hughie Cannon

*Blue Skies*    1927
Irving Berlin

*Body and Soul*    1930
Edward Heyman, Robert Sour, Frank Eyton / Johnny Green

*By the Light of the Silvery Moon*    1909
Edward Madden / Gus Edwards

*California, Here I Come*    1924
Buddy De Sylva / Joseph W. Meyer

*Carolina in the Morning*    1922
Gus Kahn / Walter Donaldson

*Come Down, Ma Evenin' Star*    1902
Robert B. Smith / John Stromberg

*Cuddle Up a Little Closer*    1908
Otto Harbach / Karl Hoschna

*Daisy Bell*    1892
Henry Dacre

*Deep in My Heart*    1924
Dorothy Donnelly / Sigmund Romberg

*Down by the Old Mill Stream*    1910
Tell Taylor

*Embraceable You*    1930
Ira Gershwin / George Gershwin

*Every Little Movement Has a Meaning All Its Own*    1910
Otto Harbach / Karl Hoschna

*For Me and My Gal*    1917
Edgar Leslie, E. Ray Goetz / George W. Meyer

*Georgia on My Mind*    1930
Stuart Gorrell / Hoagy Carmichael

*Giannina Mia*    1912
Otto Harbach / Rudolf Friml

*Give My Regards to Broadway*    1904
George M. Cohan

*Happy Days Are Here Again*   1929
Jack Yellen / Milton Ager

*I Can't Give You Anything but Love, Baby*   1928
Dorothy Fields / Jimmy McHugh

*Ida, Sweet as Apple Cider*   1903
Eddie Leonard

*I Wonder Who's Kissing Her Now*   1909
Will M. Hough, Frank R. Adams / Joe E. Howard, Harold Orlob

*I'll Be with You in Apple Blossom Time*   1920
Neville Fleeson / Albert von Tilzer

*I'm Falling in Love with Someone*   1910
Rida Johnson Young / Victor Herbert

*In My Sweet Little Alice Blue Gown*   1919
Joseph McCarthy / Harry Tierney

*In the Good Old Summertime*   1902
Ren Shields / George Evans

*In the Shade of the Old Apple Tree*   1905
Harry H. Williams / Egbert van Alstyne

*Kiss Me Again*   1905
Henry Blossom / Victor Herbert

*Let Me Call You Sweetheart*   1910
Beth Slater Whitson / Leo Friedman

*Liza*   1929
Ira Gershwin / George Gershwin

*Look for the Silver Lining*   1920
Buddy De Sylva / Jerome Kern

*Love for Sale*   1930
Cole Porter

*Love Me and the World Is Mine*   1906
Dave Reed, Jr. / Ernest R. Ball

*Love Me or Leave Me*   1928
Gus Kahn / Walter Donaldson

*Love Nest*   1920
Otto Harbach / Louis A. Hirsch

*Ma Blushin' Rosie*   1900
Edgar Smith / John Stromberg

*Makin' Whoopee*   1928
Gus Kahn / Walter Donaldson

*Margie*   1920
Benny Davis / Con Conrad, J. Russel Robinson

*Meet Me in St. Louis*   1904
Andrew B. Sterling / Kerry Mills

*Meet Me Tonight in Dreamland*   1909
Beth Slater Whitson / Leo Friedman

*Missouri Waltz*   1914
J. R. Shannon / Frederick Knight Logan

*Moanin' Low*   1929
Howard Dietz / Ralph Rainger

*Mother Machree*   1910
Rida Johnson Young / Chauncey Olcott, Ernest R. Ball

*Mother Was a Lady*   1896
Edward B. Marks / Joseph W. Stern

*My Gal Is a High Born Lady*   1896
Barney Fagan

*My Gal Sal*   1905
Paul Dresser

*My Heart Stood Still*   1927
Lorenz Hart / Richard Rodgers

*My Mammy*   1920
Joe Young, Sam Lewis / Walter Donaldson

*Oh, Promise Me*   1889
Reginald de Koven

*Ol' Man River*   1927
Oscar Hammerstein II / Jerome Kern

*On the Banks of the Wabash*   1897
Paul Dresser

*One Alone*   1926
Otto Harbach, Oscar Hammerstein II / Sigmund Romberg

*Over There*   1917
George M. Cohan

*Peg o' My Heart*   1913
Alfred Bryan / Fred Fisher

*Put On Your Old Gray Bonnet*   1909
Stanley Murphy / Percy Wenrich

*Rock-a-bye Your Baby with a Dixie Melody*   1918
Sam Lewis, Joe Young / Jean Schwartz

*St. Louis Blues*    1914
W. C. Handy

*School Days*    1907
Will D. Cobb / Gus Edwards

*Shine On, Harvest Moon*    1908
Jack Norworth / Nora Bayes

*Somebody Loves Me*    1924
Ballard MacDonald, Buddy De Sylva / George Gershwin

*Some of These Days*    1910
Shelton Brooks

*Someone to Watch over Me*    1926
Ira Gershwin / George Gershwin

*Something to Remember You By*    1930
Howard Dietz / Arthur Schwartz

*Star Dust*    1929
Mitchell Parish / Hoagy Carmichael

*Swanee*    1919
Irving Caesar / George Gershwin

*Sweet Adeline*    1903
Richard H. Gerard / Harry Armstrong

*Sweet Rosie O'Grady*    1896
Maude Nugent

*Tea for Two*    1924
Irving Caesar / Vincent Youmans

*The Band Played On*    1895
John E. Palmer / Charles B. Ward

*The Birth of the Blues*    1926
Buddy De Sylva / Lew Brown, Ray Henderson

*The Blue Room*    1926
Lorenz Hart / Richard Rodgers

*The Darktown Strutters' Ball*    1917
Shelton Brooks

*The Little Lost Child*    1894
Edward B. Marks / Joseph W. Stern

*The Man I Love*    1924
Ira Gershwin / George Gershwin

*The Sidewalks of New York*    1894
Charles B. Lawlor / James W. Blake

*They Didn't Believe Me*    1914
Herbert Reynolds / Jerome Kern

*Till We Meet Again*    1918
Raymond B. Egan / Richard A. Whiting

*Under the Bamboo Tree*    1902
Bob Cole

*Waiting for the Robert E. Lee*    1912
L. Wolfe Gilbert / Lewis F. Muir

*Wait 'Til the Sun Shines, Nellie*    1905
Andrew B. Sterling / Harry von Tilzer

*What Is This Thing Called Love?*    1930
Cole Porter

*When Irish Eyes Are Smiling*    1912
Chauncey Olcott, George Graff, Jr. / Ernest R. Ball

*When You Were Sweet Sixteen*    1898
James Thornton

*With a Song in My Heart*    1929
Lorenz Hart / Richard Rodgers

*Without a Song*    1929
Billy Rose, Edward Eliscu / Vincent Youmans

*Why Do I Love You?*    1925
Oscar Hammerstein II / Jerome Kern

*Yankee Doodle Boy*    1904
George M. Cohan

# The elect of Tin Pan Alley:
## lyricists and composers, 1880-1930

Adamson, Harold  *lyricist*  (born 1906)
Ager, Milton  *composer*  (born 1893)
Ahlert, Fred E.  *composer*  (1892-1953)
Akst, Harry  *composer*  (1894-1963)
Ball, Ernest R.  *composer*  (1878-1927)
Berlin, Irving  *lyricist-composer*  (born 1888)
Brown, Lew  *lyricist*  (1893-1958)
Buck, Gene  *lyricist*  (1885-1957)
Caesar, Irving  *lyricist*  (born 1895)
Carmichael, Hoagy  *composer*  (born 1899)
Carroll, Harry  *composer*  (1892-1962)
Clarke, Grant  *lyricist*  (1891-1931)
Cobb, Will D.  *lyricist*  (1876-1930)
Cohan, George M.  *lyricist-composer*  (1878-1942)
Conrad, Con  *composer*  (1891-1938)
Coots, J. Fred  *composer*  (born 1897)
Davis, Benny  *lyricist*  (born 1895)
De Sylva, Buddy  *lyricist*  (1892-1950)
Dietz, Howard  *lyricist*  (born 1896)
Donaldson, Walter  *composer*  (1893-1947)
Dresser, Paul  *lyricist-composer*  (1858-1906)
Dubin, Al  *lyricist*  (1891-1945)
Edwards, Gus  *composer*  (1879-1945)
Fisher, Fred  *composer*  (1875-1942)
Friml, Rudolf  *composer*  (born 1879)
Gershwin, George  *composer*  (1898-1937)
Gershwin, Ira  *lyricist*  (born 1896)
Gilbert, L. Wolfe  *lyricist*  (born 1886)

Hammerstein II, Oscar   *lyricist*   (1895-1960)
Handy, W. C.   *lyricist-composer*   (1873-1958)
Harbach, Otto   *lyricist*   (1873-1963)
Harney, Ben   *composer*   (1872-1938)
Harris, Charles K.   *lyricist-composer*   (1867-1930)
Hart, Lorenz   *lyricist*   (1895-1943)
Henderson, Ray   *composer*   (born 1896)
Herbert, Victor   *composer*   (1859-1924)
Howard, Joseph E.   *composer*   (1878-1961)
Jerome, William   *lyricist*   (1865-1932)
Kahn, Gus   *lyricist*   (1886-1941)
Kalmar, Bert   *lyricist*   (1884-1947)
Kern, Jerome   *composer*   (1885-1945)
Marks, Edward B.   *lyricist*   (1865-1945)
McCarthy, Joseph   *lyricist*   (1885-1943)
Meyer, George W.   *composer*   (1884-1959)
Monaco, Jimmy   *composer*   (1885-1945)
Morse, Theodore F.   *composer*   (1873-1924)
Norworth, Jack   *lyricist*   (1879-1959)
Porter, Cole   *lyricist-composer*   (born 1893)
Rodgers, Richard   *composer*   (born 1902)
Romberg, Sigmund   *composer*   (1887-1951)
Ruby, Harry   *lyricist-composer*   (born 1895)
Schwartz, Jean   *composer*   (1878-1956)
Shields, Ren   *lyricist*   (1868-1913)
Smith, Edgar   *lyricist*   (1857-1938)
Snyder, Ted   *composer*   (born 1881)
Stamper, Dave   *lyricist*   (1883-1963)
Sterling, Andrew B.   *lyricist*   (1874-1955)
Stern, Joseph W.   *composer*   (1870-1934)
Thornton, James   *lyricist-composer*   (1861-1938)
Van Alstyne, Egbert   *composer*   (1882-1951)
Von Tilzer, Albert   *composer*   (1878-1956)
Von Tilzer, Harry   *composer*   (1872-1946)
Wenrich, Percy   *composer*   (1887-1952)
Whiting, Richard A.   *composer*   (1891-1938)
Wodehouse, P. G.   *lyricist*   (born 1881)
Woods, Harry M.   *lyricist-composer*   (born 1896)
Yellen, Jack   *lyricist*   (born 1892)
Youmans, Vincent   *composer*   (1898-1946)
Young, Rida Johnson   *lyricist*   (1869-1926)

# Bibliography

Arnold, Elliott. *Deep in My Heart* (The Life of Sigmund Romberg). New York, Duell, Sloan and Pearce, 1949.

Baral, Robert. *Revue*. New York, Fleet, 1962.

Boni, Margaret B. (ed.). *Fireside Book of Favorite American Songs*. New York, Simon & Schuster, 1952.

————. *Songs of the Gilded Age*. New York, Golden Press, 1950.

Burton, Jack. *Blue Book of Broadway Musicals*. Watkins Glen, N.Y., Century House, 1952.

————. *Blue Book of Hollywood Musicals*. Watkins Glen, N.Y., Century House, 1953.

————. *Blue Book of Tin Pan Alley*. Watkins Glen, N.Y., Century House, 1951.

————. *The Index of American Popular Music*. Watkins Glen, N.Y., Century House, 1957.

Chipman, John H. (ed.). *Index to Top-Hit Tunes*. Boston, Bruce Humphries, 1962.

Churchill, Allen. *The Great White Way*, New York, Dutton, 1962.

Dreiser, Theodore (ed.). *The Songs of Paul Dresser*. New York, Boni and Liveright, 1927.

Engel, Lyle Kenyon (ed.). *America's Greatest Song Hits*. New York, Grosset, 1962

————. (ed.). *Five Hundred Songs*. New York, Bantam Books, 1964.

Ewen, David. *Complete Book of American Musical Theater*. New York, Holt, 1958.

————. *History of American Popular Music*. New York, Barnes & Noble, 1961.

————. *Journey to Greatness: The Life and Music of George Gershwin*. New York, Holt, 1957.

————. *Panorama of American Popular Music*. New York, Prentice-Hall, 1957.

————. *Popular American Composers*. New York, H. W. Wilson, 1962.

————. *Richard Rodgers*. New York, Holt, 1957.

————. *Story of America's Musical Theater*. Philadelphia, Chilton, 1961.

————. *The World of Jerome Kern*. New York, Holt, 1962.

Farnsworth, Marjorie. *The Ziegfeld Follies*. New York, Putnam, 1956.

Freeman, Larry. *The Melodies Linger On*. Watkins Glen, N.Y., Century House, 1951.

Fuld, James J. *American Popular Music: 1875-1900*. Philadelphia, Musical Americana, 1955.

Gammond, Peter, and Clayton, Peter. *Dictionary of Popular Music*. New York, Philosophical Library, 1961.

Geller, James J. *Famous Songs and Their Stories*. Garden City, N.Y., Garden City Publishing Co., 1940.

Gilbert, Douglas. *American Vaudeville: Its Life and Times*. New York, Dover, 1963.

————. *Lost Chords: The Diverting Story of American Popular Songs*. New York, Doubleday, 1942.

Gilbert, L. Wolfe. *Without Rhyme or Reason*. New York, Vantage, 1956.

Goldberg, Isaac. *Tin Pan Alley*. New York, Day, 1930.

Green, Abel, and Laurie, Jr., Joe. *Show Biz: From Vaude to Video*. New York, Holt, 1951.

Green, Stanley. *The World of Musical Comedy*. New York, Ziff-Davis, 1960.

Hammerstein II, Oscar (ed.) *The Jerome Kern Song Book*. New York, Simon & Schuster, 1955.

Handy, William C. *Father of the Blues: An Autobiography*. New York, Macmillan, 1941.

Harris, Charles K. *After the Ball: Forty Years of Melody*. New York, Frank Maurice, 1926.

Jablonski, Edward, and Stewart, Lawrence D. *The Gershwin Years*. New York, Doubleday, 1958.

Jordan, Philip D., and Kessler, Lillian. *Songs of Yesterday*. New York, Doubleday, 1941.

Kaufman, Helen L. *From Jehovah to Jazz*. New York, Dodd, 1937.

Kobbe, Gustav. *Famous American Songs.* New York, Crowell, 1906.

Laurie, Jr., Joe. *Vaudeville.* New York, Holt, 1953.

Lewine, Richard, and Simon, Alfred (eds.). *Encyclopedia of Theatre Music.* New York, Random House, 1961.

McNamara, Daniel I. (ed.). *The ASCAP Biographical Dictionary of Composers, Authors and Publishers.* New York, Crowell, 1948.

Marcuse, Maxwell F. *Tin Pan Alley in Gaslight.* Watkins Glen, N.Y., Century House, 1950.

Marks, Edward B. *They All Had Glamour.* New York, Messner, 1944.

———. *They All Sang.* New York, Viking, 1934.

Mattfield, Julius (ed.). *Variety Music Cavalcade.* New York, Prentice-Hall, 1962.

Meyer, Hazel. *The Gold in Tin Pan Alley.* Philadelphia, Lippincott, 1958.

Montgomery, Elizabeth R. *The Story Behind Popular Songs.* New York, Dodd, Mead, 1958.

Nathan, Hans. *Dan Emmett and the Rise of Early Negro Minstrelsy.* University of Oklahoma Press, 1962.

Paris, Leonard Allen. *Men and Melodies.* New York, Crowell, 1954.

Rice, Edward Le Roy. *Monarchs of Minstrelsy.* New York, Kenny, 1911.

Rodgers, Richard (ed.). *The Rodgers and Hart Song Book.* New York, Simon & Schuster, 1951.

Simon, Henry W. (ed.). *The George and Ira Gershwin Song Book.* New York, Simon & Schuster, 1960.

Smith, Cecil. *Musical Comedy in America.* New York, Theatre Arts Books, 1950.

Sobel, Bernard. *A Pictorial History of Burlesque.* New York, Putnam, 1956.

———. *A Pictorial History of Vaudeville. New York,* Citadel, 1961.

Spaeth, Sigmund. *The Facts of Life in Popular Song.* New York, Whittlesey House, 1934.

———. *History of Popular Music in America.* New York, Random House, 1948.

———. *Read 'Em and Weep.* New York, Arco, 1945.

———.*Weep Some More, My Lady.* New York, Doubleday, 1927.

Taylor, Deems. *Some Enchanted Evenings.* New York, Harper, 1953.

Waters, Edward N. *Victor Herbert.* New York, Macmillan, 1955.

Witmark, Isidore, and Goldberg, Isaac. *Story of the House of Witmark: From Ragtime to Swingtime.* New York, Citadel, 1939.

Woollcott, Alexander. *The Story of Irving Berlin.* New York, Putnam, 1925.

*Index*

## DATE DUE

| | | |
|---|---|---|
| MAR 20 '72 | | |
| MAR 20 '72 | | |
| OCT 13 '75 | | |
| OCT 8 '75 | | |
| JUN 14 '91 | | |
| MAY 30 NOV | | |
| MAY 26 '92 | | |
| AUG 4 '94 | | |
| | | |
| | | |
| | | |
| | | |
| | | |
| | | |
| | | |
| | | |
| | | |
| | | |